FORTRESS FRANCE

FORTRESS FRANCE

The Maginot Line and French Defenses in World War II

J. E. Kaufmann and H. W. Kaufmann

Illustrated by Tomasz Idzikowski

PRAEGER SECURITY INTERNATIONAL
Westport, Connecticut • London

Library of Congress Cataloging-in-Publication Data

Kaufmann, J. E.
   Fortress France : the Maginot Line and French defenses in World
War II / J.E. Kaufmann and H.W. Kaufmann; illustrated by Tomasz Idzikowski.
     p. cm.
   Includes bibliographical references and index.
   ISBN 0-275-98345-5 (alk. paper)
    1. Maginot Line (France)   2. World War, 1939–1945—Campaigns—France.
I. Kaufmann, H. W. II. Title.
   UG429.F8H39   2006
   940.54'2143—dc22   2005025488

British Library Cataloguing in Publication Data is available.

Library of Congress Catalog Card Number: 2005025488
ISBN: 0-275-98345-5

First published in 2006

Praeger Security International, 88 Post Road West, Westport, CT 06881
An imprint of Greenwood Publishing Group, Inc.
www.praeger.com

Printed in the United States of America

The paper used in this book complies with the
Permanent Paper Standard issued by the National
Information Standards Organization (Z39.48–1984).

10 9 8 7 6 5 4 3 2 1

To Harvey, Maria, Ed, Cam, and Lucy

CONTENTS

TABLES AND FIGURES

TABLES

FIGURES

ACKNOWLEDGMENTS

We would like to thank the following people for helping provide information and material for this work; in some cases, their help was given more than twenty-five years ago when we first began doing research on the fortifications (the individuals' fort associations are indicated in parentheses):

Bernard Bour (Ft. Mutzig); Jean-Louis and Philippe Burtscher (Ft. Schoenenbourg); Raoul Heymes (Ft. Hackenberg); Patrice Lang (Ft. Immerhof); Georges Maistret (Ft. Fermont); Y. V. Mary (Ft. Fermont); Raymond Mersch (Ft. Immerhof); Frank Philippart; Lt. Colonel Philippe Truttmann; Hans, Caspar, and Vincent Vermeullen; Colonel Viennot; and J. B. Wahl.

Those listed provided information on the Maginot Line; veterans Georges Dropsy and Andre Paquin gave us information on the operation of the forts during the war. Lt. Colonel Philippe Truttmann, the leading authority on the Maginot Line and postwar commander of Ft. Simershof, was a great help. The *Génie* of Metz, Grenoble, and Nice provided us with documentation and other information on the fortifications.

Lee Sharp, author of a series of books on the French order of battle, helped us with details on unit organization. Michelle Rodriguez at the Palo Alto College Library helped us quickly obtain copies of books we needed through interlibrary loan, and Lee Unterborn loaned us a number of books from his extensive collection. Also, Brian Chin provided us with books and magazines on French weapons and the Maginot Line. Juan Vázquez García, Bill Alcorn, and Caspar and Vincent Vermeulen sent us photos, a few of which have been included in this book.

We would like to thank Heather Staines for giving us this opportunity to expand on our first book with Praeger on the subject titled *The Maginot Line*.

Those interested in additional information in English on these and other fortifications are encouraged to contact and join the Fortress Study Group (http://www.geocities.com/CapeCanaveral/Hangar/3337/) in the United Kingdom.

Those in North America should contact the Coast Defense Study Group (http://www.cdsg.org/) or the Council on America's Military Past (http://www.campjamp.org/home.htm) if interested in fortifications. Also, those interested in research should contact SITEO, an international fortifications group (http://www.siteo.net). Additional SITEO regional locations can be found on the Web site by an Internet search.

Those interested can purchase a CDROM supplement to FORTRESS FRANCE that includes photos at http://www.merriam-press.com.

INTRODUCTION

The Maginot Line, sometimes known as the Great Wall of France, was the last of the great gun-bearing fortifications and was both praised and criticized for its role in history. It was conceived in the 1920s to shield the French frontier against an anticipated threat from a resurgent Germany in the 1930s. The goal of the Maginot Line was to prevent a German offensive from reaching the French heartland and conducting another destructive war that would last for years on French soil. Furthermore, in the event of war, the Maginot Line was to protect the newly returned provinces of Alsace and Lorraine and their industrial resources while the French army mobilized behind it.

The Maginot Line consisted of specific types of fortifications developed by the military during the 1920s. These defenses extended to cover the Alpine front with Italy in response to the bellicose Mussolini, who had designs on France. During the interwar period, according to some historians, the French developed a "Maginot mentality" that led the military establishment and the public to believe that the new fortifications would provide adequate protection and that there would be no need to prepare for an immediate counteroffensive.

This work examines the background and development not only of the Maginot Line between the wars, but also of coastal defenses developed to provide additional security to the French nation. The coast and land defenses eventually extended to cover Corsica and even Tunisia due to the growing Italian threat. The French *Génie* (army engineers) was heavily involved in these projects from their conception in the late 1920s right into the first year of the war.

In addition to examining these defenses, this work also describes the role of the French air force and navy in the overall scheme of defenses. Indeed, the French fortifications were built at the time of the birth of mechanized and armored divisions, which are also covered in the present volume.

The final two chapters analyze the role the Maginot fortifications played during the first year of the war, their effect on strategy, and their performance during the campaign. This project does not detail the battle tactics and experiences of individual soldiers and units in the French campaign of 1940, and it is not a detailed history of that campaign or the American operations against a few of the forts in 1944. For such information, we recommend a variety of books in French (listed in the bibliography). A few books in English cover the campaign, including our *Hitler's Blitzkrieg Campaigns*.

ABBREVIATIONS

AA   Antiaircraft
AC   Antichar
AP   Antipersonnel
AT   Antitank
BCR French aircraft intended for bombing and reconnaissance missions
DCR Armored division
DLC Light cavalry division (mechanized)
DLM Light mechanized division (*division légère mécanique*)
EH   Munitions entrance
EM   Men's entrance or troop entrance
FM   Automatic rifle or light machine gun
GFM For observation and automatic rifle
GO   *Gros ouvrage* or artillery *ouvrage*
JM   Twin machine gun
PO   *Petit ouvrage* or small fort
RF   Fortified region
RIF Fortress infantry regiment
SF   Fortified sector
TSF Radio

CHAPTER 1

MARCHING TO
THE WRONG TUNE

Until the outbreak of the Franco-Prussian War of 1870, the army of Napoleon III appeared to be the leading military force in Europe, but the conclusion of the conflict left the French army broken and humiliated. The victor, the army of the emerging German nation formed around Prussia, set the pattern for modern warfare in matters small and large. Thus, by the end of the century, many armies around the world emulated the Germans, adopting their spiked leather helmets and toned-down uniforms to reduce the soldiers' visibility. Prussian methods of military instruction, organization, and drill also became popular.

France, simmering with resentment and injured national pride, was one of the few holdouts. By World War I, many French soldiers still marched to war in resplendent uniforms consisting of red trousers (an 1867 pattern) and a blue tunic and greatcoat with the traditional kepi. In the West, only the Belgian army went to war with a more antiquated uniform. French weapons, tactics, and strategy changed, nonetheless. The French infantryman now carried an entrenching tool—usually the short-handled shovel known as *pelle bêche*—hanging on his belt (Bull, *World War I Trench Warfare*, p. 19). The French army also maintained a modern and updated organization based on divisions placed under corps for more efficient logistical control.[1]

With the loss of Alsace and part of Lorraine after the Franco-Prussian War, France set about fortifying its northeast frontier. What began as a defensive strategy soon became an offensive plan driven by a thirst for revenge and a burning desire to recuperate lost territories. Thus, in 1889, the French military establishment formulated Plan 1, calling for attacks on Metz and Strasbourg at the beginning of the next war. In 1911, the French high command, under the leadership of General Joffre, finally settled on Plan 17, which hinged on a massive offensive operation against the German forces occupying the territories lost in 1871. Instead of relying on new and modern weapons or sophisticated tactics, the new plan depended on an *offensive á outrance* (all-out offensive) during which French soldiers, bayonets fixed and hearts on fire with patriotic fervor, would win the day through sheer force of will and *élan*. Sadly, the French generals failed to take into account the disastrous effects of modern weapons, including machine guns, on massed formations, despite the mounting evidence provided by various conflicts prior to 1914. Their shortsightedness inflicted grievous losses on the French army in Alsace-Lorraine during the first weeks of the Great War, when Plan 17 was implemented.

The Germans, on the other hand, were better prepared. Their *Schlieffen* Plan of 1905 called for a massive concentration of force to strike against Belgium and outflank the French. However, the Belgians' refusal to give them passage rights and stubborn resistance delayed the Germans long enough to allow the French to recover and finally turn back the advancing tide at the First Battle of the Marne. The remainder of the war on the Western Front was mired in trench warfare and around field and permanent fortifications. In an effort to break the stalemate, both sides developed new tactics and strategies. The German assault on the fortress of Verdun in 1916, as badly conceived as the French Plan 17, called for striking the strongest section of the French line and "bleeding the French white," at whatever cost. The resulting slaughter lasted for many months but failed to break the stalemate. However, a French victory contributed to giving the French high command the wrong ideas for the future.

France emerged victorious from the Great War, but not without having sustained tremendous loss of life during the four years of war. In 1919, at Versailles, the French and their allies, bent on *revanche* (revenge), created a treaty intended to crush once and for all Germany's ability to threaten their security. The limitations imposed by this treaty nonetheless failed to allay the fears of the French military and political establishments. Thus, early in the 1920s France prepared once more for a possible war with Germany. During the next two decades, the French command and governmental bureaucracy created such a complex situation that it hindered the development of their own military doctrine and new weaponry.

The French military had emerged from the war with huge surplus stocks of military equipment. Like many of the nations that had invested heavily in the implements of war, France was reluctant to discard its massive war surpluses. Its government, like several others, was reluctant to invest in the development of new, improved designs to replace equipment that would soon become obsolete. As a result, the French army held on to its 75- and 155-mm guns until the next war.

The 75-mm gun was a fine weapon but presented some disadvantages, including a low trajectory that limited its range. Even though the army developed a new 105-mm howitzer with a longer range in 1936, the military leaders opted not to replace the 75-mm cannon at that time. General Maurin, inspector general of artillery at the time, insisted that with 5,400 pieces left over from the Great War, it was impractical to replace the 75-mm gun. In addition, General Pétain and his staff had decided as early as 1919 to retain both the 75- and the 155-mm gun because of the higher rate of fire of the 75-mm gun. Thus, in 1939 when the French went to war, the 75-mm gun still represented a significant part of an infantry division's artillery (Doughty, *Seeds of Disaster*, p. 96).

The development of armored vehicles and aircraft was even more critical to the French armed forces. The French created new designs but in many cases relied heavily on their surplus of older armored vehicles, including the FT-17 tank, which would remain in service in large numbers until the defeat in 1940. As for deployment and strategy, the French high command had some serious problems. Robert Doughty, in *Seeds of Disaster* (p. 26), concluded that the French refused to invest in new weapons because the weapons would become obsolete within a short time and turned their efforts toward only developing defensive weapons between the World Wars, believing that the development of new offensive weapons should take place during the next war. This went hand in hand with French strategic planning during the 1920s, which slowly shifted from offensive to defensive strategy.

WAR PLANS

Between the 1920s and the early 1930s, the French military prepared several war plans with offensive elements for dealing with a resurgent Germany. Plan P (Provisional), which replaced a transitional plan from the previous year, went into effect in June 1921 (Table 1.1). Formations of the French army in the Left Bank of the German Rhineland supported by cavalry would march into the Ruhr Basin and Main Valley and take control of Germany's main industrial center, crippling its ability to fight. Aircraft and tanks had a limited support mission. This plan was implemented in March 1923 when Germany proved unable to meet the huge reparations payments.

As French troops began to trudge back across the Rhine, a new plan, the first in a series of alphabetically lettered plans, had already replaced Plan P in 1924. This plan, called Plan A, called for securing more Rhine crossings and mobilizing additional infantry divisions to support the occupation force and allow for the expansion of the bridgehead.

In 1925, a revised plan, Plan A-*bis*, took into account the French forces involved in the Riff War in Morocco and an insurgency in Syria. After returning to the Left Bank of the Rhine, the French army adopted a defensive stance. In case of conflict with Germany, the occupation forces were to hold their positions until mobilization could take place; the French army was no longer to go on an immediate offensive.

At about the same time, the French military leadership abandoned a strategy based on a headlong rush to meet the enemy and opted instead for the creation of a line

TABLE 1-1. War plans

The army high command prepared the following war plans for mobilization between World Wars:

Plans for Offensive Actions	
Plan T (*transitoire* or transitional)	May 1920–May 1921
Plan P (*provisoire* or provisional)	June 1921–March 1923
Plan P *Modifié*	April 1923–December 1923
Plan A	January 1924–June 1926
Plan A-*bis*	June 1926–April 1929
Plans for Defensive Actions	
Plan B	May 1929–May 1931
Plan C	May 1931–April 1933
Plan D	April 1933–April 1935
Plan D-*bis*	April 1935–January 1938
Plan E	January 1938–September 1939
Plan F	October 1939

Sources: Correspondence with Lee Sharp, July 26, 2004; Hughes, *To the Maginot Line.*
Note: Plan F called for new recruits from October 1939 to form new infantry and two armored divisions.

of fortifications behind France's borders strong enough to hold the enemy until the completion of mobilization, which could take a year or more. In 1929, as the construction of the Maginot Line was set in motion and the period of active service for conscripts was reduced to one year, Plan A-*bis* was replaced with Plan B because the army could no longer expect to have a large, well-trained reserve on which to draw. To make matters worse, intelligence reported that the German army, in violation of the Treaty of Versailles, had reached up to four times its allowed strength. However, French military intelligence continually overestimated their old adversaries' resources and capabilities. In the event of a German offensive, the French occupation force of the Left Bank of the Rhineland was to withdraw (Hughes, *To the Maginot Line*, pp. 192–194).

Plan C became operational in May 1931, after the evacuation of the Rhineland. It reorganized the available forces into a mobile one, which had the capacity to move either to the frontier with Germany in the northeast or to the border with Italy in the southeast, wherever a threat materialized (Lee Sharp, e-mail correspondence, 15 July 2004). At the time, this plan went into effect, General Maxime Weygand, following up on Colonel Joseph Doumenc's ideas from the previous decade, authorized the formation of the first armored division.[2] This first armored division was the *division légère mécanique* (DLM, or light mechanized division), a converted cavalry division that became operational in 1933. General Weygand also ordered the motorization of several infantry divisions. When the Maginot Line neared completion, the French pulled out of the occupation zones to take full advantage their new ramparts.

Both Plan C and Plan D called for moving the new mobile force into Belgium. Plan D, which remained in effect between 1933 and 1935, was replaced with Plan D-*bis* in 1936 and Plan E in 1937. Plan D-*bis* relied on an invitation from the Belgian government because the new king, who had ascended to the throne in 1936, returned his country to a state of neutrality. Plan E called for the assembly of an army group for an offensive against Italy on the Alpine front after Mussolini's political realignment following his Ethiopian adventure (Hughes, *To the Maginot Line*, p. 218; Rocolle, *Illusions*, p. 155). These war plans were not entirely defensive because, until 1936, the army was still expected to advance into the Rhineland.

In 1935, as the Maginot Line approached completion and the strength and ability of the French army reached new lows, the Minister of War, General Joseph Maurin, asked: "How can anyone believe that we are still thinking of an offensive, when we have spent billions on setting up a fortified barrier?" (Hughes, *To the Maginot Line*, p. 248). The leaders of the French army did not formulate or accept Plan E until after the army began correcting its deficiencies.

EMBRACING DEFENSE

As Plan B became policy, the French high command became convinced that new weapons should be designed for defensive purposes, and that there would be time enough for the development of offensive weapons after the outbreak of war. "The French army in short, formulated a doctrine, organized and equipped its units, and trained its soldiers for the wrong type of war," pointed out Robert Doughty, author of *The Seeds of Disaster* (p. 3).

It is clear that the experience of the Great War, when the massive use of artillery combined with a system of entrenchments had eventually won the day, left an indelible impression on French military thinking.

The French military planners were convinced that firepower backed by new weapons of war, artillery, and tanks was the best way to repel an enemy assault. Although these tactics appeared to emphasize a combined arms force, in actuality they relied heavily on the infantry backed by other elements. Thus, the French had drawn the wrong lessons about tanks during the war. They also underestimated German storm trooper tactics that called for bypassing strong points.

The emphasis on defense offered the French the advantage of requiring fewer troops than a plan based on offense. As active service for conscripts dropped to one year and a half and later to only one year, the defensive option gained popularity. In addition, based on their experience in the Great War, the French military leaders concluded that a fortified position not only would require fewer troops, but also would slow enemy progress, allowing the army time to mobilize and train new conscripts.

Early in the 1920s, a military commission worked on plans for a fortified front. Meanwhile, the army formulated its infantry-oriented doctrine, which concluded that for offensive actions, a "methodical battle" involving a tightly controlled variety of units would be necessary. Subordinates must not show initiative but should follow the plans of the operation unquestioningly. Tanks and other weapons would support the foot soldiers. The same principle would apply to the defensive forces as well. This doctrine did not spring from the creation of the Maginot Line but from the conclusions drawn from experiences on the Western Front in World War I.

In 1921, a commission of thirteen officers headed by Marshal Pétain formulated the *Provisional Instructions on the Tactical Employment of Large Unit*, which were modified in 1936 under the title *Instructions on the Tactical Employment of Large Units.* The new instructions took into account mechanization, air power, and even the role of the new fortified fronts of the Maginot Line but did not alter significantly the basic doctrine (Doughty, *Seeds*, pp. 6–10). The early postwar doctrine was formulated by Marshals Henri Philippe Pétain and Ferdinand Foch and carried on by Maxime Weygand and Maurice Gamelin in the 1930s.

Pétain's ideas carried great weight because he had been one of France's most successful generals throughout the Great War thanks to his ability to set up a methodical battle employing old as well as new weapons. His tenacity at Verdun, where he proclaimed: "*Ils ne passeront pas!*" (They shall not pass!), transformed him into a national hero. In 1917, he restored confidence to the troops after putting down an army mutiny. His achievements turned him into a respected and beloved leader, even after his less-than-admirable role in the Vichy government following the fall of France in 1940. Thus, his backing gave more weight to a doctrine based on the methodical battle and the dominance of firepower. Even his erroneous belief in the 1930s that the Ardennes presented an unsurpassable obstacle to modern mechanized forces was taken as gospel truth.

Ferdinand Foch, the other French hero of World War I, had been one of the main proponents of the *élan* and vigorous offensive doctrine before the conflict. He led the French armies to the final victory. Foch also became committed to the idea of methodical battle that dominated postwar doctrine. During World War I, the chief of staff for all his major commands was General Maxime Weygand, who had gained additional experience after World War I as head of the French military mission to Poland that helped break the Russian thrust on Warsaw in 1920. He turned out to be one of France's best commanders, with an even better appreciation of new weapons than Pétain. In 1930, he became chief of the General Staff and in 1933 replaced Pétain as the vice president of the Supreme War Council and inspector general of the army. Between 1930 and 1935, he modernized the army by creating the first light mechanized division (DLM) and motorizing a third of the army's twenty active divisions. These changes coincided with the period of construction of the Maginot Line. After his retirement in January 1935 at age 68, Maurice Gamelin took his place. Gamelin was not quite as brilliant as Weygand, Foch, or Pétain, and his years of tenure as overall commander until the mid-1940s slowed the modernization of the French army and maintained the status quo of the doctrine of infantry and artillery dominance.

Although others strove to bring change, their influence was limited. In postwar France, General Jean-Baptiste Estienne, who created the first French armored formations of the war, held command of French tank forces until 1927. At a conference in Brussels in May 1921, Estienne called for a 100,000-man force consisting of 20,000 "shock" troops with 4,000 tanks and 8,000 trucks that could break the enemy's front and advance eighty kilometers in a single night. In France, confronted by the prestigious marshals and generals who believed in the rigid infantry-oriented methodical battle, his appeals for an independent tank force fell on deaf ears. Until his retirement, General Estienne had to work with the technical section, which was under the control of the infantry, to develop tanks, and he had little success in developing the new designs for tanks that he wanted (Doughty, *Seeds*, p. 138; McNair, *Les Blindés*, p. 2). Although politician Paul Reynaud supported progressive ideas like those of Estienne and called for a mobile army that could take the offensive against a resurgent Germany as early as 1924, he represented, more often than not, a minority position in the French parliament (Horne, *To Lose a Battle*, p. 65). The prevailing military doctrine continued to relegate the tank to the role of a support weapon for the infantry. The situation did not change dramatically until Weygand took command. At the time, a relatively young colonel named Charles de Gaulle expounded his own theories of modern warfare and the role of the tank. Thus, in the 1930s the French military did not fail to modernize their weapons and doctrines because of the Maginot Line. Instead, the period of military stagnation was due to a handful of stuffy old generals, ranging from the inspector of infantry to the overall army commander, General Gamelin, who insisted on clinging to the obsolete methods of the previous war.

Charles de Gaulle, a junior officer in Pétain's infantry regiment before the war, had been promoted to the rank of captain during the war. He was captured by the Germans at Verdun in 1916, after he was wounded for the third time. After the war, and several escape attempts, he returned to France and accompanied Weygand on a postwar military mission to Poland, where he received that nation's highest decoration for participating in the fight against the Red Army. De Gaulle, who was six foot, five inches tall, towered over his superiors and subordinates not only physically, but also personally and intellectually because of his leadership and military qualities. In the 1920s, after returning from Poland, he served as a professor of history at Saint-Cyr, the *École de Guerre* (War College), where he worked again with Pétain. Later, he was assigned the command of a battalion of *chasseurs* (light infantry troops), after which he was detailed to General Staff duty.

In the 1930s, de Gaulle took over General Estienne's self-appointed crusade for the reorganization of the French army. He served the secretary general of the National Defense Council between 1932 and 1937 and wrote his first book, *Vers l'Armée de Métier* (*Towards a Professional Army*, also known as *The Army of the Future*), inspired by General Estienne. In this work, de Gaulle urged the creation of a mobile army consisting of an elite force of 100,000 men in six armored divisions (Rocolle, *Illusions*, p. 113). General Weygand, like Pétain, had been de Gaulle's mentor and did not decry his efforts. Weygand, head of the French army at the time, was preoccupied with maintaining an army suffering from a shortage of conscripts resulting from a decrease in births during the years of the Great War and the reduction of the term of service to a single year of active duty. De Gaulle's new book in 1938 caused a break with Pétain (Horne, *To Lose a Battle*, p. 68), who felt that the colonel was taking other people's ideas from their time at the École de Guerre. Unlike Pétain, de Gaulle never supported a fortified frontier. His mentor, Henri Pétain, changed his mind and dropped his support of the fortified front in the 1930s. De Gaulle's "revolutionary" ideas and public stance cost him dearly because he did not advance beyond the rank of colonel until after the beginning of the war.

Another problem that de Gaulle pointed out during his assignments between 1932 and 1937 was the instability of the government. Serving fourteen governments in this short time span, he found that the administrators were not lacking in skills, but that "the political game consumed them and paralyzed them." He believed that this affected the military, causing the army to be "stuck in a set of ideas which had had their heyday before the end of the First World War." Furthermore, he pointed out, the French military leaders had grown "old at their posts, wedded to errors that had once constituted their glory" (de Gaulle, *War Memoirs*, pp. 6–7). He may have been right in some respects because this had been a traditional pattern, especially after Gamelin replaced Weygand.

Charles de Gaulle and Mechanized Warfare

The appearance of Charles de Gaulle's *Vers l'Armée de Métier* in 1934 did not cause a revolutionary change in the French army but did help put the colonel in conflict with the old generals. His German counterpart, Heinz Guderian, published *Achtung Panzer* in 1937, and his work, possibly influenced by de Gaulle's, had a much greater effect on his army than de Gaulle's had on the French army. When de Gaulle's book came out, the main sections of the Maginot Line were nearing completion. Similarly, Guderian's book came out as the German military had become heavily involved in the construction of both the East Wall and the West Wall. Thus, the existence of major fortifications was not the only factor in deterring the military from adopting these new ideas. In fact, the French moved ahead in building a large number of tanks, many superior to German models, while the Germans had struggled to match the French. The main difference was that the Germans concentrated on an independent armored force for the offensive as both de Gaulle and Guderian had called for, but the French armor was devoted mainly to supporting the infantry.

De Gaulle's concept called for forming a mechanized corps of six divisions plus a light division consisting of armored and motorized elements. The division was to include an armored brigade composed of a heavy tank regiment, a medium tank regiment, and a battalion of light tanks. The second brigade was to include two infantry regiments and a battalion of *chasseurs*, all mounted in tracked vehicles. There was an artillery brigade with two regiments of howitzers and an antiaircraft group. Finally, the division was to include a reconnaissance regiment, an engineer battalion, a signal battalion, and a camouflage battalion. De Gaulle's proposed division was a relatively balanced force of combined arms, intended for the offense based on the strength of its armored vehicles and not the foot soldiers. His light division was to serve as an advance force with faster vehicles. He also proposed an air element to support operations and create a truly combined arms force.

The troops in de Gaulle's model army were to form a professional elite enlisted for six-year terms. He did not want the divisions to be broken up to form new divisions as was the standard policy, but rather he wanted it to be an elite force ready for action at all times.

By the time the war began, the Germans had created a force of several *panzer* (armored) divisions similar to what de Gaulle had wanted, but Guderian and others did not agree with de Gaulle on concentrating a force of 3,000 tanks for a front of about fifty kilometers. In some respects, de Gaulle's ideas were calling for his own version of the methodical battle.

De Gaulle found a political ally in Paul Reynaud, who on 15 March 1935 spoke to the Chamber of Deputies. He was ardent in his speech, attempting to show the need for a mechanized army along the lines of the colonel's proposals. Soon after, he authored a bill for the creation of his seven-division corps. Reynaud's attempt met rejection, and General Maurin rebuked de Gaulle on the Superior Council of National Defense. When General Gamelin became chief of the General Staff, he also rejected the colonel's ideas. With General Weygand retired, de Gaulle had no key supporters in the high command because even Pétain had turned against him.

By 1937, Gamelin allowed the irritating Charles de Gaulle to be removed from Paris and given command of the 507th Tank Regiment at Metz, where his voice would be more distant. The next year, he published *La France et son armée* (*France and Its Army*) in what he referred to as his final warning. President Lebrun visited his unit in the first year of the war and told the colonel that he was acquainted with his ideas, but he believed it was too late to apply them. (Note that it is curious that Liddel Hart in *The Defence of Britain*, written in 1939, mentioned Reynaud's *Le Probleme militaire francaise*, which described the needs for modern warfare and made no mention of de Gaulle.) In January 1940, de Gaulle still made an appeal to several dozen government officials. At the time, the army was finally forming the first French armored divisions.

After the German offensive shattered the French front by mid-May, Charles de Gaulle took command of the newly formed 4th Armored Division and led it in vigorous attacks in an attempt to break the German offensive spearhead. On June 5, 1940, Reynaud appointed de Gaulle undersecretary of state for national defense (Buffetaut, *De Gaulle*, pp. 4–7; de Gaulle, *War Memoirs*, pp. 15–39).

PLANNING A GREAT WALL FOR FRANCE

Joffre, Foch, and Pétain succeeded each other in the post of inspector general of the army and played an important role in the decision to create a fortified barrier on the eastern frontier. During the Great War, Pétain had witnessed the strength of the French fortifications at Verdun and the German defenses known as the Hindenburg Line built late in the war. As a result, he became convinced that a continuous defensive line with depth, not unlike the German fortifications of World War I would be ideal for the security of France. However, he did not believe in investing in massive fortifications, preferring a type of trench line with light defenses laid out in depth using various kinds of obstacles to absorb an enemy offensive. However, even though some historians have concluded that the design of the Maginot Line was based on the continuous line envisaged by Pétain, the evidence does not seem to point that way.

Marshal Joffre, who succeeded Pétain as inspector general of the army, also had an important role in the development of the Maginot Line. Unlike his predecessor, he believed in the effectiveness of large subterranean fortifications, like those in the prewar rings at Verdun, Toul, Épinal, and Belfort in France and the German rings at Metz-Thionville and Strasbourg-Mutzig. He was familiar with the Germans rings because he had participated in their inspection after the war. However, although Joffre heartily endorsed the use of fortifications, he did not favor fortress rings, preferring fortified fronts along the border. The design for the Maginot Line more closely reflects the conception of Marshal Joffre rather than that of Marshal Pétain.

It must be noted that the major fortress rings of Verdun and Toul were linked by a series of forts between them, as were the rings of Épinal and Belfort. However, between Toul and Épinal the front was relatively undefended. Each pair of these fortress rings formed its own fortified front; from the flanks of this fortified front a counterattack could be launched against an advancing enemy army. The Germans also had two pairs of fortress rings opposing the French at Metz-Thionville and Strasbourg-Mutzig, which fell into French hands after the war. The first three of these rings included the new *feste*, which were even larger and more modern than the French forts. During the 1930s, the French army and government made an effort to close the gaps between fortified fronts and to extend their flanks with lighter defenses, leaving an appearance of a continuous line.

The process of determining the best way to defend France's borders and proceeding with the fortification of the frontier began soon after the war. Even though the French officials had tried to thwart Germany's offensive capabilities with the Versailles Treaty of 1919, their deep-rooted mistrust of their vanquished enemy did not abate. The return of its territories of Alsace and Lorraine after the war gave France a new eastern frontier, which rendered the surviving pre–World War I fortifications useless in the defense of the homeland since they covered the prewar border.

As they considered ways to defend the new frontier, the French military and civilian leaders, remembering the devastation caused by World War I, paid particular attention to the type of defenses to be adapted. The recovered lands included an important population center in Alsace and vital resources and industries in Lorraine that soon became a vital part of the national economy. As compensation for the heavy damages the Germans inflicted on the mines in Lorraine during the war, the French were given a fifteen-year occupation of the Saar. After that time, the people of the Saar were to hold a plebiscite to determine if they wanted to return to Germany or stay with France.

Control of a nation's industrial base had a vital effect on its ability to wage war. Thus, the return of the entire territory of Lorraine to French control contributed to the expansion of France's industrial base. If the enemy managed to close down industrial production there, or even in the north, around Lille, France's ability to wage war would be seriously impaired. It was natural, therefore, for the French to decide to fortify their eastern frontier. The Allied powers had forced Germany to demilitarize the Rhineland for similar reasons. When the Germans officially repudiated the Versailles Treaty, one of their first moves was to reoccupy the Rhineland and build a defensive line on the western frontier to protect their industrial base. Even Italy began fortifying its easily defensible mountain frontiers in the north to protect not only its territory, but also its industrial centers.

The French *Conseil Supérieur de la Guerre* (Superior Council of War or sometimes also called the Army Council), created in 1872, was the most important group to influence military policy before and after the Great War. In 1920, the responsibilities of this council regarding military policies increased. Technically, the president of the republic presided over the council but did not vote; however, the minister of war usually took the president's place during most meetings. The council members included the marshals of France and several generals. One member of the military served as vice-president. In the event of mobilization, the council's vice-president became the commander in chief. It was this council that laid the foundations for the future Maginot Line under the leadership of Marshal Pétain, who served as vice-president for over a decade.

André Lefèvre, minister of war, in March 1920 instructed the council to study the problem of defending the new frontier (Truttmann, "La Fortification," p. 24). In June 1922, Marshal Joffre took charge as president of a special commission that was assigned the task. Joffre and Pétain clashed over the best method of defense. Joffre pushed for fortified zones that included works similar to those at Verdun and other fortress rings. Pétain, on the other hand, insisted on a continuous line of light defenses relying on *parc mobile de fortifications* (fortification mobile park) that included equipment and construction materials to build field fortifications and would help give flexibility and depth to the defenses. The fact is that Pétain detested Joffre and rejected out of hand any proposal he might put forward (Rowe, *Great Wall*, pp. 25–26). In addition, both had drawn radically differing points of view during their experiences and visits to Verdun. Whereas Joffre recollected the strength and reliability of the French forts, Pétain insisted that it was his hastily erected defenses that finally checked the Germans rather than the massive forts. By August, after the two generals failed to reach an agreement, Joffre resigned, and the commission was dissolved and replaced with a new one.

General Louis Guillaumat formed the *Commission de Défense du Territoire* or Commission of Territorial Defense (CDT) early in August 1922. He continued to endorse the ideas proposed by Joffre, while General Edmond Buat sided with Pétain's faction until early 1923. Buat had risen from commanding a corps to commanding an army during the war and became chief of staff at Foch's headquarters before the conflict ended. He served as chief of the General Staff between 1920 and the end of 1923. When Buat died, he was replaced by General Marie Debeney, who became an ally of the Joffre faction, which included Marshal Foch. A consensus was finally reached in the spring of 1923, and the CDT reported on March 27.

The report presented the conclusions drawn by both factions. The authors of the report determined that the security of frontier regions required some form of defense in depth, as Pétain had suggested. However, when actual work began and costs mushroomed, the idea of any significant defense in depth fell by the wayside. The CDT also agreed that parts of the frontier regions would require permanent fortifications. However, it did not identify these locations, although it mentioned that these positions must run from Longwy to Basel, apparently in accordance to Pétain's plans for a continuous line. In addition, the CDT specified four possible invasion routes, including one along the Moselle and through Luxembourg. A second route was through the plateau of Lorraine. Both of these routes put the iron and coal resources and industrial sites of Lorraine in great jeopardy. The solution was the creation of the *Région Fortifiée de Metz* (Fortified Region of Metz, RF of Metz). In addition, the commission identified a third invasion route between the Vosges and the Rhine River, which threatened Strasbourg and the population centers of Alsace, and recommended the formation of the *Région Fortifiée de la Lauter* (RF of the Lauter). The fourth invasion route passed across the Rhine, through the Belfort Gap, so the CDT proposed a *Région Fortifiée de Haute Alsace* (RF of Haute Alsace), also known as the *Région Fortifiée de Belfort* (RF of Belfort), to close this area (Mary, *Maginot*, Vol. 1, pp. 12–13).

The proposed RF of Metz included Thionville and Metz, both of which were surrounded by the relatively new German *festen* that could be integrated into the new defenses. In the RF of Haute Alsace, the older French forts of the Belfort Ring from the Séré de Rivères era still remained. However, the Belfort region would become a low-priority area and never actually became a heavily defended RF because it was too far behind the frontier and much less vulnerable than the other regions. Although the RF of the Lauter was the most vulnerable to attack, it included only defenses of limited value, such as the first of the new German *feste* at Mutzig-Molsheim and the much older German ring of forts at Strasbourg. Except for a small amount of oil, Alsace had no major natural resources, but it included a manufacturing area and a large population in the Rhine valley that required protection.

Economic Considerations

Great Britain, Germany, France, Belgium, and Italy were the leading industrial nations in Europe before World War I and maintained their positions after the war. Unlike Great Britain and Germany, France depended more heavily on imports of resources for industry. The return of Alsace and Lorraine[3] somewhat alleviated the problem for France.

After the war, France received control over the Saar for fifteen years to use its coal resources to replace those in the badly damaged mines of Lorraine (Table 1.2). The Saar coal was not of the right quality for use as coke in the furnaces (Tables 1.3–1.5).

At Pechelbronn in Alsace, the Germans had developed oil wells and increased production during the war. These became the only postwar oil wells in France and by 1924 produced 2% of the nation's needs.

French industry concentrations

North (Rouen and Lille regions) and northeast (Metz and Mulhouse regions)

Paris region

Lyon region

Marseille region

TABLE 1-2. Estimated coal reserves (in metric tons)

Before the Great War (in metric tons)		Annual Consumption
Belgium	11 billion	25 million
France	18 billion	61 million (only 1/3 not imported)
Germany	423 billion	159 million
Great Britain	193 billion	185 million
United States	3,800 billion	?

TABLE 1-3. Estimated iron reserves (in metric tons)

Lorraine	4 billion (about half in French territory before the war)*
France	3.3 billion (including the part of Lorraine still under French control)
Germany and Great Britain had large deposits, and Belgium had none.	

TABLE 1-4. Annual production of iron ore before the great war (in metric tons)

France	19 million
Germany	26.5 million
Great Britain	15 million
United States	53 million

TABLE 1-5. Other resources used in France before the war

Copper	90% imported
Lead	50% imported
Zinc	50% imported

The prewar population was 39 million. Before the war, about 35% of the population engaged in industry or associated activities. Over 60% of the prewar imports were for industrial use. Most industries were small, with only a few factories employing five hundred or more workers.

The French colonial empire included only small amounts of iron, lead, and zinc and provided mainly agricultural products. Algeria and Tunisia had phosphate mines, but their populations provided a manpower resource for the army. Oil had become important for the new war machines, but the French colonies had none (Ogburn and Jaffe, *Economic Development*).

War in Morocco and hostilities in Syria delayed the work on border defenses and revealed a deficiency in army manpower. As the situation improved and Paul Painlevé, a skilled politician, became minister of war in 1925, the preparations for a defensive line progressed more rapidly. Painlevé created the *Commission de Défense des Frontières* (CDF, or Frontier Defense Commission), which went into operation at the beginning of 1926 with General Guillamat in charge. Generals Debeney, chief of Army General Staff; Henri Berthelot, commander of the Army of the Danube until the summer of 1919; Jean-Marie-Joseph Degoutte, commander of the Army of the Rhine from 1919 until late 1924 and later the Army of the Alps; Joseph Maurin, Inspector General of Artillery; General Étienne-Honoré Fillonneau, inspector general of *Génie* (Engineers); and several other officers served on the commission (Rowe, *Great Wall*, p. 59).

The commission produced the November 6, 1926, report a 105-page report with maps that marked the areas to be defended. This report outlined the required defenses from the coast to the Swiss border and identified the same three RFs from the previous commission's report. Zones consisting of barriers created by demolitions or other means and natural obstacles were to separate the RFs. In the northern frontier zone—extending from Hirson, at the edge of the Ardennes, to the sea—the commission recommended flooding large sectors between the city of Maubeuge and the coast. Mobile parks of fortification with materials necessary for the construction of light defenses would be placed where needed. Along the Ardennes sector, covering the remainder of the Belgian border, French troops and army engineers were to establish barriers in case of an imminent invasion, mainly by using demolitions. Flooding and other water barriers were to cover the smaller sector of the Sarre, opposite the German Saar, between the RFs of Metz and the Lauter. The commission recommended multiple lines of light defenses along the Rhine, in the RF of the Lauter and the RF of Haute Alsace. One section of the report also covered the Southeast Front with Italy. Here, five *secteurs fortifiés* (SF) or fortified sectors (RFs were also divided into SFs) were identified, including Bourg–St. Maurice, Modane, Brainçon, Tournoux, and Nice, that would cover various passages through the Alps (Mary, *Maginot*, Vol. 1, pp. 13–15; Truttmann, "La Fortification," pp. 35–39).

During 1927, the CDF modified the original trace of the fortified line. The main defenses no longer were to run up to Longwy and along the west side of the Chiers River from Longwy back to Longuyon. The planners decided to leave this salient and its economic resources undefended because they considered it too close to the border. Minor modifications were planned for the RF of Metz. The trace was also modified in the RF of the Lauter, where the line was redrawn further south on the Rhine, abandoning an exposed corner of the frontier. On the other side of the Vosges, the CDF changed its initial plans to propose expanding the defenses toward the Sarre River, just east of Sarreguemines. The final report of the CDF modified the original trace of the fortified line and called for the creation of a frontier position, a second line behind it, and finally a support line in each of the RFs. The support line would include the old German and French forts of Metz, Thionville, and Belfort. The line of heavy fortifications for the RFs of Metz and Lauter was actually built, but as a matter of economy and necessity, the fortifications for the RF of Haute Alsace never materialized.

The main type of fortifications in the line of fortifications that eventually became the Maginot Line consisted of several types of large forts known as *ouvrages*.[4] The commission studied several types of fortifications, ranging from machine gun casemates to *ouvrages*. The advantage of the first was that they were more economical. In 1924, General Normand proposed in an article a double line of concrete blockhouses that would include a machine gun at the upper level and mortars at the lower level. A line of small forts with 70-mm guns and 105-mm howitzers would provide support from the rear (Truttmann, "La Fortification," pp. 57–58).

In December 1920, a Colonel Levêque proposed two lines of these machine gun positions and *abris* (shelters) with two more lines of redoubts armed with 75-mm guns in casemates and turrets. A line of citadels would be built behind them. However, although this system would provide depth, it would require a large number of defenders (Truttmann, "La Fortification," pp. 55–56).

Pétain and other officers examined forts of the Séré de Rivières era found at Verdun and other sites, as well as the German *feste* now located in returned French territory. In February 1927, Engineer Colonel Tricaud met with the CDF to propose an improvement on the older fortifications. In 1923, he had proposed a fort known as a "palm fort," which had a number of concrete blocks for weapons casemates and turrets and a central *caserne* (garrison area). It bore a striking resemblance to the larger forts at Verdun, which had dispersed blocks. However, Tricaud's subterranean fort was more widely dispersed and not outlined with a gorge and *fossé* (moat or ditch), although it included one in front of the fort. An even more advanced version of the "palm fort" that he proposed to the commission had several well-dispersed blocks, as in the original plan, but presented a few flaws in design (Mary, *Maginot*, Vol. 1, pp. 18–19; Truttmann, "La Fortification," pp. 56–57).[25]

In October 1927, the Superior Council of War, pressed to adopt a final design for the defensive line, came to a decision after much debate. Although General Maurin and two other officers pushed for a double line of machine gun casemates, the majority decided against them. The double line, they pointed out, would not be sufficient to resist a major enemy offensive unless it was heavily defended by troops and artillery. General Fillonneau, who had rejected Tricaud's palm fort earlier in the year, saying it was too expensive, insisted on adopting the palm fort design with some modifications. He was supported by Pétain, who had originally proposed only light defenses (Mary, *Maginot*, Vol. 1, pp. 19). The palm fort combined the best elements of the older forts using the German element of dispersion of the *feste* and the French concept of no more than one turret per block. Major changes the council made were to add an entrance, a large *caserne*, and a magazine well to the rear. The council felt that the added expense would be worth it since it would require fewer men, and one of the main missions of this new line of fortifications was to hold off a German assault with a minimal force to give the army time to mobilize.

On September 30, 1927, the CDF created the *Commission d'Organisation des Région Fortifiées* or the Commission for Organizing the Fortified Regions (CORF). General Fillonneau, inspector general of Engineers, was appointed, appropriately enough, president of the CORF. He was succeeded by General Charles-Louis-Joseph Belhauge in 1929. Belhauge remained in charge of the CORF until its dissolution in 1935, earning the title of "Monsieur Fortifications" (Mary, *Maginot*, Vol. 1, p. 23). The CORF was to determine the final design and placement for the fortifications of the yet unnamed Maginot Line.

Most of the major decisions by the CDF and Superior Council of War for the location and design of the new fortifications were made between 1926 and 1929 when Paul Painlevé served as minister of war. If Belhauge was mostly responsible for designing and building the fortifications, Painlevé was the patron of the new fortified line because he endorsed and pushed the program. André Maginot, a veteran of Verdun who replaced Painlevé as minister of war in 1929, enthusiastically pushed the program through Parliament and presided over the initial construction work.

Because of his indefatigable work, Maginot became known as the father of the line that soon took his name. He appeared before the French Parliament shortly after the war.[5] The old, badly wounded veteran, who had served at Verdun as a sergeant, left an indelible impression on the members of Parliament as he hobbled before the Chamber of Deputies on his canes and made the case for the new fortifications. Before the Great War, he had held an elected office, but he had left his safe job in government to become a private in the army and was decorated for his courage. After the war, he returned to the political arena and soon earned the respect and support of the French veterans when, as minister of pensions, he championed their cause.

As Maginot stood before Parliament, he pointed out that the Versailles Treaty did not guarantee the security of a nation that had suffered more than a dozen destructive invasions in half as many centuries. He went on to warn that France must be prepared to defend itself. Maginot served as minister of war from 1922 to 1924 when the CDT met and he strove to spur to action. When Painlevé became minister of war, Maginot became president of the Parliamentary Army Commission, and the two worked well together. Maginot returned as minister of war in November 1929 and soon appeared before the lower chamber of Parliament to plead for the construction of the Maginot Line, warning that the work must be finished by 1935. He also convinced this assembly that they must approve four years of funding so there would be no yearly debates to delay the work. With the help of Albert Lebrun, the president of the Senate Army Commission and future president of France, Maginot was able to win the approval of the Senate, one of the most important victories of his career.

On January 14, 1930, André Maginot pointed out that preventing an invasion in a future war was of paramount importance, and that the defensive plans for the French borders were intended to bar the invasion routes. In addition, he said, to stop an invasion "concrete is better . . . and is less expensive than a wall of chests." He continued to focus the public's attention on the work being done, emphasizing the role and nature of the line. However, the media exaggerated his descriptions, turning the line into an impregnable fortified position that would seal the frontier, thus creating a false sense of security that later contributed to the development of the "Maginot mentality" (Rowe, *Great Wall*, pp. 17, 43–52).

Building on Experience

The French military planners who prepared the blueprints for France's new system of fortifications were heirs to a long tradition of fortification building that went back to the Middle Ages, flowered during the seventeenth century with Vauban, and culminated in the late nineteenth century with the fortresses of Raymond Séré de Rivières. The system of forts built Séré de Rivières, improved and reinforced to withstand the high explosive shells developed in the 1880s, played an important role in the Great War, when their strengths and weaknesses were tested.

The *fossé* or moat, surrounding the forts, a survival from the medieval period in the Séré de Rivières forts, was finally discarded in the plans for Maginot *ouvrages* because it was too expensive and had outgrown its usefulness. On the other hand, other Séré de Rivières era features, such as the Casemate de Bourges, that provided flanking fires with two 75-mm guns were retained. In the Maginot *ouvrages*, however, the two- and three-gun 75-mm casemates for flanking fires would be much larger. An eclipsing turret, first conceived by Commandant Alfred Galopin in 1890 for 57-mm guns, was transformed in 1905 into a turret for 75-mm guns and was improved for the Maginot *ouvrages*. A couple of the old turrets were refurbished, modified, and installed in some ouvrages in the mid-1930s. The eclipsing machine gun turrets mounting two Hotchkiss machine guns, which had a very high profile, were redesigned for the Maginot Line with stronger side and roof armor, and they maintained a lower profile in the firing position. Armored observation posts were vastly improved with the introduction of multipurpose cloches that included defensive weapons.

The Bussière eclipsing turret of 1888 was the first to replace the old Mougin rotating turrets of 1876 with two 155-mm guns. Early in the 1900s, new models of single and twin 155-mm gun Galopin eclipsing turrets were installed in several forts. The German *feste* of Metz and Thionville included turret batteries with 100-mm guns (three to four noneclipsing turrets with a single gun each). The CORF considered using guns heavier than the 75-mm gun, but in most cases the barrel would have projected beyond the embrasures and made it impossible to use a disappearing turret. The additional expense for this type of position was dropped.

The last generation of forts in Lorraine, both French and German, with their battle experience provided a basis for developing the *ouvrages* of the Maginot Line.

French Generals and Marshals and Ministers of War

Commanders of the French Army

Marshal Joseph Joffre (died 1931)
    1911: Commander in chief of the army
    Late 1916: replaced and given lesser duties

Marshal Ferdinand Foch (died 1929)
    Commanded an army during World War I
    1918: Commander in chief of Allied armies on western front

Marshal Henri P. Pétain (died 1951)
    Commanded a corps, then an army, and finally an army group in World War I
    1920: Commander in chief of the army
    1920–1931: Vice-president of the Superior Council of War
    1922: Inspector-general of the army
    1934: Minister of war

General Marie-Eugène Debeney (died 1943)
    Commanded a corps and then an army in World War I
    1924–1930: Chief of Army General Staff

General Maxime Weygand (died 1965)

    Chief of staff for Foch when he commanded an army, then an army group, and finally the Allied armies during World War I

    1920: Headed French military mission to Poland

    1923–1925: High commissioner to Syria

    1930–1931: Chief of Army General Staff

    1931–1935: Vice-president of the Superior Council of War (retired January 1935)

    1940: Recalled to active duty

General Maurice Gamelin (died 1958)

    Commanded a division during World War I

    1919–1925: Headed French military mission to Brazil

    1926–1930: Chief of staff and then commander of troops in Levant

    1931–1935: Chief of staff of the army

    1935–1939: Vice-president of the Superior Council of War

    1935: Inspector general of the army

    1940: Dismissed on May 19 as commander of the army

Ministers of war

1920: André Lefèvre

1920–1921: Baron Raiberti Flaminius

1921–1922: Louis Barthou

1922–1924: Andre Maginot

1924–1925: General Charles Nollet

1925: Paul Painlevé

1925: Edouard Daldier

1925–1926: Paul Painlevé

1926: General Adolphe Guillaumaut

1926–1929: Paul Painlevé

1929–1930: André Maginot

1930: René Besnard

1930: André Maginot

1930–1931: Louis Barthou

1931–1932: André Maginot

1932: André Trideau

1932: Joseph Paul Boncour (less than a week)

1932–1933: Edouard Daladier

1934: Marshal Henri P. Pétain

1934–1935: General Joseph Luis Maurin

1935–1936: Jean Fabry

1936: General Louis Maurin

1936–1940: Edouard Daladier

1940: Paul Reynaud

1940: General Louis Closon

Vice-President of Superior Council of War (CSG)[6]

1920–1931: Marshal Henri P. Pétain
1931–1935: General Maxime Weygand
1935–1939: General Maurice Gamelin

CHAPTER 2

THE MAGINOT LINE

THE CORF FORTS

After its first meeting at the end of September 1927, Commission for Organizing the Fortified Regions (*Commission d'Organisation des Région Fortifiées*; CORF) began to establish priorities for the regions to be fortified and to draw up plans for the communications lines, the power system for the forts, the supporting positions, and a system for re-supplying the forts. The CORF report of March 1928 laid out the requirements and priorities. The *région fortifiée* (fortified region; RF) of Metz and the RF of the Lauter were assigned first priority for construction, the RF of Haute-Alsace (Belfort) was next in line, and the third priority went to establishing the communications system for the fortifications, a system behind the front for distributing electrical power, and a supply system with depots and military roads and rail lines. One of the most important functions in its catalogue was the design of various types of fortifications—later known as CORF designs—that included all the major structures built for the Maginot Line.

Twelve types of fortifications were proposed: Forts Types 1 and 2 (the main type of *ouvrages*); *ouvrages* with 75-mm gun turrets and howitzers; a monolithic intermediate *ouvrage*; two-block intermediate *ouvrages*; intermediate *ouvrages* with four turrets of *lance-bombes*[1]; intermediate *ouvrages* with two turrets of *lance-bombes*; *ouvrages* with a *mitrailleuse* (machine gun) turret and *lance-bombes*; infantry *ouvrages* for machine guns and *lance-bombes*; casemates for two groups of machine guns; command posts for observation; and *abris* (shelters) for an infantry company. After this report was issued and CORF began selecting the positions for the fortifications and determining their size and mission, the *Service Technique du Génie* (STG) prepared the master plans, which included a number of notices or directives indicating the composition of various types of casemates, entrances, and other fortifications. CORF formulated the building standards, such as concrete thickness and components of the fortifications and allocated the resources.

The STG, on the other hand, translated the building standards of CORF into master blueprints that were sent to the regional commands of the *Génie* (Engineers) of the various directorates in each of the military regions of France destined to receive the new fortifications. In the RF of Metz, this was the *Direction des Travaux de Fortification* (Directorate for Fortification Construction, DTF) of the 6th Military Region located at Metz. The area covered for this RF was so great that the DTF had to be divided into Metz-West and Metz-East. The district engineer sections of these DTF surveyed the intended building sites and made the final adjustments to the master blueprints since CORF standards and the STG master plans were too general to suit all terrain without modifications (Truttmann, *La Muraille*, 1992, pp. 63–66).

In the RF of the Lauter, the DTF at Strasbourg of the 20th Military Region handled the construction under its jurisdiction and on the Rhine. On the Alpine front, the DTF at Nice of the 25th Military Region was responsible for the work on the Maritime Alps. The remainder of the Alpine sectors was the responsibility of the DTF at Grenoble of the 24th Military District. This arrangement accounts for the similarities and differences between the blocks of the various forts. Colonel Ph. Truttmann, one of the foremost authorities on the Maginot Line, pointed out that this organization gave the French military engineers a great deal of flexibility, allowing them to erect forts eminently suited to their surrounding terrain and their mission. The German fortifications, on the other hand, were designed by a central command and built largely from unmodified plans in total disregard of the actual situation.

The designs for the *ouvrages* evolved over time. In late 1926, the CDF (*Commission de Défense des Frontières*; Frontier Defense Commission) proposed plans for an *ouvrage puissant* (powerful fort) and an intermediate *ouvrage*. The blueprint for the *ouvrage puissant* included several features that became standard in the Maginot fortifications. Its combat blocks were detached from the entrance and linked by a central gallery to its underground *caserne* in the support area. One plan showed close groups of combat blocks consisting of two small blocks and one large block. The large block, almost ninety meters in length and about thirty meters at its widest point, included two turrets for *lance-bombes* and a pair of casemated howitzers on each flank. A short distance to the fore, on each of its flanks, was a small combat block that mounted a machine gun turret and had three machine gun casemate positions. One of the machine guns in each of these two blocks covered the flank of the fort, and another covered a howitzer casemate of the large block. The other machine gun casemate positions covered the space between the two smaller blocks. Only the machine gun turret on these two blocks and the *lance-bombes* turrets of the main block were capable of firing to the front of the fort. Flanking casemates for machine guns and artillery weapons and turrets with weapons that could fire to the front of the *ouvrage* ultimately became standard features on the combat blocks of the Maginot Line. However, CORF discarded the close grouping of blocks, the type of combat blocks, and the rigid form of the *ouvrage pouissant* in favor of a modified version of Colonel Tricaud's palm fort. The Superior Council of War also approved the modified palm fort.

The intermediate *ouvrage* proposed by the CDF was a rather standardized position with flanking machine guns in casemates and a pair of machine gun turrets. Except for the fields of fire for weapons, this blueprint was replaced with a more adaptable *petit ouvrage* (PO) that varied in size and armament; its mission was to close the gaps between the large forts.

The large forts proposed by CORF became known as *artillery* or *gros ouvrages* (GOs). In addition to being larger than the POs, they were for the most part the only forts to mount artillery weapons. Due to the diversity of the terrain from one site to another, no two identical forts were built on the line. CORF only standardized the components and features of the support area, which included the *usine* (power plant) and the *caserne* but not the overall design of this part of the *ouvrage*. The same was true for most combat blocks, which had to be adapted to their location and role.

CORF also took up the question of armaments, but its recommendations changed significantly between 1928 and the 1930s. In 1928, it proposed turrets of 145-mm guns to serve as long-range artillery (range of 18 to 20 km). For example, the advanced project plans for the massive *ouvrage* of Hochwald in the area of Strasbourg included an eastern and a western *ouvrage* (or *demi-ouvrage*), and an elevated site to the rear of these combat blocks with turrets for 145-mm or 155-mm and 75-mm guns (Wahl, *Hochwald*, p. 19). These plans followed the pre–World War I pattern of Fort Douaumont at Verdun—which had 155-mm gun turrets—and Fort Suchet (Barbonnet) in the Alps, where the older twin-gun Mougin turrets remained in use. Although CORF dropped plans for these turrets, it still considered using five naval turrets with 340-mm guns (see Chapter 4) as heavy, long-range artillery for the Maginot Line in 1931. However, this expensive project soon fell by the wayside.

After the dissolution of CORF, over ninety rail guns from the Great War era, ranging from 164 mm to 400 mm in caliber, were slated to support the forts of the Maginot Line. In the first year of the war, most of these big guns were moved into position behind the *secteurs fortifiés* (fortified sectors; SFs) of the Northeast Front, and a few were sent to the Southeast Front. Most of these rail guns took up to an hour to install in their battery firing position, and their mobility was limited by the location of the military controlled rail lines (Ferrard, *France 1940*, pp. 222–227).

When the Great Depression hit France in 1930, it imposed serious budget restraints on military spending. As a result, limits were placed not only on the type of weapons and supporting equipment to be acquired, but also, in the years that followed, on the size and number of *ouvrages* to be built. Thus, in the RF of Metz, where work was under way on defenses that extended to the left flank along the Luxembourg and south Belgian border to protect the iron-producing region of the Briey-Longwy-Longuyon arc, the building project was downsized. The original option would have encircled Longwy and followed the Belgian border on the north side (left bank) of the Chiers River with eight GOs and one PO. In 1930, the government opted for the shorter extension of the Maginot Line to the vicinity of Longuyon with only six new GOs. CORF cancelled one of the planned GOs, changed two to POs, and added a third PO.

During the next few years, as a result of the economic cuts, three GOs and three POs were cancelled in SF Haguenau, on the right flank of the RF of the Lauter, where the course of the line had already been altered. Plans to build several *ouvrages* in the SFs of the RF of Haute-Alsace and three *ouvrages* that were to control the Sarre Gap and the Vosges were called off. Finally, a number of GOs still under construction in 1934 had to be downscaled to the status of POs because of lack of funding. Thus, insufficient funding and the need to modernize the armed forces during an era of economic crisis reduced the scale of the projected Great Wall of France.

Initial Funding of the Fortifications

In 1928, the Superior War Council had requested 3,760 million francs for the first priority work. In December 1929, the government reduced that amount, approving only 2,900 million francs in credits for the construction of the fortifications. During the next year, since the RF of Metz was expanded from

TABLE 2-1. Initial funding of the fortifications (millions of francs)

	Nord Sectors	RF Metz	RF Lauter	Rhine	Alpine	Mobile Parks
Dec 1929	50	1,498	836	63	180	233
Nov 1930	50	1,898	836	63	362	233
Dec 1929 for fortifications		1,008	493	40	Allotment of funds on NE front	
Dec 1929 for equipment		345	210	18		
Dec 1929 for arms/munition		144	133	5		

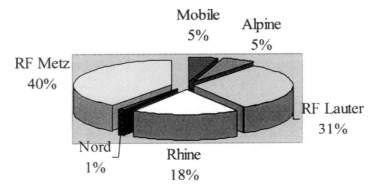

FIGURE 2-1. Nord, northern sector along Belgian border; Rhine, Rhine defenses; Mobile, mobile parks for creating field fortifications near border.

Rochonvillers to Longuyon and additional work was needed to defend the Alpine front in the southeast, the credits were raised to 3,442 million francs. The northeast front received 95% of the credits and the southeast front, only 5% (Table 2.1).

The *Génie* had done some experimental work before 1929, so when actual construction of the Maginot Line was about to begin in 1930, CORF designs were already available. Over half of the army engineers of France would be involved in this massive project for most of the decade; the project included fortifications in Corsica and the Mareth Line in Tunisia as well (Truttmann, "La Fortification," p. 42). The RFs, as the most heavily defended areas, would each receive a line of *ouvrages*.

These *ouvrages* formed the core or backbone of the defenses designed to engage in combat in the main line of resistance. By the time the government appropriated the funds and construction actually began, the number of RFs had been reduced to two: the RF of Metz and the RF of Lauter. Since the work needed to be nearly completed before the evacuation of the Rhineland in 1935 and budget restraints were instituted, not only was the RF of Haute-Alsace (Belfort) eliminated, but also the encircling *fossés*

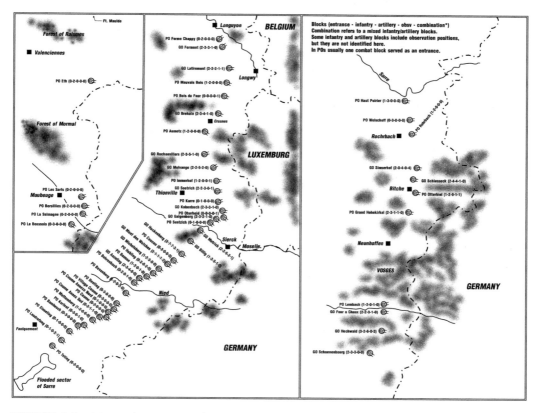

FIGURE 2-2. Map in three sections showing Maginot fortifications (the Extension is missing). [© Tomasz Idzikowski]

(moats) for the GOs were eliminated. In the few new forts where the *fossé* was actually built, it was only partially built. After years of discussion and planning, in the rush to begin the work, the first of the forts were built for outdated weapons systems and had to undergo improvements. This included small antitank (AT) gun positions for weapons that were still at the developmental stage. As a result, the first positions to be built accommodated only the 37-mm Mle 1934 AT gun and were unable to house the larger 47-mm Mle 1934 AT gun. In the case of the 75-mm turret guns, perfected a little earlier than the AT guns, the fit was less problematical. However, some of the earliest models had to be installed as is because they were too expensive to discard. When the Maginot Line went into operation, there was a still a shortage of gun turrets for the new projects.

The initial work on the Maginot Line in the Northeast Front eventually became known as the *Anciens Fronts* or (Old Fronts) (Table 2.2). On the Maginot Line Proper, the groundwork began in the RF of Metz at the end of 1929 on the sites of the *ouvrages* of Hackenberg and Rochonvillers. In the RF of Lauter, it started at Simershof and Hochwald. Hackenberg and Hochwald included sections of a *fossé* and AT walls covering the area between their two groups of combat blocks. However, the plans for extending these obstacles or building them at other *ouvrages* were soon abandoned. The

TABLE 2-2. Distribution of *ouvrages*

Sectors	Ouvrages					
	Old Fronts (NE Front)		New Fronts (NE Front)		Alpine Front (SE Front)	
	Gros	*Petit*	*Gros*	*Petit*	*Gros*	*Petit*
Escaut				1		
Maubeuge				4		
Montmedy			2	2		
Crusnes	3	4				
Thionville	7	4				
Boulay	4	11				
Faulquemont		5				
Sarre				1		
Rohrbach	2	1		2		
Vosges	2	1				
Haguenau	2					
Savoie					5	4
Dauphine					4	12
Maritime Alps					14	16
Subtotal	20	26	2	10	23	32[a]
Total	22 GOs and 31 POs Maginot Line, 5 POs Maubeuge				23	32[a]

[a]The POs of the SE Front were much smaller in scale than the POs of the NE front, and some were not even completed.

construction continued through 1934; eighteen GOs and twenty-six POs were completed. The next building period involved the *Nouveaux Fronts* (New Fronts).

By 1931, much of the work on interval positions—including CORF casemates, *abris*, and observatories—was well under way or complete, while work on subterranean sections of the GOs, which in most cases included extensive tunneling, was still in progress. During the next year, many of the individual blocks of the *ouvrages* neared completion while the weapons and armor were still being prepared. By 1933, the *ouvrages* were largely completed. In 1934, the mechanical equipment, including engines, filter systems, and lifts, were installed in the *ouvrages*. Planning for the New Fronts began in the same year. As the Old Fronts approached completion in 1935, construction on the New Fronts began, and that lasted until about 1938. The New Fronts included the extension (Table 2.3) of the left flank of the RF of Lauter with the addition of the POs in two sectors, linking up with the Sarre sector and creating the Maginot Extension in the sector of Montmédy. The sector of Maubeuge received several POs, but three planned GOs were not built. In 1935, as work began on the New Fronts, the *ouvrages* of the Old Fronts were readied for action, and an almost continuous line of AT obstacles was set

TABLE 2-3. Number of fortified sectors

Maginot Extension	1 Fortified sector
RF of Metz	4 Fortified sectors
RF of Lauter	3 Fortified sectors

along the Maginot Line Proper (Hohnadel and Truttmann, *Guide*, pp. 4–5). CORF had planned to erect two POs at Oberroedern and Bremmelbach on either side of the GO Schoenenbourg to secure the right flank of the RF of Lauter, but like many other projected *ouvrages*, they never materialized, and only a couple of casemates occupied their sites.

While it worked on the Old Fronts, the army also began laying out the Rhine defenses with the construction of two lines of casemates in 1931. These defenses were not actually part of the Maginot Line Proper because they included no *ouvrages*. The front itself was not classified as an RF even though most maps and older sources include it in the Maginot Line. One line of the Rhine defenses ran along the river and the other further behind it through the "Line of Villages." An additional line consisted of casemates blocking key points along the river and generally providing flanking fires along the Rhine. These positions lacked adequate concealment, besides camouflage, because they were built into the riverbank.

The Southeast Front, which ran along the Alps, consisted of several sectors. New designs, which included many of the CORF features, were created specifically for this front, where the mountainous terrain required special adaptations. Construction on these Alpine sectors actually began prior to work in the northeast because of the political situation in Italy and because General Nivelle reported that the military situation in the region was poor. In 1925, General Degoutte, after transferring from the Rhineland to the Alpine command, proposed some concrete solutions. He initiated a study for the construction of positions at Rimplas to dominate the valley of the Tinée and at Flaut to control the Vésubie Valley. He also recommended the strengthening of Fort Barbonnet, which overlooks Sospel and the northern approach to Nice (Truttmann, "La Fortification").

Work began on the *ouvrage* of Rimplas in September 1928 even though CORF had not yet approved the final details and was still preparing instructions. Degoutte's study did not satisfy General Debeney. By 1930, only the main gallery had been excavated, and the entrances and scarp wall were still under construction. In 1931, plans for creating and installing the artillery of this unusual fort in gun chambers cut into the rock were overruled by CORF, which insisted that the guns be placed in casemates built according to its own specifications. The CDF report of February 1929 recommended the creation of the three SFs of the southeast (Savoy, Dauphiné—named Haute Durrance at the time—and Maritime Alps). Marshal Pétain, displeased with Degoutte's initial work, insisted on standardization. To cut construction costs, the Alpine positions were to be built only at critical points and, when possible, the work was to be done on or tied into old Séré de Rivières forts like Barbonnet (Truttmann, "La Fortification"). Rimplas, which was completed in late in 1934, was unusual because it had two different gallery levels because of its location. It must be pointed out that other *ouvrages* of the Southeast Front also had unusual features not found in the northeast.

Work on most of the other Alpine *ouvrages* did not begin until 1931 and later. However, a few like St. Roch were started late in 1930 (Hohandel and Truttmann, *Guide*, pp. 5, 94). Construction on the Southeast Front, whether major or minor, was slow because it had to stop for almost half of the year due to the long, harsh Alpine winters. It took almost a decade to complete these mountain forts. Thus, some were not completed until 1938, and others were not completed at all (Mary, *Maginot*, p. 15).

Following the Mussolini-Laval accord of January 1935, the government ordered a moratorium an all construction on the Alpine front. However, the invasion of Ethiopia in the fall of that year triggered a resumption of the work, but much of the construction season was lost. After 1936, more sites that had not received primary urgency in the southeast now received priority.

In 1937, an ambitious project was launched on the Authion Plateau, which acted like a natural fort, blocking the northern approach to Sospel and Nice. Several high-altitude *ouvrages* were built on this plateau at an altitude of over nineteen hundred meters or higher. Despite the abbreviated construction season, the *ouvrage* of Restefond (at an altitude of two thousand meters) and several others were finished before the war began, in the space of only two summers. The *ouvrage* of Plan-Caval, located at an altitude of nineteen hundred, was one of the few that were not finished.

In front of the main line of resistance in the Northeast as well as the Southeast Fronts, there was a line of advanced posts or outposts called *avant postes*, smaller positions that generally did not require special designs. On the Northeast Front, near the border, they included special fortified houses that covered key avenues of approach and a variety of small concrete blockhouses with road barriers further back from the border, several kilometers in front of the Maginot Line. The *avant postes* on the Southeast Front served the same purpose but usually occupied key elevated positions, usually only a few kilometers in front of the main line and often within sight of a GO. However, only the SF of the Maritime Alps had a line of *avant-postes*. The other two Alpine sectors had no such line, although there were some advanced positions, including old forts far in front of the main line in the SF of Savoy. Unlike on the Northeast Front, these positions often consisted of a cluster of small bunkers linked by trenches or tunnels, from which the troops could observe and direct weapons on the enemy. In some circumstances, the Alpine posts could be used as firing positions.

When CORF was dissolved in January 1936, the task of designing new casemates devolved on the *Service Techniques du Génie* (STG). Many of these STG casemates and blockhouses were built in the Defensive Sector of the Sarre, the Defensive Sector of Marville between the Maginot Line Proper and the Extension, and other gaps in the line of defenses. A few even mounted 75-mm field pieces. The STG, no longer under the supervision of CORF, received instructions directly from the high command and had to prepare low-cost designs.

Later in the 1930s, almost as an afterthought, work began on a rear line, called *Ligne d' Arrêt* (Stop Line), to halt any possible breakthrough. This line, which was never completed, consisted of smaller non-CORF blockhouses built by a military labor force called *main d'oeuvre militaire* (MOM) and known as MOM bunkers. The MOM also built a number of positions in the main line of defense in the Northeast Front and most of the blockhouses and casemates of the Southeast Front.

THE OUVRAGES

The *ouvrages* of the Maginot Line can be divided into two types: artillery and infantry. The artillery *ouvrages*, the largest type, are known as GOs, whereas the smaller infantry *ouvrages* are classified as POs. The GOs share a number of standard features with layout and size that vary to fit the surrounding terrain. The POs, on the other hand, are more varied. Some POs were originally GOs that were not completed or were altered during construction. All *ouvrages* were designed by CORF and, as a rule, include:

1. A support area: *caserne* (troops barracks or quarters and facilities), *usine* (power plant), storage areas (usually in the *caserne*), and the main magazine (known as the M-1) with annexes for such items as grenades and fuses.
2. A combat area: magazines (known as M-2) for artillery blocks, a substation for converting power sent from the *usine*, and command posts. The largest *ouvrages* usually had two separate groups of combat blocks.

The size of the garrison and the location of the fort determined its final design. Some features, such as command posts and observation blocks, were located in either area, depending on the situation. Generally, the main gallery connecting the support and combat areas was long enough to warrant the use of a *metro* (subway). Smaller lateral galleries branch off the main gallery to link the combat blocks, giving them access to the subterranean facilities. In the support area, the facilities were either adjacent to the main gallery or linked by access galleries.

The subterranean facilities are generally located about thirty meters below the surface to provide maximum protection from the heaviest artillery, but there are a few exceptions to this rule. The only entrances and, usually, an emergency escape exit are located in the support area. Except for small exits in some of the combat blocks, there was no other access to the fort.

Power cables linked the support area to a fortified substation, which in turn tied into the national power grid for peacetime operation or when attack was not imminent. Those power lines usually were buried underground in the area near the *ouvrage*. Some GOs were connected to neighboring *ouvrages* through underground cables. A small transformer station, usually made of brick, was located in the vicinity of the fort. A military road gave access to the fort, and in many cases, depending on the type of entrance and the location, a 0.60 narrow-gauge military railroad also served the *ouvrages*. Usually, a regular or temporary *caserne* was located nearby so that the garrison would not have to live underground until an actual threat materialized.

The distance between the support area and the combat area varies from several hundred meters (usually about a half kilometer) to less than one hundred meters, depending on the terrain. As a result, the main gallery can extend for a kilometer or more, from one end of the support area to the last access gallery of the combat blocks. In a few GOs, like Mont du Welches, the support area and the combat blocks are intermingled; in others, like Grand Hohekirkel, they are adjacent to each other. When the main gallery was short, a *metro* was unnecessary. In several GOs, like Hackenberg, where there are two separate groups of combat blocks, the main gallery splits to link each section to the service area. The GO of Hochwald is so large that it has two support areas, one for each group of combat blocks.[2] This small sample of *ouvrages* highlights the uniqueness of each *ouvrage* because of its adaptation to the local situation (Table 2.4).

The GO usually has two entrance blocks with facades that face the rear. The larger entrance is the munitions entrance (*entrée des munitions*, EM), and the smaller is the

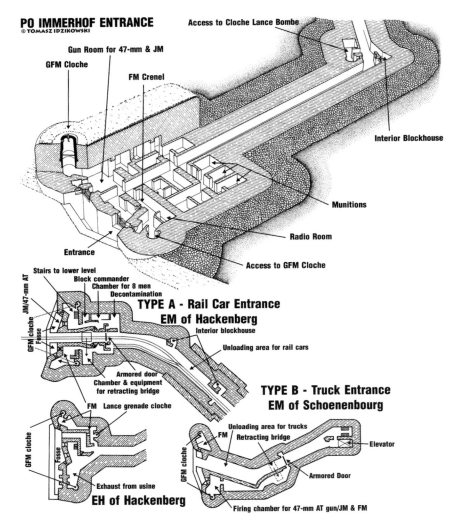

FIGURE 2-3. Examples of types of entrances of Maginot *ouvrages*. [© Tomasz Idzikowski]

men's entrance (*entrée des hommes*, EH). In a few GOs, a single mixed entrance served both men and munitions. There are two basic types of EMs: Type A for handling rail cars from the military railway, especially laid out to serve it, and Type B for trucks. Type A could also accommodate trucks. A *fossé* protects the EM's exposed façade; its name, fossé *diamant* (diamond moat), is derived from its distinctive angular shape.

Machine gun and AT gun positions behind the moat covered the entrance. On top of the block, an observation/machine gun cloche covered the approaches to the entrance. The standard cloches were bell-shaped, fixed turrets that could mount a 50-mm breech-loaded mortar and automatic rifles. In addition, a special *lance-grenade* cloche was installed to shower the area with grenades (or mortar bombs). However, none of these 60-mm weapons was ready for installation in time for the war. A small concrete bridge spanned the moat into a vestibule that was secured by a heavy steel grating. At

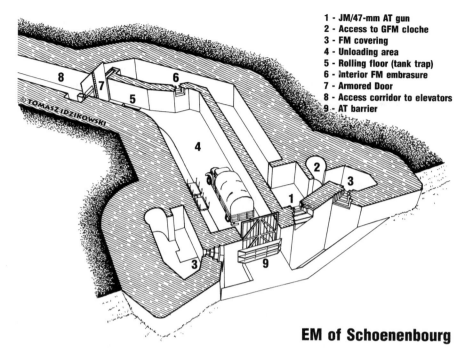

1 - JM/47-mm AT gun
2 - Access to GFM cloche
3 - FM covering
4 - Unloading area
5 - Rolling floor (tank trap)
6 - Interior FM embrasure
7 - Armored Door
8 - Access corridor to elevators
9 - AT barrier

© TOMASZ IDZIKOWSKI

EM of Schoenenbourg

FIGURE 2-4. Type B entrance of Schoenenbourg. [© Tomasz Idzikowski]

TABLE 2-4. Examples of *gros ouvrages* main galleries

Gros Ouvrage	Length of Main Gallery between Combat and Support Areas[a]	Total Length of Main Gallery
Fermont	550 meters	1,250 meters (1.25 km)
Brehain	700 meters	1,400 meters (1.40 km)
Rochonvillers	1,200 meters[b]	2,250 meters (2.25km)
Molvange	Combat area overlapped support area	1,750 meters (1.75 km)
Soetrich	125 meters	625 meters (0.62 km)
Galgenberg	Combat area overlapped support area	425 meters (0.42 km)
Métrich	150 meters	1,250 meters (1.25 km)
Hackenberg	425 meters[c]	2,250 meters (2.25 km)
Mont des Welches	Combat and support areas together	200 meters (0.20 km)
Simserhof	500 meters[c]	1,600 meters (1.60 km)
Hochwald	2 support and 2 combat areas	4,000+ meters (over 4.km)

[a]Lengths are approximations within fifty meters.
[b]A combat block located between support and combat areas.
[c]Main gallery splits to serve two combat areas.

the end of the entrance corridor, a "rolling" armored door split into two sections and slid into the adjacent walls, allowing access into the block. In one panel of the door, there was a man-size door. The grating gate could block access to the fort while the armored door remained open to allow fresh air to flow into the *ouvrage*. A machine gun position covered the length of the vestibule. In Type A entrances, a tank trap in front of the armored door was exposed when a small metal rolling bridge was cranked back into the wall. In Type B entrances, a heavy AT barrier in front of the grating gate swung outward across the concrete bridge to allow vehicles to enter. The shape and number of defensive positions such as weapons embrasures, interior blockhouses, and cloches defending the EM varied depending on the location.

Access to the subterranean support area from the entrance blocks was accomplished in three different ways. The most desirable type from an EM was a level approach to the main gallery; however, in many cases it was impossible to achieve. In that case, the main underground gallery was reached by an inclined access gallery. These generally had an incline of 25% (50% in the Alpine *ouvrages*). The access galleries with the steepest incline required special rail cars to trans-ship supplies from the entrance block to the underground main gallery. If an inclined access gallery was not feasible, the munitions supply carts were lowered from the EM to the main gallery by elevators. Generally, there was only one subterranean level in the *ouvrages*, unlike the many fantasized drawings showing multiple levels.

The type of access from the EM to the main gallery is related to the topography of the area defended. Thus, in the area between Longuyon—where the GO of Fermont was located—to the area near Thionville—where the GO of Kobenbusch was placed— almost all of the EMs had elevators to access the main gallery. Only a couple of *ouvrages* had inclines. The elevator option was selected because most of the terrain defended by the GOs consisted of rolling hills that did not offer sufficient depth to the rear of the *ouvrage*, near the base of a hill, to accommodate a level entrance. In the area between Galgenberg and Anzeling, most of the GOs, except Anzeling, Billig, and Mt. des Welches, had level entrances. The three exceptions had inclined access galleries. The selection of this particular design was dictated by the terrain, which offered sharper relief so that the support areas and EMs could occupy a rear area at an elevation well below the site occupied by the combat blocks.

Hackenberg and Métrich are good examples of forts situated on very large, high hills (or mountains, depending on the definition of the terms). Anzeling had an inclined entrance because it occupied a low ridge that nonetheless dominated its surroundings. In the RF of Lauter, the GOs, with the exception of Four-au-Chaux and Schoenenbourg, had level entrances because the Vosges presented a much more dramatic relief than the area around Metz. This made it possible to select commanding sites for *ouvrages* with the optimum conditions required to create the most desirable features for the fortifications. Only Schoenenbourg required elevators in the EM because it was located in a relatively flat area, although there was sharper relief not far behind it, where an *abri* was located.

The EH had a smaller, "L"-shaped entryway. At the point where the entrance made a 90° turn, there was a blockhouse position for an *fusil-mitrailleur* (FM) that could fire through the grating gate of the entrance. The armored door stood behind the point where the hallway turned, out of the line of direct enemy fire. A small removable metal footbridge spanned the *fossé*. From this entrance, access to the subterranean works was either level or by stairs, the latter was preferred because it presented an additional obstacle. In fact, it is not uncommon for EHs to be located higher than the EM. In both EHs and EMs where access to the gallery was at a different level, the troops used stairs because the elevators were intended strictly for the transport of munitions and important persons. In mixed entrances, direct or level access was preferred because this type of entrance served as both a troop and a munitions entrance. In most cases, entrance blocks were large, especially the EMs and mixed entrances. The EHs were generally not large. In some POs, such as Lembach and Haut Poirier, the entrance consisted of little more than a defended armored door smaller than the average EH.

The EM linked directly to the main gallery, giving direct access to the main magazine, the M-1. The EH, on the other hand, usually led to the caserne and *usine*. However, because the location of the *usine* varied widely in the GOs, the EH did not always end there. Ducts in the façade of the EM or EH allowed the escape of fumes from the *usine*. In some cases, the *usine* was too far from either entrance, and a special "chimney block" was needed.

In general, the *usine* of a GO consisted of several chambers with four diesel engines, storage tanks for diesel fuel, oil, and cooling water. In addition, a substation in the *ouvrage* housed a set of converters that stepped down the voltage for use in the *ouvrage*. The same converters stepped the voltage up for transmission across the *ouvrage* to the combat block area, where it was converted at another substation. The converters in the usine also had to increase the voltage for use by the electric trains of the GOs. When the generators were in use, the noise level was extremely high in the confined chambers, which reeked with the pungent smell of diesel. The *usine* was very much like the engine room of a ship, except that the temperature was much cooler because of the underground location. Due to the depth at which the galleries were built, a bone-chilling dampness permeated the entire fort, increasing the gloom. When the fort was on a war footing and its outside power supply was shut off, its diesels engines were activated. Two of the four diesels provided all the needs of the entire GO. However, Hochwald was so large that each of its two support areas had a separate *usine* with four diesel engines.

The *casernes* of a GO varied in size, depending on the required garrison. They included sleeping quarters with triple bunks for the troops to share because there were not enough to accommodate the entire garrison at the same time. Separate chambers for the noncommissioned officers and officers were located nearby, as was a small private room for the commanding officer. Latrines with septic tanks and showers were near the troop chambers. A state-of-the-art kitchen and food and wine storage areas were also located in the *caserne*. Several rooms housed an infirmary with an operating room and a small recovery room. Some of the larger *ouvrages* also included a dentist office. The troops could spend some of their free time in a recreation room or canteen with a radio for entertainment. The miscreants ran the risk of cooling their heels in one of the tiny cells in the small detention area.

The filter room where the incoming air could be purified in case of gas attack was located near the *caserne* and the *usine*. There were additional filters in most of the blocks of the *ouvrage*. Moreover, the garrison carried gas masks in case of an emergency. Fresh air was drawn into the fort through armored air vents mounted on casemate walls or roofs. Stale air was forced out through the cloches and other embrasures. During normal operations, the armored doors of the *ouvrage* were left open, and the air could flow through the closed grill gate. When the fort was in action, the armored doors at the entrance and the airtight doors (armored or metal) inside the entrance block and in the access galleries were shut. The electrically operated ventilators, which could be operated manually in an emergency, brought air in from the air vents and maintained a state of overpressure inside the *ouvrage* to prevent outside gases from seeping in. When the weapons in the firing chambers and cloches were fired, the tubes connected to them carried the gases to the outside.

In case of a gas attack, the air entering though the air vents moved through the filter system and was purified, then distributed throughout the *ouvrage*. Since the filters had to be replaced after a certain number of hours of operation, they were not in constant use. In the event the filtering system failed, technicians chemically would test for poison gas; if they found any, they would sound the alarms in the *ouvrage* so the troops could don their gas masks.

During construction, a well was drilled, usually in the support area, to keep the garrison supplied with water.[3] A large water tank was situated near the well. One utility the *ouvrage* lacked was a large enough area to store the trash and garbage generated by a garrison during an extended occupation.

In or near the support area, a secret escape chamber allowed access to the surface. It was normally filled with sand, which emptied into another chamber below when the hatch was opened. As the sand seeped away, it revealed a vertical tunnel with a ladder that led toward the surface, where a hatch covered with a thin layer of soil and vegetation was pulled open.

Since groundwater seeped into the galleries, a drainage system was installed beneath the gallery floor. The water drained to the lowest end of the *ouvrage*, usually in or near the support area, where a drain carried it out. A firing embrasure covered much of the length of this drain because it was generally large enough to serve as an emergency escape.

Most GOs had a large main ammunition magazine of several chambers. Chicane-type entrances to the magazine storage cells protected against accidents. The main magazine, the M-1, was designed with safety features such as curved access galleries branching off the main gallery that allowed rail cars to be rolled in but deflected the force of an accidental explosion. The train engine did not operate in the M-1 because of fear that sparks might trigger an accidental explosion. A sprinkler system in the ceiling of the M-1 cells that held the powder was the first line of defense against an accidental fire in the magazine. In the *ouvrages* where this system was not available, firefighting equipment was supplied. A few GOs and the POs, which rarely had artillery weapons, had no M-1. Also, located off the main gallery near the M-1 were annexes for storage of sensitive items like fuses and grenades, a garage for the train, and workshops. A large armored door sealed the main gallery from the M-1 or the caserne. This door was equipped with a mechanism that, when manually tripped, automatically slammed the door shut in the event of an explosion in the magazine. A small passageway went around the armored door.

The facilities in the support area and the main gallery were damp and chilly, but the individual chambers were generally well illuminated. The lights in dimly lit galleries were installed along the walls. An array of power and communications cables, usually set on shelves, ran below them, and there was a duplicate set along the opposite wall. The rails of the *metro* ran in the middle of the main gallery. The power arm of the electric engine drew electricity from an overhead cable to which it was connected. However, there was no overhead power source above the rail spurs going into the M-1 and the access galleries of most of the combat blocks. Here, the troops had to push the wagons or use a mobile power arm. The train, not intended for movement of troops, served mainly to deliver munitions and food to the combat area. The number of train stations depended on the length of the main gallery. In general, these stations were mere sidings where the train could pull off.

At the point where the main gallery reached the area of the combat blocks, the cables from the *usine* in the service area fed power to a substation with converters that stepped down the power for the blocks and the subterranean facilities supporting them. GOs with very long galleries and two combat areas had two or more of these substations. A large fort, like Hackenberg, had as many as four.

Most of the mechanical equipment and machinery, such as the turrets, the train, the elevators, and the lighting system, were operated with electrical power. If the power system failed, the *ouvrages* resorted to emergency lighting, mainly kerosene lamps. The turrets could be rotated and raised manually. The train, however, depended on electrical power, but individual rail cars could be pushed by the soldiers if needed. Each artillery block was provided with its own magazines of ready ammunition (the M-3) so it could maintain combat operations.

At least one set of niches in the walls of the main gallery provided room for explosive charges that could be detonated to seal the passage in the event the enemy penetrated into the subterranean sections of the fort. There were also one or two other armored doors in the main gallery beside the one near the M-1. The access galleries were usually fitted with a set of more lightly armored airtight doors.

There was no standard location for the fort's command post, although its optimal emplacement was near an observation block, except at Hackenberg, where the command post was situated on a separate level, above the main gallery and below the two observation blocks on the highest ridge occupied by the *ouvrage*. The command post included offices for the commander of the fort and for the commanders of the infantry, artillery, and engineers of *ouvrages*. The calculations for firing the guns and sending the firing instructions to the blocks were done in a larger work area adjoining a communications room. The command posts included topographic maps and photomosaic maps of the terrain around the *ouvrage* so plotters could quickly identify the location of targets as reports flowed from the observation positions. The firing data for all gun positions were preplanned. However, the guns covered nonmilitary terrain; they could not be test fired and zeroed in on possible targets before the war.

The combat blocks were the most important element of the *ouvrages*; without them, the *ouvrages* served no purpose.[4] There were several types of combat blocks based on their use and form. Usually, they contained infantry- or artillery-type weapons for engaging the enemy. These blocks, built of ferro-concrete, were built as a casemate (generally for flanking fire), as a turret block, or as a combination of the two. Most blocks mounted one or more types of nonrotating steel domes known as *cloches* because of their bell-like shape. They became one of the distinguishing features of the Maginot fortifications. A few blocks had no casemate or turret but several cloches that, in many cases, formed a position known as an observation block.

The combat blocks for artillery and infantry usually normally consisted of two levels that accommodated crews of twenty to thirty men. The upper level of a casemate block mounted the weapons and included a place for the ready supply of ammunition and an M-3 magazine.[5] At the lower level, there usually was a rest area for the troops, the command post for the block, and filters. In a casemate block, a small exit with interior defenses might be found in one of the two levels. The artillery turret block also consisted of two levels. The equipment for operating and retracting the turret occupied both levels, and the M-3 magazine was on the upper level.[6] There were also a number of mixed blocks with turrets and casemates. The 81-mm breech loaded mortar in casemate was the only weapon to be installed on the lower level.

The combat block was linked to the main gallery by a stairway and an access gallery. An elevator installed in the artillery blocks transported the munitions from the lower level to the second. Spent casings from 75-mm and 135-mm rounds dropped into a room at the gallery level via a tobogganlike chute.

In addition, artillery blocks had large M-2 magazines at the gallery level, which usually consisted of two chambers, and a smaller M-3 magazine. Ammunition containers were moved from the M-2 to the lifts along monorails attached to the ceiling. In the combat block above, the system of monorails continued, moving the containers to the M-3 and to the turret's *monte-charge* that carried the ammunition up to the guns or to the gun positions in casemates.

The observation blocks generally mounted no weapons, except if they included a *guêt-fusil mitrailleur* (GFM) or *jumelage de mitrailleuses* (JM) cloche, and generally contained only cloches of various types for observation. Many combat blocks played the dual role of observation and combat; in some *ouvrages*, there were no observation blocks at all. In the last case, the fort had to rely solely on the combat blocks for observation or observatories in the intervals.

WEAPONS, CLOCHES, AND TURRETS

The fighting power of the *ouvrages* rested in their weapons and in the casemates, cloches, and turrets that protected them. Although heavy artillery had been considered for the *ouvrages* during the early planning stages, the scheme was soon dropped because the *ouvrages* occupied positions in the main line of resistance rather than behind it, rendering heavy artillery impractical. The GO of the Barbonnet in the Alps, which was built alongside an older fort with heavy artillery in turrets, is one of the few exceptions. However, since it was actually located behind the main line of *ouvrages* of the Maritimes Alps, its heavy artillery did not pose the same problem. In general, though, the Maginot forts were intended to engage in direct combat against enemy forces attempting to breach the line. Relatively rapid firing weapons capable of engaging infantry and tanks allowed the *ouvrages* to fulfill their role as combat positions. Supporting positions and the French air force behind the Maginot Line had the mission of engaging enemy artillery.

The *ouvrages* not only lacked heavy artillery, but also had no antiaircraft weapons. In 1928, the CORF rejected the 37-mm antiaircraft gun for the new forts because open positions on the surface of the *ouvrages* would have left them vulnerable to bombardment. On the other hand, the creation of permanent positions, like those of the Greek

Metaxas Line built several years later, may have jeopardized the hard protective shell of the Maginot forts. It was deemed preferable, therefore, to leave air defense to field units and the air force.

The weapons selected for the Maginot forts included infantry weapons and light and medium artillery. The infantry weapons consisted of automatic rifles, machine guns, mortars, and AT weapons. The automatic rifle adopted was a standard weapon of the French army after the 1920s. The FM 1924/1929 (Model 1924 modified in 1929) was the automatic rifle used in almost every *ouvrage* block and interval casemate. In some cases, it was adapted to a special stand to be used as an antiaircraft weapon. These weapons fired a 7.5-mm round at a rate of two hundred to four hundred rounds per minutes with a range of up to two thousand meters (effective range about five hundred meters). This weapon was modified in 1930 by General Reibel, who created a drum-fed machine gun known as the *Mitrailleuse* MAC 1931 (MAC, Munitions Factory of Chatellerault) that fired 750 rounds per minute when firing alternately in pairs with a range of up to 4,900 meters (effective range about 1,200 meters). The fortress version of this weapon was slightly different from the one used by the air force and motorized units. It consisted of a pair of these weapons mounted together, creating a so-called *jumelage de mitralleuse* (JM). The local defense of the Maginot forts was ensured by a number of FM and JM in casemates and cloches. When mounted in a casemate, the JM was connected to the casemate wall by tubes: one carrying the gases out of the gunroom and the other dropping expended shell casings into the *fossé*.

Another standard infantry weapon of the Maginot Line was the 50-mm Mortar Mle 1935. This breech-loaded weapon had a range of about eight hundred meters and was able to fire ten to fifteen rounds per minute. It was primarily used in cloches, and in some cases, it was also installed in casemate and turret (mixed-arms [armes mixtes, AM]) positions. A 60-mm Mortar Mle 1931, with an automatic loader, with a higher rate of fire for use in a special grenade-throwing cloche in entrance blocks was planned but not developed in time for the war.

The standard crew-served AT gun was the 47-mm AC (antichar or AT) Fortress Mle 1934. It had a rate of fire of twenty rounds per minute with an effective range of one thousand meters. It was meant to replace the 37-mm AC Fortress Mle 1934 but turned out to be too large for most of the existing casemates. The 25-mm AC Fortress Mle 1934 had a similar range as the other two weapons, about half the penetrating power, and a faster rate of fire. It was small enough to be used in special cloches and the machine gun turrets.

The 13.2-mm Hotchkiss Mle 1930 was a heavy machine gun with a limited AT capability. It had a range of about 2,500 meters (effective range 800 meters) and a rate of fire of 450 rounds per minute. It served as an antiboat gun in some Rhine casemates and as an AT weapon on some of the casemates in the Vosges but was not used in the *ouvrages*.

One other infantry weapon used in the Maginot fortifications was known as the *goulotte lance-grenades* (a grenade launcher) and consisted of a tube placed at a 45° angle in a casemate wall. A mechanical piece at the end of the tube inside the casemate was opened, and a standard defensive grenade, Type F1, was placed inside. In normal use, the grenade's safety ring was removed, but the fuse did not become active until after the curved handle popped off as the grenade left the soldier's hand as it was thrown toward a target. In the fort, the entire grenade, with the safety ring still on, was placed inside the apparatus. When it was activated, the grenade launcher removed the ring as the grenade was pushed into the tube. The grenade then slid out into the *fossé*, where it detonated. This apparatus was the standard protection for casemates with a *fossé*.

The heaviest piece of artillery used in the *ouvrages* was the 75-mm cannon. This modified version of the famous "75" from World War I was a gun-howitzer with a higher trajectory and longer range than the original weapon.[7] It had the same barrel as the field gun, but it had a special fortress mounting that allowed it to serve as both a howitzer and a gun-type weapon in the artillery casemates. Its maximum range was twelve kilometers. Fourteen of these weapons were used in five casemates of the first three GOs built, and another sixteen were employed in Alpine *ouvrages* and in casemates in Corsica.

While the Maginot Line was still under construction, a modified version of this weapon, the 75-mm Mle1932, was developed. The new model had a slightly shorter barrel (2.42 meters as opposed to 2.72 meters) and did not protrude from the embrasure as far as the Mle 1929, allowing the embrasure to be covered with a pair of armored shutters. The new mounting included a platform that moved with the gun so the crew could load the weapon quickly. A semiautomatic sliding breech replaced the older Nordenfeld breech in later models (75-mm Mle 1933), increasing the rate of fire. Twenty-one of these weapons were mounted in seven artillery casemates of the Maginot Line and only two in the Alpine sector. The Mle 1932 remained in two casemates of two *ouvrages*, while the newer Mle 1933 was installed in five casemates of three *ouvrages*. All three types of 75-mm cannons had a maximum rate of fire of from twenty-five to thirty rounds a minute and a normal rate of twelve rounds per minute. The Mle 1932 and Mle 1933 had a maximum range of about 11,900 meters.

An old shortened version of the 75-mm gun was used in some casemates that served as coffre for a couple of the largest *ouvrages*. These guns, which had the barrel of the old 75-mm Mle 1905, served as an AT weapon.[8] It was designated as a 75-mm 1932 R (for *Raccourci*) and had a range of about 9,100 meters.

The 135-mm Mle 1932 *lance-bombe* (bomb thrower) was a special fortress weapon designed for the *ouvrages*. This weapon, which lies between a howitzer and a mortar, is classified as a heavy mortar by the Germans and as a howitzer by English sources (a classification attributed to a number of heavy German mortars). Unlike most mortars, this weapon left a shell behind after firing the projectile. Its range was only 5,600 meters. Its minimum range was 320 meters, so it was an anti-infantry weapon for longer ranges than those of the other mortars used in the forts. Only seven of these were mounted in seven casemates of five *ouvrages*. Two more were found in the Alps. This weapon had a rate of fire of only six to eight rounds per minute, making it the slowest-firing piece of artillery in the *ouvrages*.

The 81-mm Mle 1932 mortar was a unique weapon designed for the Maginot Line. It was breech loaded, and its rate of fire varied from twelve to sixteen rounds per minute; it had a maximum range of 3,600 meters, with a minimum range of 100 meters. Its range was controlled at the breechblock by regulating the escaping gases emanating from firing the weapon in the two large cylinders above the tube. In the Maginot Line, a total of eighty-six mortars were mounted in casemates, sixty-eight of which were in the Alpine positions.

The 75-mm Mle 1931 mortar designed for the Alpine front had a range of only 5,900 meters. Not a true mortar, it was similar to a short-barreled 75-mm gun with the ability to elevate to 35°. Unlike true mortars, it could be depressed to level or even −3°, and a

Artillery Weapons of Ouvrages

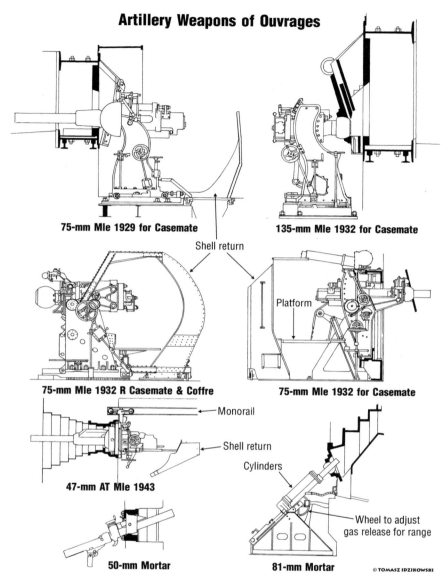

FIGURE 2-5. Various types of artillery used in the Maginot Line. [© Tomasz Idzi-kowski]

telescopic sight could be used for direct firing. Like the 135-mm *lance-bombes*, the round it fired had a shell, which was discarded into the shell return behind the weapon. This weapon resembled a mortar because its range could be regulated by adding up to five firing charges. The difference was that these charges were placed in the shell casing that was attached to the round just before firing. It was largely used in Alpine casemates instead of 135-mm *lance-bombes* since it had a range of 5,900 meters as opposed to 5,700 meters and served as a long-range anti-infantry weapon. It also could be depressed to cover areas the 135-mm weapon could not reach.

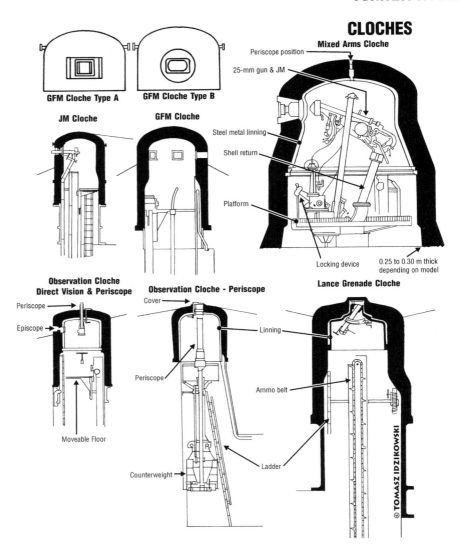

CLOCHES

FIGURE 2-6. Examples of various types of cloches used in Maginot *ouvrages*. [© Tomasz Idzikowski]

The artillery weapons for the turrets were the same as for the casemates with additional modifications in the mounting: 75-mm cannon, 135-mm *lance-bombes*, and 81-mm mortar. All these pieces had short barrels, so they did not protrude beyond the embrasure, allowing the turret to retract into the ground. The longest gun barrel was that of the 75-mm gun, which measured 2.42 meters, requiring the largest of the Maginot Line turrets.

The 75-mm Mle 1933 used in casemates served the turrets with mounting for two guns. Although there is some disagreement about its rate of fire, it is safe to say that it varied between twenty and thirty rounds per minute. Sixteen turrets in twelve forts of the main line mounted this weapon, as did five turrets in *ouvrages* of the Alps. The

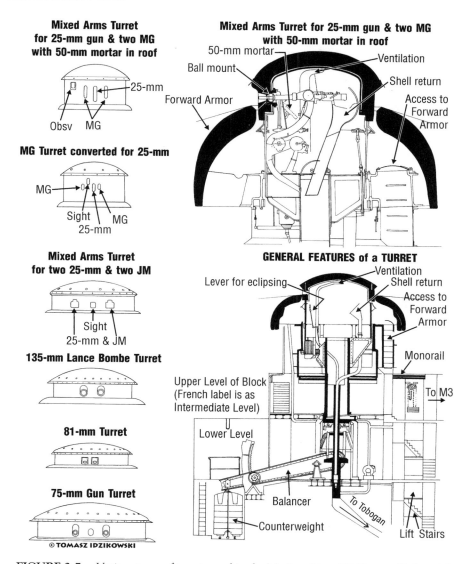

FIGURE 2-7. Various types of turrets used in the Maginot Line. [© Tomasz Idzikowski]

75-mm Mle 1932 R was also used in turrets. Both models had the same range as those designed for the casemates. Twelve turrets in nine forts mounted this weapon. One turret in the Maginot Extension mounted a 75-mm Mle 1905 R from the World War I with a range of 8,200 meters and a slightly lower rate of fire.

The 135-mm *lance-bombes* Mle 1932 was similar to the casemate weapon, but it was mounted in pairs, like the 75-mm weapon in turrets. Sixteen turrets in thirteen forts had these weapons; only one (at Monte Grosso) was in the Alps. The situation was the same for the 81-mm Mle 1932 mortar. In addition, mounted in pairs in turrets, it had the same characteristics as the casemate-mounted weapon. Twenty-one turrets in nineteen *ouvrages* mounted these mortars (Table 2.5) (Ferrard, *France 1940*, pp. 229–232;

TABLE 2-5. Weapons distribution in maginot line *ouvrages* (not including interval positions)

| | Casemate Weapon | | | | | | | Turret Weapon | | | |
| | 75-C Model | | | | | | | 75-C Model | | | |
	29	32	32R	33	135-H	81-M	75-M	32R	33	135-H	81-M
Extension								2[a]	2		
RF Metz	9	6	5	9	3	14		16	24	22	28
RF Lauter	5	6	4		4	2		8	6	10	14
Total	14	12	9	9	7	16		26	32	32	42
Total 66 turrets NE front. Subtotal of types of turrets:								13	16	16	21
SE front	12	2		8	2	68	26		10	2	
Total[b]	26	14	9	17	9	84	26	26	42	34	42

Source: Mary, *La Ligne Maginot*, 1981.

Note: Numbers vary for types of 75-mm cannons on southeast front (Alpine front). NE Front was Maginot Extension RF Metz, and RF Lauter plus other sectors that were not part of the Maginot Line from Dunkirk to Basel. G, guns; H, howitzer; M, mortar.

[a]Old 75 Mle 05 guns.

[b]Total number of weapons in Northeast and Southeast Fronts.

Hohnadel and Truttmann, *Guide*, backcover; Mary, *Maginot*, Vol. 2, pp. 92–105; Truttmann, "La Fortification," pp. 88–121; Vermeulen and Vermeulen, *Atlas CORF*).

Most of the artillery pieces and heavy infantry weapons are classified as water-cooled weapons, although similar field weapons are not. A small water reservoir was found in most combat blocks, but the actual water cooling system for the weapons in turrets consisted mainly of small containers that held a few liters of water, very similar to portable plant sprinklers used by gardeners. They were strapped to the turret column so the gunners could spray the gun barrels to cool them down.

Except for the 81 mm, which had no powder shell, there was a shell return behind the artillery pieces in casemates in which expended shells were dropped to the lower level and fed into a toboggan-type chute that carried them down to the gallery below. There was the same type of chute in turret blocks; these received the expended shell casings and returned them to the block, where they continued down to the gallery level through a toboggan.

In addition to the standard weapons, older weapons were mounted in one Maginot *ouvrage* and some of the CORF casemates, but they were few in number and not standard. They included four old 95-mm naval guns mounted in the *ouvrage* of Janus in the Alps and older naval 47-mm guns in a few interval casemates.

Several types of cloches were used in the Maginot Line *ouvrages* and most interval casemates. The most common types included the GFM (or observation and automatic rifle) cloche, the JM (twin machine gun) cloche, the AM cloche, and observation cloche.

There were two versions of the GFM cloche: Model 1929 or Type A and Model 1934 or Type B. They came in several sizes, ranging from a diameter of 1.60 to 1.88 meters. The thickness of the steel varied from 0.20 to 0.30 meters. Only the smaller models of Type A were 0.20 meters thick.[9] The number of crenels varied from three to five. Each of these types was designed to mount an FM in any of its crenels. The Type A GFM cloche could also accommodate a 50-mm mortar at a fixed angle of 20° when a special plate was installed in its embrasure. The mortar's range was adjusted with a valve located near the breech. The observer used either an episcope similar to those used in tanks (no magnification) or binoculars Type D (8× magnification). These optical devices had a special piece to fit in the embrasure. In all cases, the embrasure remained sealed, protecting the occupants. In many cases, after the cloches were installed on the *ouvrage*, a small opening was drilled in their ceiling to accommodate a small periscope. The GFM cloches mounted small Type J-2, F-1, and F-2 periscopes (7×, 1.1×, and 1.1× magnification, respectively). The cloche was accessed from the block below by means of a ladder. The floor of the cloche was cranked up and down to adjust for the height of the occupant; if needed, it could be lowered to the chamber below. This moving floor was a common feature in all the cloches of the Maginot *ouvrages* (Table 2.6).

The Type A GFM cloche had distinguishing rectangular embrasures. In addition to thicker armor, the Type B cloche had a new type of embrasure that looked like a truncated cone screwed into position and that offered more protection. The weapons and observation equipment were mounted on a ball mount. The only drawback of this new type of embrasure was that it did not accommodate the 50-mm mortar. Some Type A cloches were converted to Type B in 1939 (Mary, *Maginot*, Vol. 2, pp. 65–68).

The main problem with the GFM cloches was that they protruded above the blocks of the *ouvrages*, giving the Maginot positions a distinctive look. During the war, several succumbed to the deadly German 88-mm guns because of their high visibility.

TABLE 2-6. Fields of fire for casemate and turret artillery

Weapons Casemate	Elevation		Traverse	No. per Casemate[a]
	Max	Min		
75-mm 29 Cannon	+40°30′	−9°	45°	3[b]
75-mm 32 Cannon	+40°30′	−9°	45°	3
75-mm 33 Cannon	+45°	−10	45°	3
75-mm 32 R Cannon[c]	+34°	−17°	45°	2
135-mm *lance-bombes*	+40°30′	0°	45°	1
81-mm mortar	Fixed at 45°		45°	2
75-mm 31 mortar[d]	+35°	−3°	45°	1 or 2

Weapons Turrets	Elevation		Traverse	No. per Turret
	Max	Min		
75-mm 33 Cannon	+40°	−2°	360°	2
75-mm 32 R Cannon[c]	+35°	−5°	360°	2
135-mm *lance-bombes*	+45°	+9°	360°	2
81-mm mortar	Fixed at 45°		360°	2

Source: Truttmann, "La Fortification."
[a]This represents the normal number of weapons; in some cases, fewer were employed per casemate.
[b]In the Alps, usually two per casemate.
[c]These 75-mm weapons are classified as true howitzers, while the others are cannon-howitzers.
[d]This was not a true mortar and was used only in the Alps.

The JM cloche Model 1930 came in three sizes with armor protection that varied from 0.20 to 0.30 meters. These cloches offered a limited field of fire for the JM and generally covered an avenue of approach toward a block from a flank or even from the front. The maximum traverse for the JM in the cloche was 45°, the same as in a casemate. After 1934, a new AM cloche was used instead of the JM cloche; and in 1936, several JM cloches were transformed into AM cloches.

The AM cloche Mle 1934 was used on the new fortifications built to extend the Maginot Line into the Sarre and the Extension past Longuyon. It came in a large and small size and included two embrasures similar to the cone-shaped ones in a Type B GFM. The embrasures were only a short distance apart so that together they gave 90° of coverage. Like the JM cloche, the AM was embedded as much as possible in concrete protection. The AM cloche included a 25-mm gun sandwiched between a JM. The gunners could shift this set of weapons from one crenel to the other. In the ceiling, there was a periscope for observation. In the few JM cloches that were converted into AM cloches, the embrasure was replaced with Type B GFM embrasures. A set of JM with a 25-mm gun and a periscope-type L-2 or L-3 (1.25× magnification) were installed inside. This type of cloche was distinguished by its single firing embrasure.

The cloche *lance-grenades* was almost flush with the ground and had an opening for a 60-mm mortar. Although the weapon was not developed in time for the war, a number of these cloches had already been installed in combat blocks before the war. The mortar was meant to protect the surface of the block with a shower of bombs and was to have been fed automatically by a chain hoist.

The final category of cloches was for observation and came in two versions. One type, placed almost flush with the ground, had a single opening protected by an armored cover that swung to the side. Through this opening in the ceiling emerged one of the larger heavy periscopes of type B or C (12× and 25× magnification, respectively). The other type of observation cloche included three narrow observation crenels and had a small periscope of Types M, N, and P2 (8×, 8×, and 2×, magnification, respectively—the last for nighttime observation) and P-8 (8× magnification) through the ceiling.

The turrets of the *ouvrages* came in seven different models. The largest was for the 75-mm Mle 33 cannon-howitzer with a diameter of 4.00 meters; the smallest was for a machine gun turret with a diameter of 1.98 meters. The size of turret crews varied from several men in a 75-mm gun turret to as few as two in a machine gun turret. Additional troops served in the upper and lower levels of the turret block, operating the mechanisms that raised, retracted, and rotated the turret and sending the ammunition to the turret level. On the turret columns, a special mechanism, known as *monte-charge*, carried the shells to the turret. Some *monte-charges* were ammunition lifts, and others were chain or conveyor-belt ammunition hoists. In the 75- and 135-mm turrets, the crew ejected the expended shells into a bin behind the guns; from this bin they dropped to the bottom level of the block.

An *avant-cuirasse* (frontal armor) consisting of large curved plates, thickest in the top half, surrounded the turret and fit on a large shelf above the turret control room. After the armor was in place, the gap between the shelf wall of the block and the armor plates was filled with concrete. When the turret retracted into its well, its roof rested on top of this frontal armor, which gave it added protection. The walls of most turrets were 0.30 meters thick, except those of an older type of AM turret, which was 0.28 meters thick. The roof of the thicker turrets was 0.35 meters thick. All the turrets were eclipsing models that required more equipment than older turrets, which only rotated. At the lower level of the block, a large counterbalance supported the turret column on one end and counter-weights were on the other, which allowed it to raise and retract the turret.

The turret for the 75-mm Mle 33—the largest on the Maginot Line—had a roof 0.35 meters thick, a diameter of 4.00 meters, and weighed 265 tons, over 65 tons more than the next largest turret, which mounted the 75-mm Mle 32 R. It held the turret chief, the gunner, and two loaders and included a position between the guns where the gunner could actually sight the guns for direct fire. A shell return behind the guns carried the expended casings to the block below, where a toboggan chute carried them down to the gallery below the block. Twelve of these turrets were found in nine *ouvrages* of the RF of Metz, three in three *ouvrages* of the RF of Lauter, one in the Maginot Extension, and five in four *ouvrages* of the Alpine front.

The turret for the 75-mm Mle 32 R was smaller than the other 75-mm gun turret, with a diameter almost a meter smaller and a roof 0.30 meters thick. The most unusual feature of this turret was that the gunner who aimed it was seated midway up the control column, in the upper level of the block and not in the turret. Eight of these turrets were installed in six *ouvrages* of the RF of Metz, and four more were found in three *ouvrages* of the RF of Lauter.

The next largest turret, the turret for the 135-mm *lance-bombes* required two loaders. All maneuvering and aiming was done on the upper level of the turret block since the weapons could not be aimed through the turret. As in the 75-mm gun turrets, a shell return dropped the casings to the block below. The turret was situated in a slight depression because its weapons had a high angle of fire. Eleven of these turrets were mounted on nine *ouvrages* of the RF of Metz and five in four *ouvrages* of the RF of Lauter. The *ouvrage* of Mont Grosso also mounted one of these turrets, the only one on the Alpine front.

The mortar turret for a pair of 81-mm mortars was only 2.35 meters in diameter. Two pairs of gas cylinders above the mortar tubes—fixed at 45° and regulating the range of the mortar—occupied much of the turret. However, there was sufficient room for the two loaders who fed the ammunition that arrived on the *monte-charge* from the control room below. As in the 135-mm turret, the crew executed maneuvering and firing directions from the control room, where they also armed the mortar bombs by attaching the detonators, fins, and charges. Mortar fire could not be directed from inside the turret. On the surface, the turret sat in a depression deeper than that of the 135-mm turret, which reduced its profile. Fourteen of these turrets were installed in thirteen ouvrages of the RF of Metz and another seven in six ouvrages of the RF of Lauter.

The smallest turrets were for machine guns, weighed 96 tons, and had a diameter of 1.98 meters. Some were located on a slightly elevated position to increase the field of fire and reduce some of the dead space created by the terrain. In these turrets, there was enough room for a gunner, who was the turret chief, and the gunner's assistant. The gun-ner controlled the electrical rotation of the turret with a set of pedals. In case of power failure, the turret was maneuvered with hand controls. The barrels of the JM fit into two small embrasures. A third embrasure was for a telescopic sight. In many of these turrets, a fourth embrasure was drilled through the turret wall on the opposite side of the opening for the sight, which made it possible to use an AM combination, similar to the one in the

AM cloche made for a JM and 25-mm cannon. Of the sixty-one turrets in the Maginot Line (none in the Alpine front), fifteen were drilled for the AM combination.

Two types of AM turrets came into service on the new fronts built after 1934. One type, with a wall only .18 meters thick and a roof .28 meters thick, was the weakest in the Maginot Line. Larger than an 81-mm turret, it actually was an old turret for a pair of 75 Mle 05 guns. It was weaker than the machinegun turret with a roof .30 meters thick and walls .30 meters thick (Koch, "La tourelle mitrailleuse Modèle 1935," *39–45 Magazine*, pp. 55–58). This AM turret had enough space to mount two pairs of AM with an observation crenel between them. Several of these turrets were converted into AM turrets after 1934. Twelve were in *ouvrages* of the New Fronts, on the left flank of the RF of Metz, in the Maginot Extension, and around Maubeuge.

The second type of turret was a heavier model, 2.55 meters in diameter (0.35 meters smaller than the other turret) and mounted a single AM set and a 50-mm mortar in the roof. One of these turrets was installed at the *ouvrage* of Anzeling, one at Le Boussois, five on casemates around Maubeuge, and five at other positions, including on the front to the north.

These were the standard weapons for *ouvrages* and casemates and were found in Maginot-type positions from the North Sea to Corsica.

Optics for Fire Control and Surveillance

The cloches, turrets, and casemate positions all had some form of optical equipment. The single large periscope of the special observation cloches, with no direct vision crenels and almost flush with the surface, was raised and lowered by the observer. These special cloches used one of two types of periscope: B and C. The latter offered a range of magnification from 2.4× to 25×. Types B and C were the largest periscopes in use. The periscopes in the observation cloches with crenels for observers were outfitted with Types M and N periscopes with a magnification power of 8×. The F-1 and F-2 in the GFM offered little magnification power. The Type L, employed in the AM cloches, was not much more powerful than the F series.

Periscope Type K, used in the machine gun turret, had a magnification of 4×. In the gun turrets, a telescope was used for direct fire control. Type L 650, with magnification of 4×, was installed in the 75/33 gun turret, and a similar L 655 was in the 75/R32 turret. A similar L 679 was found in the AM turret. Finally, the much less powerful L-4 periscope equipped the AM turret with a 50-mm mortar.

The gun casemates positions included a telescope Type G or H with magnification of 3.5× and 1.2×, respectively. The 75-mm Mle 31 weapon had an L 634 periscope with magnification of 4×, and the 75-mm Mle 29 and 75-mm Mle 32 had similar L 647 and L 656 periscopes, respectively. Types L 652 and L 653 telescopes with a magnification of 2.5× were found in the AT gun casemates. The JM in casemate (and cloche) was equipped with a Type L 638 or L 676 with a magnification of 2.3×.

Other optical equipment included the Type D binoculars and episcope L 639 for the GFM cloche, a Type O telescope for infantry casemates with magnification of 3.5×, which was never delivered to the forts. The R-2 periscope, intended for surveillance of the area around the *fossés*, also was not installed in the *ouvrages*.

All this equipment made it possible for the garrison to carry out its assignments with minimal direct exposure to enemy fire. Nonetheless, the exposed GFM cloches and casemate walls eventually proved vulnerable to weapons such as the high-velocity German 88-mm gun (Truttmann, *La Muraille*, pp. 588–589).

As can be seen from Tables 2.7 and 2.8, most GOs consisted of eight to nine blocks, including two entrance blocks. Only a few had twelve or more blocks, and the largest had two separate sections of combat blocks. Of all the completed GOs, Hackenberg had the largest number of blocks, but Hochwald, with two separate caserne areas, covered the largest area and in fact has often been mistakenly identified as two separate *ouvrages*.

TABLE 2-7. Features of the ouvrages

Chart of *Gros Ouvrages* from Longuyon to Soultz, Maginot Line Proper

Ouvrages RF Metz	Garrison	M-1 Cells	EM	EH	Artillery Block 75[a]	81	135	Inf. Block	Obs. Block	Mix Block	Block Total
Fermont	600	2[b]	A-e	1	1-c 1-t	1-t	—	1-c 2-t	1	—	9
Latiremont	600	4	A-e	1	2-c	A-t	—	1-t 1-cl	A	1	8
Brehain	630	4	A-e	1	2-t	1-t	1-t	1-cl 2-t	1	—	10
Rochonvillers	680	5	A-i	1	A-c 2-t		A-c 2-t	3-t	1	1	11
Molvange	735	5	A-i	1	3-t	1-t	1-t	2-t	2	—	11
Soetrich	600	3	B-e	1	2-t	B-c	1-t	1-t A-t B-c	A	2	8
Kobenbusch	530	No	A-e	1	1-c 1-t	1-t	—	1-c 2-t	1	—	9
Galgenberg	445	2	B-l	1	—	1-t	1-t	2-c 1-t	1	—	8
Métrich	795	6	A-l	1	1-c A-t 1-t	1-c 1-t	1-t	A-c 1-tc 1-t	2	1	12
Billig	545	No	M-i	—	1-c 1-tc	1-t	—	2-c 1-t	1	—	8
Hackenberg	1,080	9	A-l	1	2-c 1-t	2-t	1-t 1-tc	4-c 1-cl 1-t 2-tc	2	—	19
Mt. Welches	520	No	B-i	1	A-t B-t	A-c 1-t	—	A-c B-c 1-t	1	2	7
Michelsberg	515	No	M-l	—	1-t	1-t	1-t	1-c 1-t	—	—	6
Anzeling	760	5	A-i	1	2-t	1-t	1-tc	1-t 2-tc			9

TABLE 2-7. Continued

Chart of *Gros Ouvrages* from Longuyon to Soultz, Maginot Line Proper

Ouvrages RF Metz	Garrison	M-1 Cells	EM	EH	Artillery Block 75[a]	81	135	Inf. Block	Obs. Block	Mix Block	Block Total
Simserhof	820	7	A-l	1	B-c D-c 1-t	C-t E-t	A-c F-c 1-t	A-tc C-c E-c F-tc	B D	6	10
Schiesseck	700	No	B-l	1	1-t	1-c 1-t	A-t	B-c 2-cl 1-t	1 A B	2	11
Grand Hohekirkel	185	No	B-i	1	A-t	—	—	2-c 1-t	A 1	1	6
Four A Chaux	220	No	B-i	1	1-t	1-t	1-t	A-c 1-t	A 1	1	8
Hochwald	1,070	7	A-l	2	1-c B-c 1-t	1-t C-c D-t	A-tc C-c	2-c[c] B 2-t D	A	4	14 plus 9 Cas.
Schoenenbourg	630	No	B-e	1	A-t 1-t	1-t	—	2-c 1-t	A	1	8

Garrison: Number of men for which the *ouvrage* was designed (the number is approximate).

M-1: Number of cells for ammunition; No indicates no M-1 was built.

EM, munitions entrance; EH, men's entrance. All GOs had one EM: Type A for rail cars, Type B for trucks, or a mixed entrance (with no EH). On the chart, they are listed as A-, B-, or M- plus the following letter designations: l = level entrance, i = inclined entrance, e = elevator down to main gallery.

Artillery blocks: 75 mm (c = casemate, usually for 3 guns; t = 2-gun turret); 81 mm (c = casemate, usually for 2 mortars; t = 2-mortar turret); 135 mm (c = casemate for 1 gun, t = 2-gun turret).

Inf. Block, infantry blocks: Machine gun and/or AT gun (c = casemate, cl = cloches only, t = machine gun turret, tc = turret and casemate).

Obs. Block, observation block: Includes cloches for observation.

Mix. Block, mixed block: Combination of other types of block, such as infantry and artillery. A letter designation is used for the columns that include the elements of that block. For example, in the column for mixed blocks, the number 2 appears. In the column for 81-mm mortar is A-t, and in the column for observation block is A. This means the block is an artillery and observation block with an 81-mm mortar turret and one or more observation cloches. Under the column for 75-mm gun appears B-t, and under infantry block appears B-c. This means that there is a mixed artillery infantry block with a 75-mm gun turret and a casemate position with infantry weapons.

Cas.: Refers to nine separate flanking casemates in the AT ditch at Hochwald.

Blocks Total: Total number of entrance, combat, and observation blocks.

[a]Some *ouvrages* (Billig, Hochwald) had casemates with two guns. Also, casemate positions with a 75-mm gun covering AT ditch not included.

[b]In some *ouvrages* like Fermont, not all the cells were completed (two of five in this case).

[c]Special counterscarp blocks with two 75-mm howitzers and machine guns.

However, a number of its blocks, including a redoubt and observation block, remained unfinished.

In general, the *ouvrages* were classified based on the garrison size and weapons positions. Some GOs were manned by as few as two hundred men. The Class 3 PO included an 81-mm mortar either in turret or casemate position. A number of the POs originally planned as GOs consisted only of a few blocks because financial restraints or other problems had cut short their construction. In many cases, there were plans to expand some POs into GOs during a second building cycle, which never materialized.

TABLE 2-8. Class of *Ouvrage* on Northeast Front

Class of *Ouvrage*	Size of Garrison	RF of Metz *Ouvrages*	RF of Lauter *Ouvrages*
GO 1	600 to over 1,000 (average 600)	Fermont, Latirement, Brehain, Rochonvillers, Molvange, Soetrich, Métrich, Hackenberg, Anzeling.	Simsherof, Schiesseck, Hochwald, Schoenenbourg
GO[a] 2	550 or fewer (average 450)	Koebenbusch, Galgenberg, Billig, Mt. des Welches, Michelsberg	Grand Hohekirkel, Four au Chaux
PO[a] 3	100 to over 200 (average 190)	Immerhof, Annex Sud Coume, Bovenberg,[b] Laudrefang[c]	Otterbiel[c]
PO 4	More than one block	Mauvias Bois,[c] Aumetz,[c] Hobling,[a] Bousse,[a] Brehrenbach, Denting, Village Coume, Mottemberg,[a] Kerfent,[c] Bambesch,[a] Teting[a]	Haut Poirier,[c] Welschoff,[a] Rohrbach,[c] Lembach[a]
PO 5	Single block	Bois du Four,[c] Karre, Oberheid, Sentzich, Coucou, Coume Annex Nord, Coume,[c] Einseling[d]	

Source: Mary, *Maginot*, Vol. 3, pp. 81–138; Wahl, *La Ligne Maginot en Alsace*, pp. 241–243.

[a]These GOs by this official classification system are referred to as medium instead of *gros*. This type of PO was considered to be a mixed infantry and artillery position because it contained artillery, usually in the form of an 81-mm mortar.

[b]This *ouvrage* had a large garrison of over 200, but the only artillery position built was a casemate for two 75-mm guns, and it was never linked to the *ouvrage* because work was not completed.

[c]Planned as an artillery *ouvrage* but not altered or planned for the second cycle as an artillery *ouvrage*, and the work was not done.

[d]Plans were to convert it into a Class 3 in the second cycle by adding an 81-mm mortar turret.

Plans also called for converting some of the Class 4 and 5 POs into Class 3 POs during the second construction cycle with the addition of 81-mm mortar positions.

The initial function of the PO was to fill the gaps between GOs. The RF of Metz numbered fourteen GOs and twenty-four POs, seven of which were planned as GOs. If the original plans had been realized, there would have been a total of twenty-one GOs and seventeen POs. A map of the region reveals that the large gap between the GOs of Latiremont and Bréhain would have been occupied by two more GOs instead of the POs of Mauvais Bois and Bois du Four. Likewise, in the large gap between Bréhain and Rochonvillers, the PO of Aumetz, originally intended as a GO, would have filled the interval. On the other hand, a single PO was located between the GOs of Molvange and Métrich, as planned. Although no GOs were built past Anzeling in the SF of Boulay and in the SF of Faulquemont, there were plans to turn the POs at Bovenberg, Coume, Kerfent, and Laudrefang into GOs, but they never materialized. Of the five POs in the RF of Lauter, only two were intended to be POs instead of GOs. Although there were plans to build a PO on either side of Schoenenbourg to secure the right flank, the two small *ouvrages* were never built (Table 2.9).

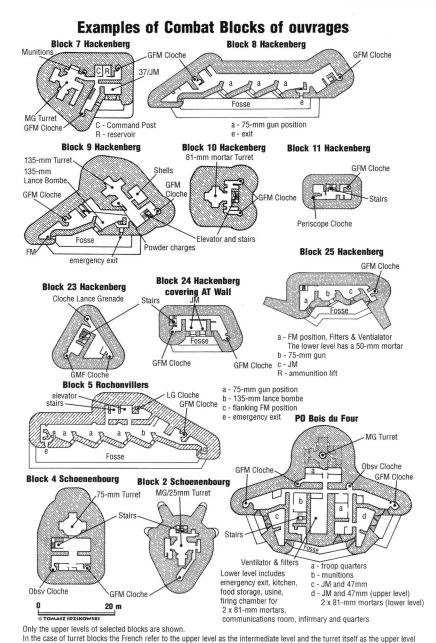

FIGURE 2-8. Examples of various types of blocks in Maginot forts. [© Tomasz Idzikowski]

The POs differed from the GOs in that they were infantry forts and consisted of one or more combat blocks for infantry weapons. Some included a turret with machine guns, and later works even had an AM turret that mounted a combination of machine guns and a 25-mm gun. Some POs consisted of a single monolithic block; a few, Class 3, had an artillery block consisting of 81-mm mortars in casemate or turret positions. In many

TABLE 2-9. Types of concrete protection

Protection Type		Reinforced Concrete	Resists Shells of
1 Walls	D	1.70 meters	150 mm
	R	1.00 meters	
Roof slab		1.50 meters	
2 Walls	D	2.25 meters	240 mm
	R	1.00 meters	
Roof slab		2.00 meters	
3 Walls	D	2.75 meters	300 mm
	R	1 to 1.3 meters	
Roof slab		2.50 meters	
4 Walls	D	3.50 meters	420 mm
	R	1.30 meters	
Roof slab		3.50 meters	

D, walls in the line of direct enemy artillery fire even if earth covered;
R, rear walls not expected to be in the direct line of enemy artillery.

cases, the POs had no separate entrance block, and their support and combat areas were usually together. In this case, one of the combat blacks also served as the entrance. Most POs occupied a much smaller area than the GOs; in many cases, their subterranean sections were not as deep. In some instances, the terrain did not permit the excavation of deep galleries, forcing the builders to abandon plans for a GO at some sites.

The standards for the defensive strength of the ouvrages set by CORF depended on the amount of concrete and steel used. Placing the subterranean facilities at depths of up to thirty meters gave reasonably good protection. The blocks were exposed to the surface on at least one side. The roof, if it mounted cloche and turrets, was also visible. The roof and the frontal walls exposed to direct enemy artillery fire required sufficient protection to resist the heaviest shells, whereas the other sides, whether exposed or not, needed less protection.

For this reason, four categories of reinforced concrete protection were established. The thickest concrete protection, 3.5 meters thick, was able to resist hits by 420-mm weapons—the largest caliber of the German artillery in World War I—and was employed for the frontal walls and ceilings of GOs (Table 2.10). The thinnest concrete protection, 1.00 to 1.75 meters thick, was used mainly on exposed rear walls of some casemates. The reason for building thinner walls stems from the Battle of Verdun in 1916, when it took the French several months to recapture Fort Douaumont from the Germans despite heavy artillery bombardment from the rear, where it was most exposed. To prevent a similar situation from arising again, the designers of the Maginot *ouvrages* opted for thinner rear walls that would crumble more easily.

In some POs with subterranean galleries close to the surface, like Immerhof, a five-millimeter thick metal sheet was attached to the ceilings and outer walls to prevent flaking under bombardment. Many gun chambers of the blocks of both types of *ouvrages* had similar sheets. The GOs and some isolated exposed artillery observation positions received Protection 4 (Table 2.11). Most PO blocks, abris, and some isolated observatories were given Protection 3. Many isolated casemates used Protection 2.

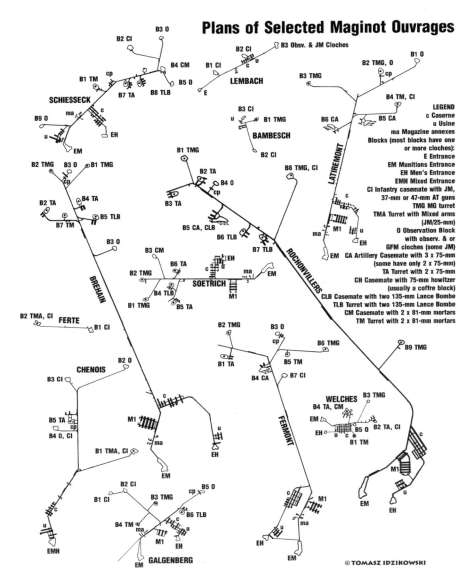

Plans of Selected Maginot Ouvrages

LEGEND
c Caserne
u Usine
ma Magazine annexes
Blocks (most blocks have one
   or more cloches):
E Entrance
EM Munitions Entrance
EH Men's Entrance
EMH Mixed Entrance
CI Infantry casemate with JM,
   37-mm or 47-mm AT guns
TMG MG turret
TMA Turret with Mixed arms
   (JM/25-mm)
O Observation Block
   with observ. & or
   GFM cloches (some JM)
CA Artillery Casemate with 3 x 75-mm
   (some have only 2 x 75-mm)
TA Turret with 2 x 75-mm
CH Casemate with 75-mm howitzer
   (usually a coffre block)
CLB Casemate with two 135-mm Lance Bombe
TLB Turret with two 135-mm Lance Bombe
CM Casemate with 2 x 81-mm mortars
TM Turret with 2 x 81-mm mortars

© TOMASZ IDZIKOWSKI

FIGURE 2-9. Plans of several Maginot forts. [© Tomasz Idzikowski]

The regulation standards for the building of the galleries were established in 1929. The galleries and interior portions of the *ouvrages* varied in depth according to the geology of the area. In many mountainous regions, especially the Alps, where the forts were built into hard rock, a depth of twelve meters was considered sufficient. In limestone regions, the standard depth was sixteen meters, while in areas where the subsurface was softer and had consistent layers of average density, the required depths ranged from eighteen to twenty meters. When the subsurface consisted of soft clays, the regulation mandated depths of twenty-five to thirty meters (Truttmann, "La Fortification," pp. 239–240). Softer subsurfaces were particularly subject to shifting;

Selected Maginot Ouvrages part 2

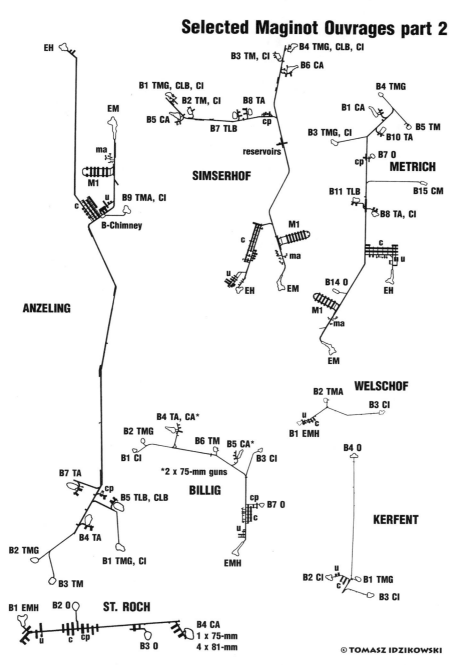

FIGURE 2-10.   Plans of several Maginot forts. [© Tomasz Idzikowski]

clays, on the other hand, tended to expand and contract. These conditions could damage the galleries much more severely than the enemy's superheavy artillery. However, this type of damage would take ten to fifty years to show, as in the case of the GO of Métrich, where subterranean shifting has pushed up and broken gallery floors.

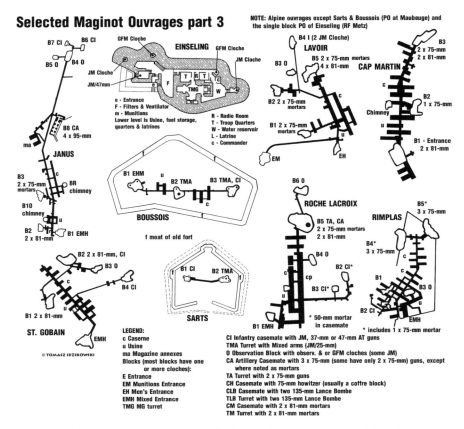

FIGURE 2-11. Plans of several Maginot forts. [© Tomasz Idzikowski]

TABLE 2-10. Armor protection

Resists Shells of	Armor (Steel) Components: Thickness of Turret Roofs	Equal to Protection Type
150 or 240 mm	GFM cloches: 200 to 250 mm	1 or 2
	JM cloches: 200 mm	
240 mm	AM cloche[a]: 300 mm	2
300 mm	JM cloche: 250 mm	3
	Turret mixed arms (old 1905 turret)[b]: 285 mm	
300 or 420 mm	GFM cloches: 300 mm	3 or 4
	JM cloches: 300 mm	
	AM cloches: 300 mm	
420 mm	Turret for machine gun, 81, 75R32, 135: 300 mm	4
	Turret for 75/33[c]: 350 mm	
	Turret mixed arms[c]: + 350 mm[d]	

Source: Truttmann, "La Fortification," p. 206.
[a]Small model.
[b]Sides 185 mm
[c]Sides 300 mm.
[d]One of the two types of mixed arms turrets was the old 1905 turret. See note b.

SYSTEMS OF COMMUNICATION

In the northeast, a network of underground telephone cables merged at small bunkerlike buried control centers. These small chambers not only contained the cable links and relays, but also had a switchboard that the interval troops could use to communicate

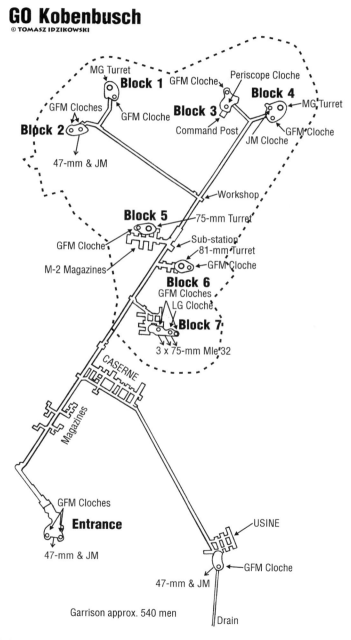

FIGURE 2-12. Plan of GO of Kobenbusch. [© Tomasz Idzikowski]

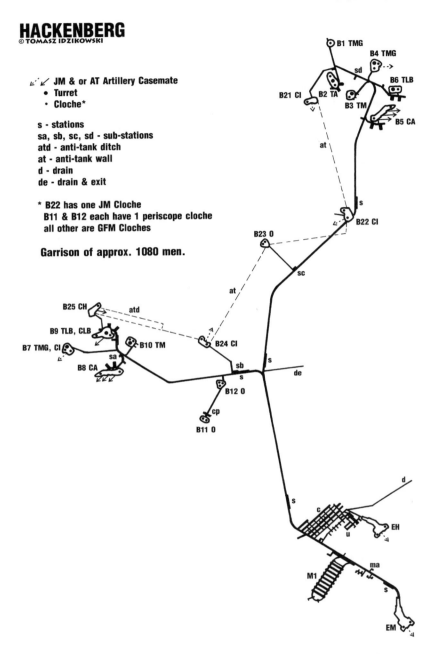

HACKENBERG
©TOMASZ IDZIKOWSKI

↗↙ **JM & or AT Artillery Casemate**
• **Turret**
• **Cloche***

s - stations
sa, sb, sc, sd - sub-stations
atd - anti-tank ditch
at - anti-tank wall
d - drain
de - drain & exit

* **B22 has one JM Cloche**
B11 & B12 each have 1 periscope cloche
all other are GFM Cloches

Garrison of approx. 1080 men.

FIGURE 2-13. Plan of GO of Hackenberg. [© Tomasz Idzikowski]

with sector headquarters and fortifications in the line. The *transmetteur sans fil* (TSF; wireless transmitter) radio system, also used on both fronts, had a limited range of about twenty kilometers. The antennas for this radio system were usually strung along the upper face of the entrance of infantry casemates or in the *fossé* of the entrance block of most artillery casemates, facing the rear. Some casemate combat blocks with a radio room also sported such an antenna. The TSF made it possible to communicate with isolated positions, such as observatories, and served as an alternate source of communication if the underground telephone lines were cut. The casemates with a deployed antenna included a room for a receiver that was linked to the Central TSF room, which relayed messages by an internal telephone system to the proper command post (Lambert, *TM 32 Le Telephone*, pp. 15–17, 58–59). The radio transmitter with a receiver was usually located in an entrance block since communications was mainly to the rear, as in the case in the GO of Immerhof. In some combat blocks, there was only a receiver.

In each *ouvrage*, there was a communications center with telephone switchboards for controlling and directing calls within the fort and outside. Underground telephone cables, buried about two to three meters deep, provided external links to various headquarters, other fortifications (forts, casemates, and observatories), and the interval troops who could tie into the system by using the switchboards in the numerous chambers spaced about five kilometers apart along the underground line. The telephone was the fastest and most efficient way to communicate between the combat blocks and various headquarters within an *ouvrage*.

The telephone was not the only method of communication in the *ouvrages*. Voice tubes were used in the cloches. To control the artillery, the artillery command post and the artillery casemates mounted order transmitters. In the weapons turrets, there was also an order transmitter on the turret column that linked the crew with the artillery command post. Two models of transmitters with round, clocklike faces and needles that pointed to the firing directions, resembled those used on warships. Both types were electrically powered but also had a battery backup for emergencies. They made it possible to send firing orders to artillery blocks during the height of battle when the noise of battle might interfere with voice commands. An operator selected the type of fire mission on this transmitter and sent it to the turret or casemate block, where a red light flashed and a bell rang. The gunners in the turrets received their orders the same way from the control room below.[10]

MODIFICATIONS FOR THE NEW FRONTS AND ALPINE SECTORS

The relative standardization of features of the *ouvrages* on the Old Fronts of the Maginot Line Proper did not extend quite as rigorously to the forts in the Southeastern Front, the Maginot Extension, and the Maubeuge region. This is because construction started late on the Alpine front and halted at the time of the dissolution of the CORF in 1936. When the work resumed, much of it was placed under the control of sector commanders and their engineers. When work began on the New Fronts in 1935 in the Northeast Front, CORF made changes to its design to produce more economical and improved fortifications.

The few *ouvrages* of New Fronts consisted of three POs on the left flank of the RF of Lauter that extended it into the Sarre and five POs in Maubeuge area. To extend the Maginot Line further along the southern Belgian border, the army created the Maginot Extension, which consisted of two GOs and two POs in the SF of Montmédy linked to the Maginot Line Proper by the weaker Defensive Sector of Marville. This last sector

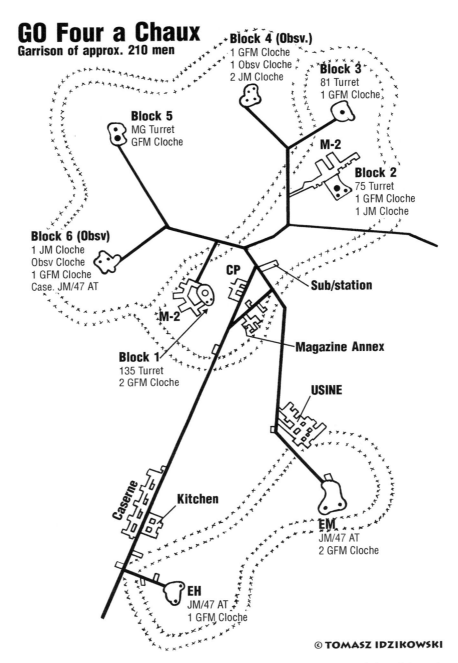

GO Four a Chaux
Garrison of approx. 210 men

Block 4 (Obsv.)
1 GFM Cloche
1 Obsv Cloche
2 JM Cloche

Block 3
81 Turret
1 GFM Cloche

M-2

Block 2
75 Turret
1 GFM Cloche
1 JM Cloche

Block 5
MG Turret
GFM Cloche

Block 6 (Obsv)
1 JM Cloche
Obsv Cloche
1 GFM Cloche
Case. JM/47 AT

CP

Sub/station

M-2

Magazine Annex

Block 1
135 Turret
2 GFM Cloche

USINE

Caserne

Kitchen

EM
JM/47 AT
2 GFM Cloche

EH
JM/47 AT
1 GFM Cloche

© **TOMASZ IDZIKOWSKI**

FIGURE 2-14.   Plan of GO of Four a Chaux. [© Tomasz Idzikowski]

included about two dozen STG casemates and a number of smaller casemates and blockhouses.

The Montmédy sector consisted of a line of twelve interval casemates placed be-tween four *ouvrages*. The only two GOs built on the New Fronts were Veslones and Le Chesnois. The PO of Thonnelle had been intended as a GO, but plans for four turret

PO SENTZICH
© TOMASZ IDZIKOWSKI

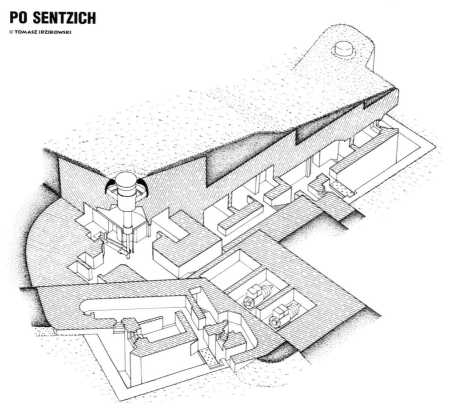

FIGURE 2-15a. PO Sentzich. [© Tomasz Idzikowski]

blocks—two for 75-mm guns, one for 135-mm *lance-bombes*, and one for 81-mm mortars—were cancelled. The two-block PO of La Ferté, one of the weakest of the Maginot Line, marked the end of the line at Villy. The two GOs included an artillery turret with 75-mm guns, but that of Le Chesnois was an old turret with the World War I era 75-mm Mle 05 instead of the new 75-mm Mle 33, which limited its ability to effectively support the weak *ouvrage* of La Ferté (Cima, *Ligne* CD).

Three new POs extended the left flank of the RF of Lauter: the PO of Haut Poirier, the only *ouvrage* in the Defensive Sector of the Sarre; the PO of Welschoff; and the PO of Rohrbach in the SF of Rohrbach. The last two forts were covered by the artillery of the GO of Simserhof, unlike Haut Poirier, which had no artillery protection. The PO of Rohrbach was originally meant to be a GO with a 75-mm Mle 33 turret, two turrets of 135-mm *lance-bombes*, and an artillery casemate that would have extended its artillery coverage (Cima, *Ligne* CD).

In the Maginot Line Proper, the artillery forts were usually designed to protect with artillery fire not only the adjacent POs, but also the nearest GO on their right and left flanks. Thus, each GO had the capacity of sweeping off intruders from the top of its neighbors without damaging them since the forts were impervious to the weapons of the caliber mounted in the Maginot Line forts. In the New Fronts of the Maginot Line, on

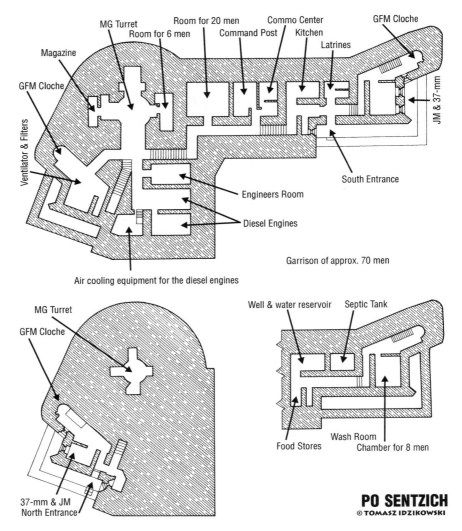

FIGURE 2-15b. Plan of PO (monolithic block) of Sentzich. [© Tomasz Idzikowski]

the other hand, the forts could barely support each other because two of the planned GOs were actually built as POs.

The New Fronts were not part of the Maginot Line or Extension. Originally, the Maginot Line was not built along the frontier of Belgium, which had been France's ally until 1936, for fear of giving the appearance of lack of support for this nation. In addition, the heavily populated industrial region of Lille was difficult to fortify. Furthermore, in the area north of the Maubeuge sector, the topography was not favorable for the construction of heavy fortifications with subterranean works without incurring heavy expenses. Finally, a large part of the border included, according to Pétain, the "impassable" Ardennes, which he thought would not require heavy defenses.

Nonetheless, the army proposed new *ouvrages* for this front early on. In the 1920s, the Commission of Territorial Defense (CDT; *Commission de Défense du Territoire*) had

PO Immerhof Block 3: 81-mm Mortar Turret and Infantry Casemate

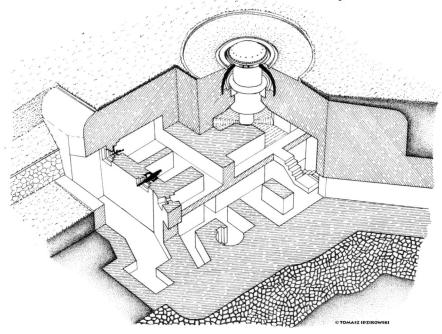

FIGURE 2-16.   Block 3 of Immerhof. [© Tomasz Idzikowski]

identified five defensive salients that included Maubeuge, Valenciennes, Lille, and Dunkirk and could be held by using natural obstacles such as forests and areas subject to flooding. The SFs of Escaut and Maubeuge were created in 1933, and money was appropriated the next year to create the fortifications of the New Fronts. At Maubeuge, four POs were built onto the older forts of Seré-de-Rivières. When Belgium's new king declared neutrality in 1936, the completion of the new defenses took on a new urgency.

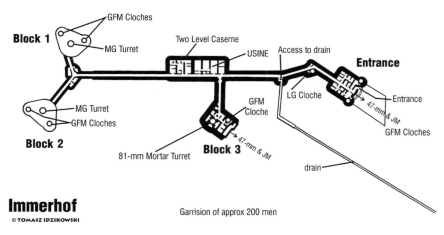

FIGURE 2-17.   Immerhof. [© Tomasz Idzikowski]

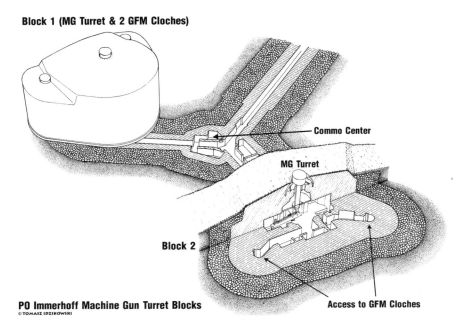

Block 1 (MG Turret & 2 GFM Cloches)

Commo Center

MG Turret

Block 2

PO Immerhoff Machine Gun Turret Blocks
© TOMASZ IDZIKOWSKI

Access to GFM Cloches

FIGURE 2-18. Immerhof Blocks 1 and 2. [Tomasz Idzikowski]

Thus, four POs were completed by 1937. However, as usual, funds were in short supply, and the *ouvrages* of Sarts and Boussois, first intended as GOs with artillery turrets, were built as POs. All four were additions built on older forts. Further to the northwest, the PO of Eth was the last Maginot-type PO on the north (Cima, *Ligne* CD; Depret, "Le Secteur Fortifié de Maubeuge," pp. 52–57; Mary, *Maginot*, pp. 217–225).

The construction of the *ouvrages* of the New Fronts took place after the dissolution of the CORF; of seven planned GOs, only two were actually completed as such. These GOs had a new type of mixed entry block. Instead of a rolling bridge, they were designed for trucks and had an armored door that operated somewhat like a portcullis that rose vertically from beneath the floor to seal the entranceway. Behind it, a grille normally closed the entrance. Only the two GOs in the Maginot Extension had this type of entrance. The combat blocks were not much different from those on the Old Fronts, but some of the infantry blocks included AM turrets and AM cloches. Most of these new infantry blocks comprised an entrance block and three or more cloches. However, the 25-mm guns could not replace the artillery protection these new forts needed. Even the two flanking casemates for 75-mm guns, not linked to the fort, built to protect the flanks of the *ouvrage* of La Ferté proved inadequate.

The Southeast Front was very different from the Old and New Fronts of the northeast. In two of the three Alpine SFs, there were no fortified lines; instead, groups of *ouvrages* were built in the valleys that allowed access from Italy. Some of these forts were put on mountaintops and others on mountain flanks and in valleys, sealing off a line of advance for the enemy. In the SF of the Maritime Alps, something on the order of a fortified line was created, but as in the other two sectors, the fortifications were placed along valley approaches. The terrain affected not only the location of the forts,

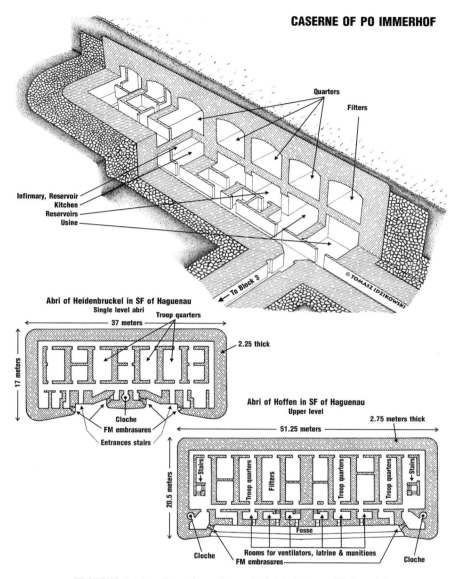

CASERNE OF PO IMMERHOF

Quarters
Filters

Infirmary, Reservoir
Kitchen
Reservoirs
Usine

To Block 3

© TOMASZ IDZIKOWSKI

Abri of Heidenbruckel in SF of Haguenau
Single level abri
Troop quarters
37 meters
2.25 thick
17 meters
Cloche
FM embrasures
Entrances stairs

Abri of Hoffen in SF of Haguenau
Upper level
2.75 meters thick
51.25 meters
Stairs
Troop quarters
Filters
Troop quarters
Troop quarters
Stairs
20.5 meters
Fosse
Cloche
Rooms for ventilators, latrine & munitions
FM embrasures
Cloche

FIGURE 2-19. Barracks at Immerhof. [© Tomasz Idzikowski]

but also their overall design and even methods for communication and logistical support.

The *ouvrages* of the Alpine sectors were very different from those of the northeast, although the ubiquitous GFM cloche that graced their superstructures and other types of cloches, turrets, and sundry features characteristic of CORF fortifications gave them the characteristic Maginot aspect. The main differences between the Alpine forts and those of the northeast lay in their design and layout.

A case in point is the GO of Rimplas, the first *ouvrage* to be built in the sector. Its initial planning and design was done by *Génie* in Nice before CORF had set the

Castillon

© TOMASZ IDZIKOWSKI

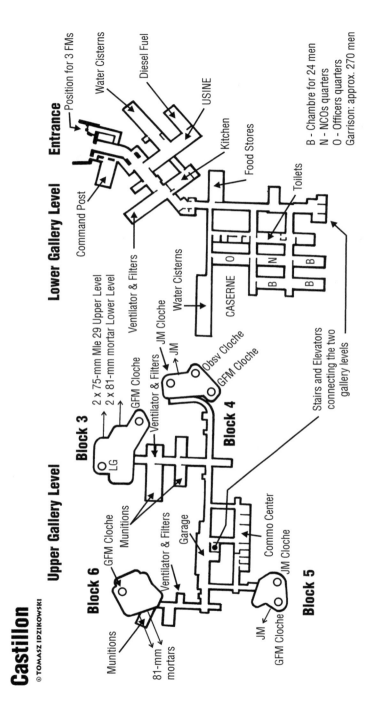

Upper Gallery Level

Lower Gallery Level

Entrance

Position for 3 FMs

Water Cisterns

Diesel Fuel

USINE

Kitchen

Food Stores

Command Post

Ventilator & Filters

JM Cloche

Water Cisterns

2 x 75-mm Mle 29 Upper Level
2 x 81-mm mortar Lower Level

GFM Cloche

Ventilator & Filters

JM

Obsv Cloche

GFM Cloche

Block 3

LG

Block 4

Stairs and Elevators
connecting the two
gallery levels

CASERNE

Toilets

O

N

B

B

B - Chambre for 24 men
N - NCOs quarters
O - Officers quarters
Garrison: approx. 270 men

Block 6

GFM Cloche

Munitions

Ventilator & Filters

Garage

Commo Center

JM Cloche

Block 5

JM

GFM Cloche

Munitions

81-mm
mortars

FIGURE 2-20. Plan of GO of Castillon in the Alps is unusual because it had two underground gallery levels. [© Tomasz Idzikowski]

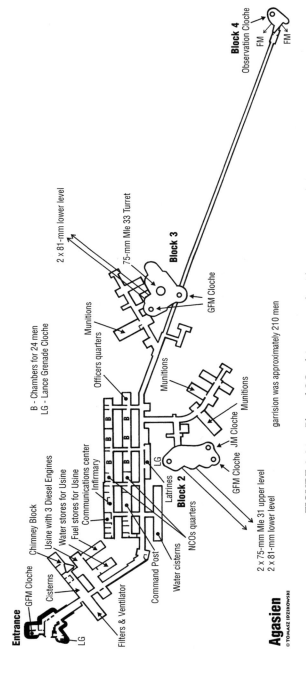

Entrance

GFM Cloche
Chimney Block
Cisterns
Usine with 3 Diesel Engines
Water stores for Usine
Fuel stores for Usine
Communications center
Infirmary
LG
Filters & Ventilator
Command Post
Water cisterns
NCOs quarters
Latrines

Block 2

B - Chambers for 24 men
LG - Lance Grenade Cloche

Officers quarters
Munitions
Munitions
Munitions
JM Cloche
GFM Cloche
LG

2 x 75-mm Mle 31 upper level
2 x 81-mm lower level

garrison was approximately 210 men

Agasien
© TOMASZ IDZIKOWSKI

2 x 81-mm lower level
75-mm Mle 33 Turret

Block 3

GFM Cloche

Block 4
Observation Cloche
FM
FM

FIGURE 2-21. Plan of GO of Agaisen in the Alps. [© Tomasz Idzikowski]

63

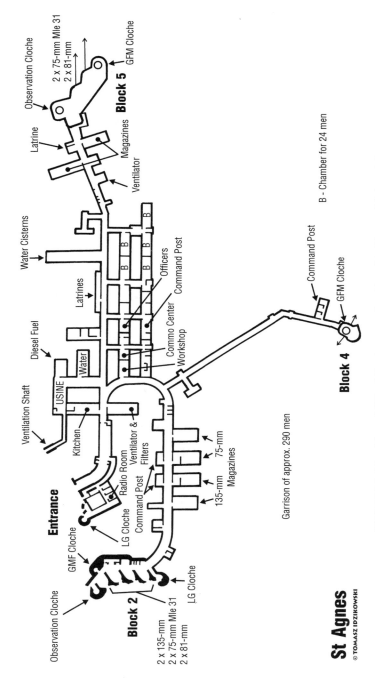

FIGURE 2-22. Plan of GO of St. Agnes in the Alps. [© Tomasz Idzikowski]

St Agnes
© TOMASZ IDZIKOWSKI

Observation Cloche
GMF Cloche
LG Cloche
Entrance
Command Post
Radio Room
Ventilator & Filters
Command Post
Block 2
2 x 135-mm
2 x 75-mm Mle 31
2 x 81-mm
LG Cloche
135-mm
Magazines
75-mm

Kitchen
USINE
Ventilation Shaft
Diesel Fuel
Water
Latrines
Water Cisterns

Commo Center
Workshop
Command Post
Officers
B
B
B
B
B
B

Ventilator
Magazines
Latrine
Observation Cloche
2 x 75-mm Mle 31
2 x 81-mm
GFM Cloche
Block 5

Garrison of approx. 290 men

Command Post
GFM Cloche
Block 4

B - Chamber for 24 men

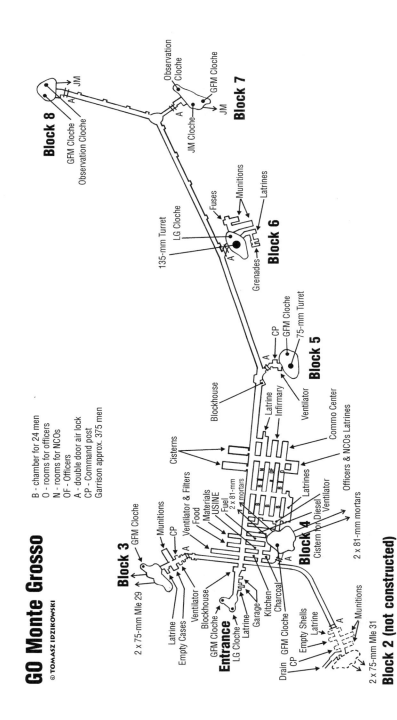

GO Monte Grosso
© TOMASZ IDZIKOWSKI

B - chamber for 24 men
O - rooms for officers
N - rooms for NCOs
OF - Officers
A - double door air lock
CP - Command post
Garrison approx. 375 men

Block 8

Observation
Cloche
GFM Cloche
Block 7
JM
Observation Cloche
JM Cloche
A
JM
A
JM
GFM Cloche
Observation Cloche

Block 6
Munitions
Latrines
Fuses
LG Cloche
135-mm Turret
Grenades
A

Block 5
CP
GFM Cloche
75-mm Turret
A
Ventilator
Infirmary
Latrine
Commo Center
Officers & NCOs Latrines
Latrines
Ventilator
Blockhouse
Cisterns

Block 4
Cistern for Diesel
2 x 81-mm mortars
A
Ventilator
Materials
USINE
Food
Fuel
2 x 81-mm mortars
B
OF
B
N
D

Block 3
GFM Cloche
Munitions
CP
Ventilator & Filters
A
2 x 75-mm Mle 29
Latrine
Empty Cases
Ventilator
Blockhouse

Entrance
GFM Cloche
LG Cloche
Latrine
Garage
Kitchen
Charcoal
A
Drain
GFM Cloche
CP
Empty Shells
Latrine
Munitions
A
2 x 75-mm Mle 31

Block 2 (not constructed)

FIGURE 2-23.   Plan of GO of Monte Grosso in the Alps [© Tomasz Idzikowski]

65

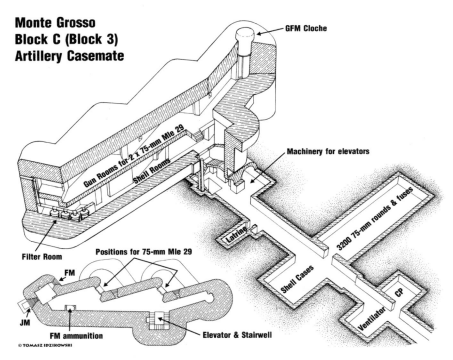

**Monte Grosso
Block C (Block 3)
Artillery Casemate**

GFM Cloche

Machinery for elevators

Gun Rooms for 2 x 75-mm Mle 29

Shell Rooms

Latrine

3200 75-mm rounds & fuses

Shell Cases

CP

Ventilator

Filter Room

Positions for 75-mm Mle 29

FM

JM

FM ammunition

Elevator & Stairwell

© TOMASZ IDZIKOWSKI

FIGURE 2-24. Plan of Block 3 of Monte Grosso in the Alps. [© Tomasz Idzikowski]

standards. Its triple entrance, which did not consist of the standard CORF block, included three accesses: one for men, one for cable cars, and the largest of the three for vehicles carrying ammunition and supplies. A similar entrance was found at the GO of Saint Agel.

Subsequent plans were standardized by CORF. The Alpine entrances were generally smaller than in the northeast and consisted of a single mixed entryway with the exception of the GO of Lavoir, which had an EM and EH, and the GO of Saint Ours Haut, which had none. There was no rolling bridge for defense against tanks in the vestibule, but like the forts of the northeast, they had a defensive blockhouse at the end of the corridor in front of the armored door. Instead of a concrete bridge over the *fossé* and grating gate, an armored drawbridge was lowered or raised as needed. The bridge was perforated so that it could be employed like the grating it replaced to close the fort and leave the armored doors at the entrance open so air could circulate. Adjacent to the drawbridge for the munitions entrance was a smaller doorway for men. Like the EHs of the northeast, the corridor made a 90° turn in front of a blockhouse for an FM. All the Alpine entrances served trucks because military railroads were not practical in the mountain locations. In a number of cases, special military roads were built if roads did not exist.

Other significant differences in the Southeast Front were that the support area was adjacent to the combat areas and the gallery was not long enough to necessitate a *metro*. Because these forts were smaller than those of the northeast, additional M-2 magazines replaced the M-1 magazine.[11] In some cases, the galleries had more than one level; in

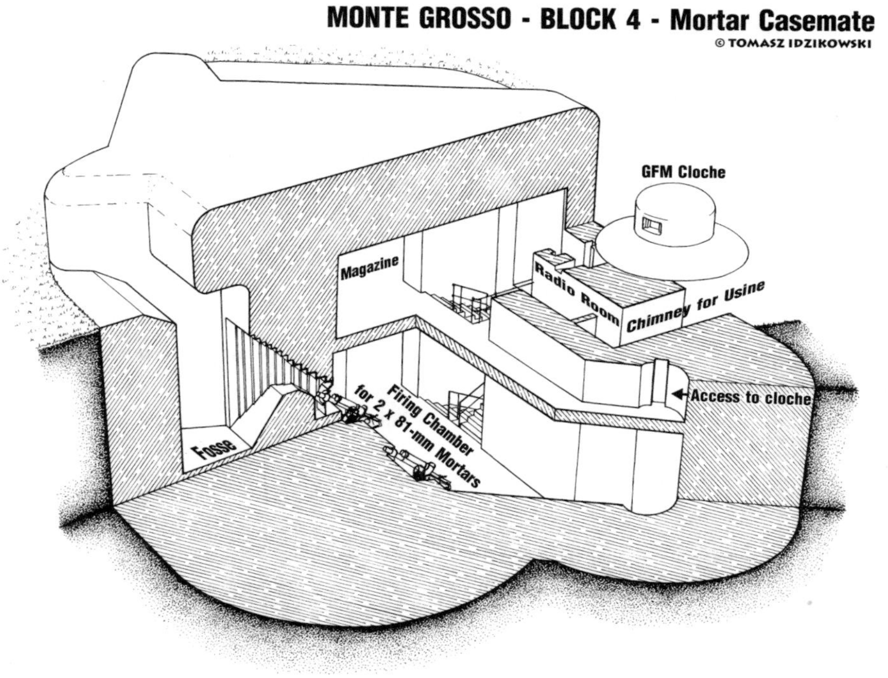

FIGURE 2-25.   Plan of Block 4 of Monte Grosso in Alps. [© Tomasz Idzikowski]

other cases, they branched off toward the combat blocks. Some blocks were reached through an incline, while others were accessed through vertical shafts by elevators and stairways, like in the Northeast Front. The *usine* of GOs had three generators instead of four like in the northeast. Although there was no more than one turret per combat block, most of these forts had a large amount of artillery. The garrisons of most of the GOs numbered well under two hundred men; only about half a dozen, like Rimplas, Mont Grosso, and Castillon, had over three hundred.

There were no special military power lines to link the Alpine *ouvrages*, and communication was problematic. The radio was supplemented with a light-signaling system developed late in the nineteenth century. Special crenels were designed for this purpose. Buried telephone lines were rare since the terrain did not favor excavation. In addition, the field switchboards were only partially buried.

The same types and models of weapons were used in the Alps as in the Northeast, except for the addition of a 75-mm mortar. However, the combat blocks in the Alps mounted a mixture of arms instead of one type of artillery. This was largely due to the mountain locations, which made it difficult and expensive to build separate blocks for various types of artillery. Thus, Block 1 of Saint Antoine had two 75-mm and four 81-mm mortars. Block 2 of Roche Lacroix mounted two 75-mm and two 81-mm mortars and a turret with 75-mm guns. Two artillery blocks at Rimplas included two 75-mm guns and a 75-mm mortar, and Roquebrune had two artillery blocks with two 75-mm and two 81-mm mortars. The largest block was the four-level Block 2 of Sainte Agnès, with two 135-mm *lance-bombes*, two 75-mm mortars, and two 81-mm mortars.[12]

With the exception of Block 5 of Sainte Agnès and the turret of Block 6 at Monte Grosso, the Alpine fortifications did not mount the 135-mm *lance-bombes*. Built on the top of Monte Grosso, the GO of the same name was one of the few Alpine forts that resembled the forts of the Maginot Line Proper. This *ouvrage* with a single entrance was originally meant to have two flanking gun casemates with two 75-mm weapons, only one of which was actually built. It included a turret block with 75-mm guns and a turret block with the 135-mm *lance-bombes*. There was also a nonstandard 81-mm mortar casemate with two pairs of mortars on two sides. No machine gun turrets and only a few artillery turrets were installed in the Alps because they were impractical unless they were located on mountaintops where they could have a 360° turning radius. This is why Mont Agel, located on a strategic position, had two turret blocks with 75-mm guns and a 145-mm gun turret in the plans. Further to the north, in the SF of Dauphiné, Roche Lacroix had a turret for 75-mm guns that dominated the valley below. However, the area behind the turret block was masked by the terrain and the structures of the *ouvrage*, which limited its ability to cover more than 180°. No other *ouvrages* on the Alpine front had turrets.

Due to the lack of turrets, many artillery casemates in the Alps faced in the direction of the enemy, a feature that distinguished them from similar positions on the Maginot Line Proper. These casemates had a higher than average amount of concrete protection and armor reinforcement to withstand direct hits from enemy heavy artillery fire.

There were few single-block POs like Bas de Saint Ours in the Alps. Many of the POs had up to three blocks, including a small entrance block, but they were relatively small, with garrisons well under one hundred men in most cases. Some of the combat blocks only had a casemate for an FM or JM or a cloche for similar weapons and observation.

CHAPTER 3

CLOSING THE GAPS FROM THE NORTH SEA TO THE MEDITERRANEAN

The very first major post–World War I fort to be built was not on the Northeast Front, as one might expect, but on the Southeast Front, where work began at Rimplas in 1928. On the Northeast Front, the two *régions fortifiée* (RFs; fortified regions) of the Maginot Line Proper were built first. They were shortly followed by the three *secteurs fortifié* (SFs; fortified sectors), forming the Rhine defenses on its right flank and the Maginot Extension on its left flank. The only heavily fortified area north of these defenses was Maubeuge. The groundbreaking on four of the Maginot Line's major forts—Rochonvillers, Hackenberg, Simserhof, and Hochwald—took place at the end of 1929 and early in 1930.

Rimplas was finished by early autumn of 1934, and four additional Alpine forts were completed within the next few weeks. Except for Rimplas, the other *ouvrages* of the Southeast Front were begun in 1930 or later. The *gros ouvrages* (GOs) of Cap Martin, Roquebrune, and Mont Agel went into operation during the summer and fall of 1933, and a couple of *petit ouvrages* (POs) were operable early the next year. This was only possible because the milder climatic conditions near the Mediterranean did not hamper construction. Further north in the Alps, building was slowed by unusually long and severe winters, so that by 1939 considerable work remained undone in three of the SFs of the Southeast Front. On the *anciens fronts* (Old Fronts) of the northeast, the *ouvrages*, generally larger and more extensive than those of the southeast, were largely completed by 1934. In the same year, work started on the underground telephone lines, the 0.60—gauge military railroad, the power lines linking the *ouvrages* to the National Grid, and the support facilities that included supply depots. In 1935, the Commission for Organizing the Fortified Regions (*Commission d'Organisation des Région Fortifiées;* CORF) completed plans for the New Fronts, drawing from the experience acquired during the construction of the *ancien fronts*, allowing for improvements and some budgetary cuts.

Few fortifications were erected between Maubeuge and the Maginot Extension and in the four sectors between the Rhine defense and the Southeast Front, along the Swiss border. It would have been impossible to fortify the entire perimeter of the nation, even in ideal economic conditions. Such a mammoth construction project would have made it impossible to build up and modernize the French armed forces. However, all the border sectors required and received some type of protection, no matter how little, especially in the latter half of the 1930s. Even the already fortified areas required additional defenses, but budgetary restraints prevented this work.

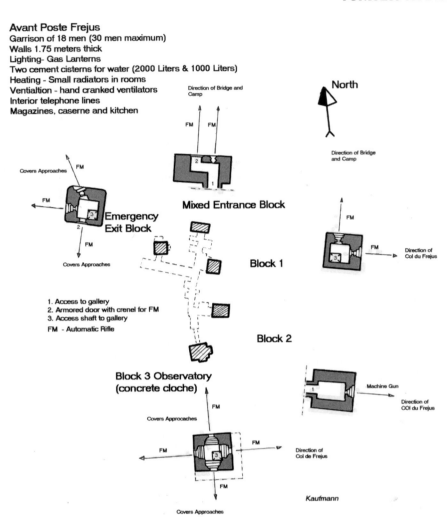

Avant Poste Frejus
Garrison of 18 men (30 men maximum)
Walls 1.75 meters thick
Lighting- Gas Lanterns
Two cement cisterns for water (2000 Liters & 1000 Liters)
Heating - Small radiators in rooms
Ventialtion - hand cranked ventilators
Interior telephone lines
Magazines, caserne and kitchen

1. Access to gallery
2. Armored door with crenel for FM
3. Access shaft to gallery
FM - Automatic Rifle

FIGURE 3-1. *Avant Poste* Frejus. This is an example of one of the many multiblock *avant postes* found in the maritime Alps. [Joseph Kaufmann]

COMMISSION FOR ORGANIZING THE FORTIFIED REGIONS AND OTHER INTERVAL POSITIONS

A line of *avant postes* (advanced positions or outposts) consisting of small blockhouses and obstacles was built in front of the Maginot Line. In addition, single- and two-story fortified houses were placed near the border. The single-level houses generally had a bunker position at each end, whereas the two-level houses consisted of a concrete blockhouse surmounted by an upper floor. The whole house was camouflaged to look like a civilian residence. These positions would be the first to meet an enemy assault, sound the alarm, and impose the first delays on the enemy.

CORF-designed interval casemates with *jumelage de mitralleuse* (JM), 47-mm, anti-tank (AT) guns and a *guêt-fusil mitrailleur* (GFM) cloche filled the gaps between the

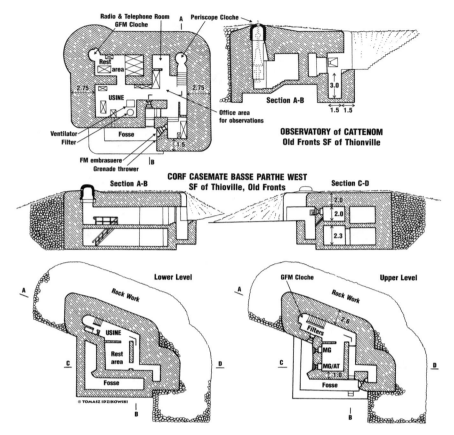

FIGURE 3-2. CORF casemate of Parthe West. [© Tomasz Idzikowski]

ouvrages. Some of these casemates also included a JM cloche. There were three types of interval casemates: a single casemate that had positions for weapons on one flank, a double casemate that had weapons on two flanks, and an armored casemate that had no *fossé* or positions for heavy weapons. The third type had two doors and an embrasure for a *fusil-mitrailleur* (FM) to cover them with flanking fire and two or three cloches (usually including a JM cloche).

Underground telephone cables linked all the CORF interval positions to the *ouvrages*. Filters and generators allowed these positions to operate independently. Often, a subterranean passage linked pairs of CORF interval casemates built in close proximity. An interval casemate usually held a platoon-size force of twenty to thirty-five men and an officer. There were almost eighty interval casemates in the RF of Metz and about the same number in the RF of Lauter. CORF observatories were similar to the interval casemates, but they were located at points from which they could direct the fire of an *ouvrage*. Eleven of these observatories were in the RF of Metz, but only two were in the RF of Lauter, both located on the lower ground of the right flank.

A few non-CORF casemates that included positions for a pair of 75-mm field guns or only a single 75-mm gun were built to strengthen the defense of an area that lacked the support of an artillery fort. After the dissolution of CORF, the *Service Technique du*

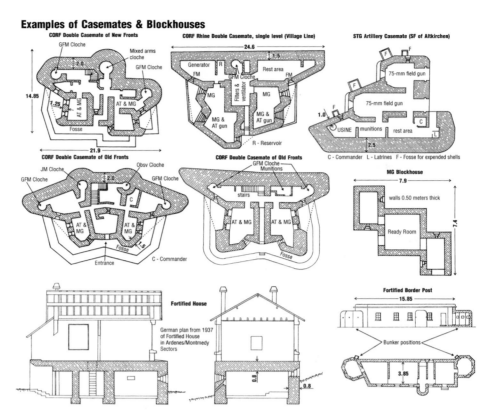

FIGURE 3-3. Plans of interval casemates, blockhouses, and frontier fortified houses. [© Tomasz Idzikowski]

Génie (STG) also built a number of casemates and blockhouses to fill the gaps, but regional military engineers and the *main d'oeuvre militaire* (MOM) were responsible for most of the work. At the onset of the war, local army commanders ordered the construction of many nonstandard blockhouses to tighten the intervals. These blockhouses, usually named after the army commander who had them built (Billotte, Garchery, etc.) often lacked the strength to resist artillery or aerial bombardment.

Abris (shelters) that could hold a full company of infantry were built just to the rear of the casemates and ouvrages of the main line of resistance these consisted of casemates and ouvrages. These positions, which also served as command posts, came in two types: large monolithic structures, usually of two levels, and the cavern type with two small entrances with stairways leading down to the subterranean facilities. In the RF of Metz, there were thirty-three, and in the RF of Lauter, there were twenty-three.

The great majority of CORF positions, with the exception of several special CORF blockhouses and the casemates on the Rhine River, were self-sufficient since they had their own power source (a generator), a filter system, and other amenities. They usually maintained enough supplies to hold out for up to two weeks if isolated. The blockhouses on the Rhine River were designed to close the gap in the RF of Lauter in the Vosges. They were simpler than most CORF works and lacked their own generators for power,

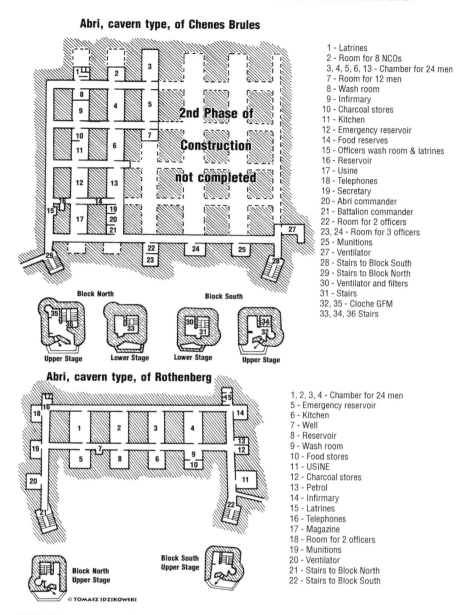

Abri, cavern type, of Chenes Brules

1 - Latrines
2 - Room for 8 NCOs
3, 4, 5, 6, 13 - Chamber for 24 men
7 - Room for 12 men
8 - Wash room
9 - Infirmary
10 - Charcoal stores
11 - Kitchen
12 - Emergency reservoir
14 - Food reserves
15 - Officers wash room & latrines
16 - Reservoir
17 - Usine
18 - Telephones
19 - Secretary
20 - Abri commander
21 - Battalion commander
22 - Room for 2 officers
23, 24 - Room for 3 officers
25 - Munitions
27 - Ventilator
28 - Stairs to Block South
29 - Stairs to Block North
30 - Ventilator and filters
31 - Stairs
32, 35 - Cloche GFM
33, 34, 36 Stairs

Block North   Block South

Upper Stage   Lower Stage   Lower Stage   Upper Stage

Abri, cavern type, of Rothenberg

1, 2, 3, 4 - Chamber for 24 men
5 - Emergency reservoir
6 - Kitchen
7 - Well
8 - Reservoir
9 - Wash room
10 - Food stores
11 - USINE
12 - Charcoal stores
13 - Petrol
14 - Infirmary
15 - Latrines
16 - Telephones
17 - Magazine
18 - Room for 2 officers
19 - Munitions
20 - Ventilator
21 - Stairs to Block North
22 - Stairs to Block South

Block North
Upper Stage

Block South
Upper Stage

© TOMASZ IDZIKOWSKI

FIGURE 3-4. Examples of cavern type abri at Chenes Brueles and Rothembourg. [© Tomasz Idzikowski]

but they had a filter and ventilation system to protect against gas. CORF observatories, *abris* serving as battalion headquarters, and a few casemates included a *transmetteur sans fil* (TSF; wireless transmitter). Many of the casemates, like the infantry casemates in the *ouvrages*, included a small searchlight in an armored casing mount that could be directed and operated with a remote control inside the casemate. In addition, there usually were small concrete niches near the casemates for mine storage.[1]

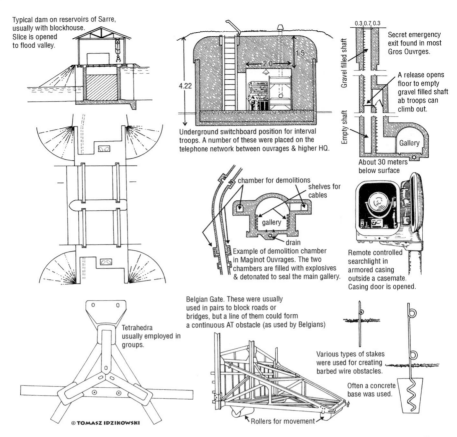

FIGURE 3-5. Drawings of features found in the *ouvrages* and positions supporting them, including obstacles. [© Tomasz Idzikowski]

In the Southeast Front, there was only one CORF interval casemate. The rest of the interval casemates filling the gaps in the Alpine sectors were designed by the army and built by the MOM. No CORF *abris* were built in the Alps, but many of the POs could be considered *abris* since they were incomplete and had few weapons positions. MOM built a number of smaller *abris* and a number of command posts in the Maginot Line and elsewhere. The majority of the MOM and STG positions were erected after the deactivation of CORF, at the end of 1935.

POSITIONS SUPPORTING THE REAR AREA

Supporting positions such as depots for munitions supplies and permanent *casernes* for peacetime garrison were placed behind the Maginot Line. However, smaller temporary *casernes*—some of which included rather large masonry structures—for the garrison in the main line were located near the forts. A few German forts from the World War I era were restored to serve as depots, headquarters, or other functions. The German *feste* at Thionville, Metz, and Mutzig were also used for support. The gun turret blocks (usually four turrets to a block) of some of the German *feste*, such as Fort

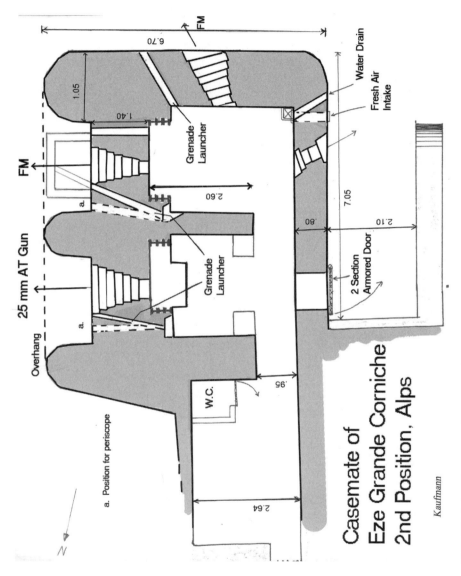

FIGURE 3-6. Casemate of Eze Grande Corniche second Position Alps. It shows an example of a second line casemate in the southeast. [Joseph Kaufmann]

Kaufmann

Koenigsmacker and Fort Guentrange at Thionville, were outfitted with new artillery pieces of the same caliber but longer range. The turrets mounted a single 105-mm gun able to support the *ouvrages* and other positions on the Maginot Line. A line of four of these nonretracting turrets was often shown firing in propaganda films and newsreels and was identified as a fort of the Maginot Line. A few of the old forts at Verdun were also renovated, but they were unrelated to the Maginot Line system.

On the Alpine front, some of the old forts were actually turned into *ouvrages*. Thus, the two-block GO of Barbonnet was built into the flank of Fort Suchet. The old fort included two obsolete Mougin turrets that mounted two 155-mm guns and served as supporting artillery. The *ouvrage* of Mont Agel was built into a preexisting fort to which two 75-mm gun turrets were added. There were also plans to add a 145-mm gun turret. Although considered a Maginot fort, Mont Agel was well behind the main line of forts in the maritime Alps sector.

The Rhine Defenses

There were no *ouvrages* in the Rhine defenses, for which the only ties to the Maginot Line were the CORF-designed casemates. Although in some Rhine sectors the defenses numbered as many as three lines, in most there were only two. The river line consisted mainly of single-level casemates, many of which occupied exposed positions on the riverbank and had to rely on camouflage nets for concealment.

There were four types of these river casemates. They could be single or double with casemate positions on one or two flanks and a GFM cloche. The main weapon was the JM and FM with a 13.2-mm heavy machine gun that served as a light AT or antiboat weapon. Except for the cloches, the weapons positions were built for flanking fires. The casemates had only Protection 1 since the planners did not believe they would need to withstand shells of a larger caliber than 155 mm. Although classified as CORF casemates, they more akin to the special CORF blockhouses in the Vosges because they had air filters but no generators. The troops used gas lamps for lighting (Burtscher, *Coeur*, pp. 20–23). There were about fifty of these casemates along the Rhine River.

The casemates of the second and third lines were larger and more standard CORF casemates with all the normal features for independent operations but generally consisted of only one level only. Double casemates with weapons positions on two flanks were used in the third line. They included a GFM cloche, sometimes a JM cloche and a JM and a 47-mm AT gun for covering the flanks. About forty of these casemates served as the main line of resistance together with a dozen or more double casemates of the type used on the river (Burtscher, *Coeur*, p. 15; Mary, *Maginot*, Vol. 3, pp. 143–149).

The third line, known as the Village Line, was to hold back any enemy force that managed to penetrate beyond the second line, which was not actually a line, but groups of non-CORF casemates, blockhouses, and special CORF *abris* protecting routes leading away from the river so it was possible for the enemy to penetrate between these groups. These *abris*, not as large as the two types found in the main line, consisted of a single position with a GFM cloche. There were three basic versions of these shelters. Only about a dozen of these *abris* were found in this second line and a few more on the Rhine (Mary, *Maginot*, Vol. 3, pp. 143–149).

The Rhine defenses also included STG- and MOM-designed structures that were added in 1935 and later. Some of the blockhouses employed older naval 47- and 65-mm guns and 25-mm AT guns. In addition to building fourteen casemates along the river at Strasbourg, the *Génie* of Strasbourg returned some of the old German forts that ringed the city into limited service in 1935 and later. Artillery positions were added at Forts Ulhrich and Ney-Rapp; blockhouses for machine guns and observation at Forts Pétain, Foch, and Ducrot; two casemates for 75-mm guns at Fort Ducrot; and positions for the old 65-mm naval guns at six other forts. These old forts, once served by large garrisons, were only manned by a platoon-size force when the war began (Burtscher, *Coeur*, pp. 48–56).

The Sarre Gap

The lowland between the RF of Metz and the RF of Lauter received light defenses. Initially, it had been considered as a possible route for the French army to advance against the Germans after mobilization. This plan remained active until the war; in 1939, the French actually used it to invade German territory. Interest in increasing the defenses of the sector grew when a January 1935 plebiscite returned the Saar to Germany. The fact that the Rhineland was supposed to remain demilitarized did not assuage the French distrust of their neighbor.

The French army intended to flood large areas between St. Avold—Sarralbe and Sarreguemines by releasing water from large reservoirs in the region into the Sarre River and its tributaries. Blockhouses on or near the dams controlled the reservoirs and the water flowing from them. A number of STG casemates and blockhouses, including a few MOM casemates for a 75-mm field gun, formed a line along the Nied and Moderbach Rivers between St. Avold and Puttelange, where the inundations were expected to be minimal.

The *Commission d'Études des Zones Fortifiées* (CEZF), created by the army in 1939 and directed by General Belhague (replaced by General Philippe in 1940), planned a second line along the Albe River. This second line was to include about twenty STG casemates, most of which were not built. Along the Sarre River, east of Puttelange, most of the positions consisted of smaller blockhouses added later by the army and a few CORF casemates at Wittring between the Sarre River and the RF of Lauter, where the new PO of Haut Poirier was built in 1935. In 1940, the year the campaign began, the spring rains had been lighter than normal, and the planned water barrier failed to reach the anticipated levels.

REINFORCING THE INTERVALS

After 1934, locally designed blockhouses began to appear in the intervals of the Maginot Line and elsewhere. The designs of these fortifications, mostly rather simple, were named after the military region where they stood. If they were erected outside the Maginot Line, they were often named after the area army commander. In the RF of Metz, about fifty Region Fortifiee Metz (RFM) Model 1935 blockhouses with an old naval 47-mm gun, designed for frontal fire, and having sufficient concrete protection to resist 105-mm guns appeared. The RFM Model 1936 blockhouse also mounted the new 25-mm AT gun and machine guns for flanking fire, but it had greater concrete protection and could resist weapons of up to 155-mm caliber. About seventy of these blockhouses were built. The RFM Model 1937, mounting a 25-mm gun and a machine

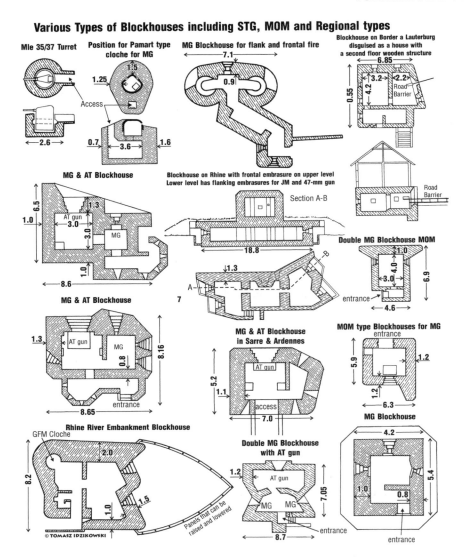

FIGURE 3-7. Various types of STG, MOM, and regional blockhouses. [© Tomasz Idzikowski]

gun, also for flanking fires, was also built in this RF. Another Model 1937 had a pair of machine guns for frontal fire. These new models used armored shields to protect embrasures. Finally, in 1936 an RFM artillery casemate that included a GFM cloche mounted two 75-mm field guns (Mary, *Maginot*, Vol. 2, pp. 130–133).

The designs from the RF of Lauter included a casemate for two 75-mm field guns and a simpler one for a single 75-mm field gun; these were built in the Vosges and the Sarre sectors. Only a few of these gun casemates were actually built. During 1939, additional nonstandard concrete positions and even log bunkers were erected.

During the 1930s, in addition to these positions, an almost continuous line of AT obstacles extended for most of the length of the two RFs, running along the main line of resistance and connecting most of the *ouvrages*. These obstacles consisted of several rows—usually six rows at a depth of about twelve meters—of AT rails projecting above the ground at different heights up to 2.4 meters. In some places, there were AT ditches as well. This line was interrupted by roads, which were usually barred by a pair of Cointet obstacles,[2] which could be rolled and locked into position. These obstacles were ideal for blocking bridges. Another commonly used obstacle was a more standardized, older type of armored barrier that consisted of an arm that could be raised (*Denkschrift*, p. 346; Truttmann, "La Fortification," p. 77). A barrier of barbed wire obstacles encircled the combat areas of the *ouvrages* and many interval positions. It usually consisted of about four rows of metal stakes with wire strung through each row, across each column, and diagonally to create a barrier that generally followed the line of AT obstacles. Finally, several thousand AT mines were placed in the line of obstacles and a special stake known as a "Piquet Olivier" was attached to an explosive that served as an AT obstacle.

Equipment Used for the Construction of the Fortifications

The construction of the *ouvrages* required a large amount of excavation, followed by the enlargement of subterranean and block positions and the setting of concrete and stone. In some cases, if the gallery level did not reach the standard depth of twenty-five to thirty meters, the entire area was excavated with heavy construction equipment, as was done at the GO of Immerhof. In most cases, the galleries had to be tunneled out by work crews with picks, shovels, and drilling equipment and using mining techniques. After the galleries were excavated, bricks and stone masonry vaults were erected, and concrete was poured over them from portable mixers to line the walls.

When the various blocks were finished, their shafts were excavated down to the gallery level, and the elevators were installed. Heavy lifting equipment was needed for lowering the various elements of the elevators and their shafts. Heavier concrete mixers were required to pour the foundations, walls, and roofs of the block after the forms and reinforcement had been set up. Usually, the construction material, including that for the stonework placed around the foundation and the earth covering the concrete walls, was hauled in by truck. Vehicle-mounted cranes or mobile lifting equipment were brought in to lift the cloches and turrets into place.

Although the machinery lightened the work, most of the construction required backbreaking manual labor. A civilian labor force was hired to work under the supervision of the army. A large number of foreign workers who found employment with the civilian firms that worked on the fortifications created a security problem.

The deployment of obstacles around and between the *ouvrages* also required a large labor force, especially for the AT ditches, which were excavated with pick and shovel. Sometimes, steam shovels and other heavy equipment speeded the process. The AT rails were planted with portable pile drivers or with mobile motorized pile drivers. The work was done by the MOM or by soldiers.

The telephone system was installed by civilian companies; for the cables, these companies cut three-foot deep trenches with motorized trenching machines. The large cable reels were hauled in by tractors that laid out the cable, and the trenches were backfilled manually or with machines.

The installation of the equipment inside the *ouvrages* included tasks that ranged from wiring the internal telephone system to the installation of the diesel engines. The installation of the armored components such as embrasures, doors, cloches, turrets, and associated machinery was usually accomplished during the last construction phases. The final layers of concrete work on the exposed roofs of the blocks were poured after the cloches and turrets were installed. In the case of the turrets, the surrounding forward armor (the large plates that formed an armored protective skirt) also had to be covered in concrete. The emplacement of the heavy weapons was among the final steps that led to an *ouvrage* becoming operational. The military had to finish much of the work.

THE NEW FRONTS OF THE NORTH

The New Fronts included not only the area between the Maginot Line Proper and the North Sea, but also the Sarre and the left flank of the RF of the Lauter. Besides STG casemates and blockhouses, not much was added to seal the Sarre Gap effectively, with the exception of a lone PO on its right flank: the Haut Poirier situated near Achen. A few CORF casemates closed the gap between Wittring and Achen. Between Wittring and a point to the west of Sarable, the Sarre River Valley was to be flooded. Only light blockhouses were built on both sides of the area to be inundated. In a few places like Herbitzheim, a number of small, poorly designed MOM blockhouses were built to defend the dam. This sector eventually became a subsector of the SF of Rohrbach of the RF of the Lauter.

Originally, the PO of Haut Poirier was designed to become a GO after the addition of Blocks 4 and 5 with 75-mm gun turrets that would cover the entire sector to the west of the fort and the border beyond Sarreguemines. Block 6 was to include a 135-mm *lance-bombe* turret that would cover most of the subsector of Kalhouse to the west.[3] All three blocks, planned for the second cycle of construction, were canceled because of the cost. Instead, the two POs of Rohrbach and Welschoff were built on the Rohrbach plateau of the SF of Rohrbach. Both, like Haut Poirier, had three combat blocks and one block that mounted the new mixed-arms turret. However, neither had the small entrance block found at Haut Poirier. Rohrbach was also planned as a GO with similar blocks to those of Haut Poirier, but they too had to be canceled. The PO of Welschoff, located between Rohrbach and Haut Poirier, was to include an 81-mm mortar turret, also cancelled. These POs were completed by 1938. Thus, the New Front created on the left flank of the RF of the Lauter had no artillery forts.

The Defensive Sector (SD) of the Sarre relied heavily on the network of rivers between Téting and Sarralbe and their associated water obstacles for its defense. It was reinforced by numerous light blockhouses, about thirty STG casemates, and four casemates for a 75-mm gun in the adjacent SFs. The STG-designed casemates were simpler and cheaper than those designed by CORF but lacked the equipment needed for independent operations. The artillery casemate was smaller than the STG infantry casemate. In 1939, CEZF tried to create a second line of defense to the rear, mainly along the Albe River, but made little progress beyond creating some new STG casemates with 25-mm AT guns.

Several innovations materialized in the SD of the Sarre, which included a variety of observatories, including a small pentagonal armored position that could be placed on a concrete block. Old tank turrets and bodies—mainly from the Renault FT 17—found their use as well. The turrets were embedded in concrete to form armored machine gun positions. In addition, an STG turret Models 1935 and 1937 mounting a Hotckiss Model 1914 machine gun was specially designed for the fixed positions in this SD. These turrets were accessed through a hatch at the bottom that opened from the concrete base. They also had a hatch on the roof. Six hundred of these new turrets were placed on both fronts (Wahl, *La Ligne Maginot en Alsace*; pp. 52–53). Older armor pieces like the Digoin cloches, which had narrow observation slits, and the Pamart cloches from World War I, shaped like elephant heads, were also put to use in other sectors for observation. The Pamart cloche could mount a Hotchkiss machine gun.

The Montmédy Bridgehead was an important addition to the New Front, which extended from Villy to Montmédy. Between this bridgehead and the Maginot Line Proper lay the SD of Marville. On English maps, these sectors were identified as the Maginot Extension. Work on the Montmédy Bridgehead began well before it did in the SD of Marville, which was only started in 1936, and included about twenty-five STG casemates and numerous other fortifications. This front closed off much of the southern Belgian border to a possible German advance through Luxembourg.

In the Montmédy Bridgehead, the SF of Montmédy received four *ouvrages* that, due to cost cutting, were less effective than the older Maginot forts. The Maginot Line ended at Villy with the small, two-block PO of La Ferté flanked on each side by two casemates, mounting a single 75-mm gun each, to cover the approaches. The PO only had one mixed-arms turret. The original plans for the Montmédy Bridgehead also called for three GOs because in this area the distances between forts were greater than in most of the main line, and the extra firepower was needed to ensure the forts' ability to support each other.

The GO of Chenois, which was next in line, included a single 75-mm turret block with an old refurbished 1905 turret instead of the two planned 75-mm gun turrets. Block 6 was cancelled. Block 1 included a mixed-arms turret. Chenois was followed by the PO of Thonnelle, which stood east of the town of the same name. This was also supposed to have one block with an old 1905-model turret, one block with a newer model, and one block with an 81-mm turret. However, only four of the seven blocks originally envisioned were actually built, including the entrance. The most heavily armed block included only a mixed-arms turret, rendering this fort heavily dependent on its neighbors for artillery support.

In the interval between the PO of Thonnelle and the GO of Chenois, to the west of the town, was an STG casemate mounting a 75-mm field gun that covered the terrain in front of the PO. A second STG artillery casemate between the PO of Thonnelle and the GO of Vélosnes covered the PO with defensive fire as well. Finally, the GO Vélosnes, very similar to the Chenois but with a modern 75-mm gun turret—the only one in the Extension—included a block with a mixed-arms turret. Twelve CORF interval casemates occupied the gaps between the forts. However, this sector remained lightly fortified despite the addition of the four *ouvrages*.

Positioning the Forts of the Maginot Line

The Maginot *ouvrages* were placed so that they could control and dominate the area surrounding them. In the Maginot Line Proper, they were also positioned in

RF of LAUTER:

HP – 5 km – Wel –3 km – Roh – 8 km – **Sim** – 3 km – **Schi** – 2 km – Ott – 7 km – **GH** – 20 km – Lem – 1.5 km – **FC** – 4 km – **WHoch** – 2 km – **EHoch** – 4.5 – **Sch**

75 T&C (Sim)

75 T (Schi)

75 T (GH)

75 T (FC)

75 C (WHoch)

75 C (EHoch)

75 T (Hoch)

75 T (Sch)

(HP – Haut Poirier, Wel – Welshof, Roh – Rohrbach, Sim –Simserhof, Sch –Schiesseck, Ott–Otterbiel, GH – Grand Hohekirkel, WHoch & EHoch – West & East Hochwald, Sch –Schoenenbourg)

RF of METZ

A-1 – 2 km – **A-2** – 6 km – **A-3** – 4 km – **A-4** – 3.5 km – **A-5** – 5 km – **A-6** – 5.5 km – **A-7** – 6 km – **A-8** – 4 km – **A-9** – 3 km – **A-10** – 2.5 km – **A-11** – 2.5 km –

75T&C (A-2)

75C (A-3)

75 T (A-6)

75 T (A-8) C

75 T (A-9)

75 T (A-11)

75 T (A-13)

75 T &C (A-17)

A-12 – 3 km – **A-13** – 1.5 km – **A-14** – 1 km – **A-15** – 0.5 km – **A-16** – 5 km – **A-17** – 3.5 km – **A-18** – 3.5 km – **A-19** – 2 km – **A-20** – 2.5 km –

75 T (A-9)

75 T (A-11)

75 T &C (A-13)

75 T (A-17)

75 T (A-18) C

75 T&C (A-19)

75 T (A-21)

75 T (A-22)

75 T (A-25)

A-21 – 1.5 km – **A-22** – 2 km – A-23 – 2.5 km – **A-24** – 1 km – **A-25** –1 km – A-26 – 4 km – A-27 – 4 km – A-28 – 1.5 km – A-29

------ 75 T (A-18)C ------

------- 75 T&C (A-19) ---------------

75 T (A-21) --

-----------75 T (A-22) ---

-------- 75 T (A-25) --

(A-1 – Chappy, **A-2 – Fermont**, **A-3 – Latiremont**, A-4 – Mauvis Bois, A-5 – Bois Four, **A-6 – Brehain**, A-7 – Amuetz, **A-8 – Rochvillers**, **A-9 – Molvange**, A-10 – Immerhof, **A-11 – Soetrich**, A-12– Bois Karre, **A-13 – Kobenbusch**, A-14 – Oberheid, **A-15** – Galgenberg, A-16 – Sentzich, **A-17– Metrich, A-18 – Billig, A-19- Hackenberg**, A-20 – Coucou, **A-21 – Mont Welches, A-22 – Michelsberg**, A-23 – Hobling, A-24 – Bousse, **A-25 – Anzeling**, A-26 – Berenbach, A-27 – Bovenberg, A-28 – Denting, A-29 – Village Coume, A-30 to A-38 omitted). NOTE: All *ouvrages* of the RF of Metz were identified with the numbering system of A-1 through A-38. The forts of the RF of the Lauter did not use this method.

In the Maginot Extension, the gap between *ouvrages* was much larger and the artillery coverage for each fort was much less.

LaFerte – 7 km – **Chenois** – 5.5 km – Tonnelle – 7 km – **Velosnes**

|---------------- 75 T (Chenois) -----------------|

|------------------ 75 T (Velosnes) ----------------|

NOTE: The distance in kilometers placed between each *ouvrage* on the charts above are not spaced to give a proper scale. The chart only shows the area of coverage of the 75-mm weapons of each fort so the length of the lines can not be used as a scale.

such a way that they could support each other. In the RF of the Lauter, the forts built in groups because the Vosges formed too large an obstacle between groups. Haut Poirier, Welsches, and Rohrbach, the last three *ouvrages* of this RF, which guarded the left wing of the Plateau of Rohrbach, lacked artillery and could not mutually support each other. In the RF of Metz, the first groups of *ouvrages* were set to form a continuous barrier with a small gap in the Moselle Valley. At the time this RF was extended on the left flank to cover the Luxembourg border, the lack of adequate funds made it impossible to build a sufficient number of GOs. Thus, the spacing between GOs was increased, and several forts originally planned as GOs were built as POs. Figure 3.1 is a comparison of the groupings. It shows the approximate distance (within 0.5 kilometer) between the centers of the forts and identifies the 75-mm weapons in supporting range of other forts.

The sectors beyond the Maginot Extension formed the SD Ardennes, where some work was begun in 1936 along the Meuse River, and other construction along the front did not begin until 1939. These sectors relied mainly on the Ardennes, which had forested, hilly terrain that could be easily blocked. Several dozen small bunkers were erected on the west bank or behind the Meuse River between Villy and Givet. Several casemates formed a bridgehead east of Mezières. In 1939, the CEZF tried to create in the SD Ardennes a second line of defenses, similar to the one in the Sarre. Unfortunately, this project suffered from the same lack of success.

The STG casemates designed for the CEZF lines were generally smaller than the STG casemates of the first line and included positions for 25-mm AT guns and a Type C cloche. This type of cloche was similar to the GFM cloche Type B but was sent directly from the manufacturer without being finished. Since it was strictly for observation, it included a periscope position and three narrow crenels for observation but none for weapons. However, it did not have an interior lining or a mobile floor. It was the same size as the small Type B with Protection 2. There were plans to replace the observation crenels with crenels for weapons of the type used in Type B. Lamentably, these cloches were not installed in all of the STG casemates in time for the war (Mary, *Maginot*, Vol. 3, p. 41).

The border area between the Maginot Line and the North Sea was initially neglected in France's defense schemes because Belgium was an ally. Officially, French officials claimed that they did not want to give the Belgians the impression that France was abandoning them by fortifying this front. In addition, they maintained that the construction of heavy fortifications in many sectors to the north of Maubeuge presented serious problems. In reality, some work was actually done after 1930 on this front, but by the end of 1931, a French senator complained that the work was not satisfactory and demanded the fortification of the front between the Ardennes and the North Sea.

In his article "Le Secteur Fortifié de Maubeuge," Julien Depret pointed out that the senate approved funds for the fortification of Maubeuge and a few other areas, including a zone of inundations, in 1932. Marshal Pétain objected, claiming it was better to use mobile parks and to take up positions in Belgium. Although the marshal's ideas were more diplomatic, they were impractical. In 1933, Daladier, the minister of war, was able to designate Maubeuge and Escaut as SFs, and the parliament, overcoming its fear of offending the Belgian government, approved and authorized the funding of the

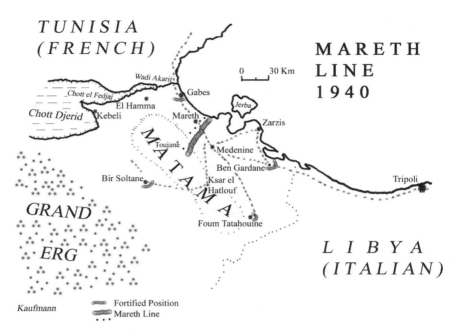

FIGURE 3-8. Mareth Line 1940. Some consider this a southern extension of the Maginot fortifications in Tunisia, but the structures have little in common with those of France. This line was garrisoned in 1940, and in 1943 the Italians and Germans modified it. It became part of their defenses against the British eighth Army. [Joseph Kaufmann]

project. Thus were born the last of the New Fronts prepared by CORF, a line that was dubbed as the *Ligne Daladier* by Julien Depret to distinguish it from the remainder of the Maginot Line (Depret, "Le Secteur Fortifié de Maubeuge (1)," *39–45 Magazine*, no. 155, pp. 52–58).

Eventually, the SF Maubeuge became the most heavily defended area north of the Maginot Line since it stood on the direct invasion route through Belgium, one the Germans had taken in World War I when they had to pass the Belgian fortresses of Liège and Namur. To check another German advance through that open terrain in Belgium, north of the Meuse River, the French decided to build several *ouvrages* around Maubeuge. These *ouvrages* were built on old Séré de Rivères forts between 1934 and 1937. Shortage of funds prevented the construction of any of the planned GOs, but four POs were completed. Each of these POs had two blocks, except Boussois, and included one block with a new mixed-arms turret mounting two pairs of 25-mm guns/JM. Boussois consisted of three blocks, one of which held the modified single mixed-arms turret with a combination of a 25-mm gun and a 50-mm mortar. The blocks of the new *ouvrages* occupied a position near the angle formed by the front and flank of the old forts. The underground gallery running across the center of the old fort linked the new blocks to one another. At the PO of Sarts, the usine, command post, and other features found in Maginot *ouvrages* occupied the lower level of the two blocks since a thirty-meter deep gallery could not accommodate them. At the POs of Bersillies, Salmagne, and Boussois, the standard thirty-meter deep gallery housed the *caserne* and *usine*. The army canceled plans to complete two 75-mm turret blocks for both Sarts and Boussois.

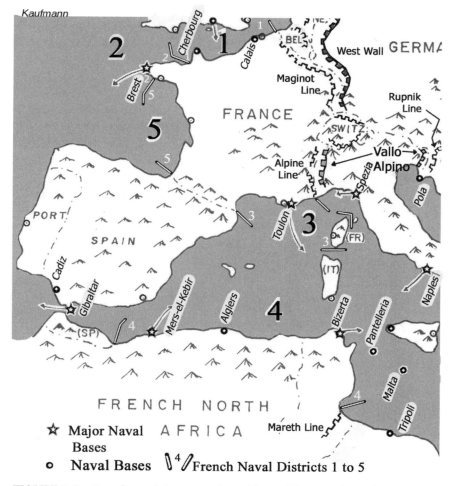

FIGURE 3-9. French naval districts and naval bases. This map shows the location of major naval bases and the five French naval districts. [Joseph Kaufmann]

In addition to these POs, CORF built a number of casemates between the POs around the city of Maubeuge (Mary, *Maginot*, Vol. 3, pp. 65–68; Wahl, *La Ligne Maginot en Alsace*, pp. 86–97). Some of these casemates had an unusual design, which included not only a mixed-arms cloche, but also a mixed-arms turret mounting one set of JM with a 25-mm gun and a 50-mm mortar. One of these special casemates, Héron-Fontaine, stood to the west of the PO of Sarts; four more to the east of the PO of Boussois formed the end of the line of CORF positions. Also between 1934 and 1937, before the *ouvrages* were completed, thirteen additional CORF casemates were built across the north end of the Mormal Forest as planned in 1932.

On the New Fronts, beyond the Maginot Line Proper, new types of CORF casemates included a GFM cloche or a mixed-arms cloche with a 25-mm gun. Their entrances resembled the *ouvrage entrées des hommes* (EHs; men's entrances) because they usually included an L-shaped hallway protected by an interior firing position for an FM. To the north of the forest line, near the border, along the position of Maubeuge, and south to the Ardennes sector, there were a number of locally built bunkers designed by the STG and the *Génie* of Valenciennes and Maubeuge. Known as RM1 blockhouses (Military Region 1 blockhouses), some had Protection 2 and mounted 25-mm guns. They were mostly added after Belgium returned to neutrality in 1936.

The PO of Eth was built in the SF of Escaut. Further north, old Fort Maulde anchored the end of the line that extended along the border from Maubeuge after 1936. Across the east edge of the Raismes Forest, north of Valenciennes, stood twelve CORF casemates built according to the plan of 1932. Like the POs of Maubeuge, the PO of Eth had two blocks, one of which included a mixed-arms turret. It also had an underground gallery that linked it to the Casemate of Jenlain 600 meters down the slope of the hill occupied by the fort. This gallery was smaller than the main one, which linked the two blocks that stood about 250 meters apart, also served as the drain for the fort.

Several STG and RM1 blockhouses were built in front of the line of CORF casemates in the Raismes Forest, along the Canal du Jard, between Maulde and Condé. The remainder of the line between the town of Condé and the PO of Eth contributed no major obstacles to the defensive line formed by blockhouses. Old Fort Maulde, which was not actually a Maginot *ouvrage*, included two STG flanking casemates mounting two 75-mm guns. These casemates were built onto the rear corners of the rectangular fort and an observatory near the front. An unusual STG casemate was built to the rear in 1937. It mounted one 155-mm grande puissance Fillioux (GPF) gun for frontal fire. The renovation of Fort Maulde took place in early 1937 under the direction of the STG. However, work on a subterranean gallery linking the flanking casemates of the fort to the casemate for the 155-mm GPF and on two nearby casemates did not begin until 1939. By the time the war started, it remained unfinished (Depret, "La defense de l'Escaut," *39–45 Magazine*, no. 186, 44–46; Depret, "Le Fort de Maulde," *39–45 Magazine*, no. 172, pp. 51–53; Wahl, *Maginot*, pp. 79–81).

Defending the Lille-Roubaix industrial complex was not a practical proposition due to its proximity to the border. As a result, little work was done in the SD of Lille before the war. The SD of Flanders, which continued to the coast, relied heavily on inundations east of Dunkirk for its defense. About two dozen STG blockhouses were built in the remaining sixty kilometers of the sector, mostly between 1937 and 1939. When the war began, the French military plans called for advancing the defensive position into Belgium to shorten the line and improve the defenses of the northern front between Dunkirk and Maubeuge.

The French high command ordered the construction of additional fortifications along the Swiss border, between the SF of Altkirch and the SF Jura. Although these two fronts were lightly defended, the terrain added to their strength, allowing the designation of SF. The defenses consisted of STG casemates in flanking positions, a few of which mounted 75-mm guns, and blockhouses. The Model 1935/37 turrets and other types of positions for observation were used here as on the northern sectors. Old forts, like Fort Joux in the southern part of the SF of Jura and Fort Écluse in the SD of Rhone, formed much of the main defenses, guarding the routes into Switzerland.

Although it was not part of the Alpine defenses, the island of Corsica was considered a section of the Southeast Front because its location in relation to Italy required some defenses. The island's defenses consisted of seventeen CORF casemates, two blockhouses, and five *cavern abris* built into the hilly terrain. The main positions were concentrated in the south, where they covered the approaches from Sardinia. Ten casemates, one of which included artillery, and five *abris* protected the town of Bonifacio on the southern tip of the island. Five more casemates defended the port of Porto Vecchio, further up the coast. The two casemates that stood at the entrance to the bay mounted artillery. In the north, a blockhouse and a casemate secured the town of Bastia. On the other side of the peninsula, two similar positions defended St. Florent. Bastia was on the main ferry terminus for crossing to Piombino and Leghorn in Italy.

Corsica offered a peculiar problem for the French because its east coast was almost as long as the entire Alpine frontier on the mainland. Yet, the French could only afford to build a minimal number of fortifications and defend the island with a small garrison. Thus, the French air force and navy became the two keys to maintaining control of the island. Ironically, Corsica presented the same threat to Italy's island of Sardinia, as Sardinia did to Corsica. Indeed, the French could also threaten much of Italy from Rome to the Franco-Italian border from this island. The Italians, on the other hand, threatened the most direct routes from Toulon and Marseille to the French colonies of Tunisia and northeastern Algeria from Sardinia. Thus, Corsica served as a counter-threat to help secure the line of communications to Africa.

The French dedicated little effort to the defense of their far-flung empire. The task of defending France's territories was relegated to the small formations of the French Foreign Legion, French colonial and "native" units, and the French fleet. However, the French navy was not in a position to defend France's overseas territories because, by the time the war began, it had only one aircraft carrier. Likewise, the air force, which played an increasingly important role in the defense of mainland France, could not spare its best aircraft to support France's colonies. In fact, French Indochina, the Pacific Islands, the West Indies, the African colonies, and Syria/Lebanon were not high on the priority list when it came to defenses and fortifications.[4] The only notable exception was French North Africa, where Italian forces in Libya could easily threaten neighboring Tunisia as well as Algeria and Morocco. These three colonies were the most valuable and populous of the French empire and a source of manpower for many of France's colonial and native divisions. To secure the region, the French army built a line of fortifications deep inside Tunisia to take advantage of the terrain and desert obstacles. The main route of advance was along the coast, which was effectively blocked with a new line of fortifications called the Mareth Line. Although they had features vaguely reminiscent of the Maginot Line, these fortifications were not designed by CORF and did not include any structures larger than casemates.

The Mareth Line ran behind the Wadi Zigzaou[5] covering a distance of about fifty kilometers from the Gulf of Gabes to the vicinity of Cheguimi and the Djebel (mountains) Matmata. The sea secured its left flank. Its right flank rested on a rocky plateau known as Dahar located between the Great Eastern Erg[6] and the Matmata Mountains. The French commander in Tunisia did not consider closing the gap between the Mareth Line and the Great Eastern Erg, which could allow the enemy to outflank the line, until 1938. The fortified line occupied a point where all major routes from Italian Libya into Tunisia converged, leading toward Mareth, with the sea on one side and the sand on the other. Although the position had been studied before 1934, it was not until January

1934 that the office of the *Génie* at Tunis and the local military engineer office at Gabes began planning the defenses in earnest. According to General Pierre Daillier, author of *Terre d'Affrontements*, infantry officers selected the sites for the strongpoints with a view to creating fields of fire that would control the front, a principle that was developed during the Great War (Daillier, *Terre d'Affrontements*, pp. 38–41).

However, the French government did not authorize any credits for the construction until 1936, when Italy allied itself with Germany, becoming a looming threat to French security in North Africa. The amount spent on the entire Mareth Line and its forward positions was comparable to the sum expended on the four-block *ouvrage* of St. Agnès in the Alps. The Mareth casemates cost only a fraction of the CORF interval casemates and were considerably less sophisticated. In fact, building only ten CORF-type casemates would have expended the budget for the entire line.

General Morin supervised the planning and construction of the Mareth Line until 1938, when he was replaced by General Dumont (Daillier, *Terre d'Affrontements*, pp. 39–41). The casemates the two men designed for the Mareth Line in some cases may have looked like those built in France, but they seldom surpassed the equivalent of Protection 1 in concrete thickness. In addition, they had no protective *fossé*; instead, a double door ("Dutch door") allowed escape in case the lower part of the door was blocked by rubble.[7] The large rearward-facing façades of the command posts, which were tunneled into the rock in many cases to create additional rooms, resembled those of the Maginot *ouvrages*.

In September 1936, during a meeting concerning Tunisia and headed by General Georges, it was determined that the fortifications of Mareth, the port of Bizerte, Medenine, Ben Gardane, and Foum Tathouine must be completed. The last three positions were located in advance of the Mareth Line. Ben Gardane was located on the right and Foum Tathouine on the left flank of the point at which the lines of communication began to funnel between the Matmata Mountains and the sea, toward Mareth.

The fortified region was divided into an eastern and western sector.[8] Two lines about 1.5 kilometers apart were planned for the Mareth Line: the main line of resistance and a stop line behind it. An SD was added in the rock-strewn Dahar Plateau, across the Matmata. The plateau later became part of an SD extending across the Matmata to Kebili, on the edge of the Chott Djerid. Wadi Akarit drained Chott Djerid and Chott El Fedjaj, forming a continuous line across Tunisia.[9] Despite this major obstacle, the French failed to fortify heavily the Abkarit Wadi, instead concentrating their efforts on the Mareth Line about 50 kilometers to the south because it protected Gabes.

The Mareth Line consisted of *Points d'appui* (support positions) in the main line and the stop line to provide fire support and serve as strongpoints. The strong points in the main line included flanking machinegun casemates and AT gun positions, whereas in the stop line the artillery positions were sited to cover the intervals between strongpoints in the main line. A few of the flanking casemates for machine guns covering the intervals had connecting galleries. The strongpoints on the plain and hillsides included AT positions. Barbed wire obstacles encircled the strongpoint; these were laid out for all-around defense. These obstacles were doubled in front and on the sides of the strongpoints. In addition, a line of AT obstacles, vertical rails like those used on the Maginot Line, ran across the entire front. The sides of the wadi itself were cut to make them steeper.

In the Matmata, Ksar el Hallouf covered an AT ditch that created a continuous obstacle since the main line ended on the foothills of these mountains. This main line of resistance included twelve strongpoints. Eleven more were built behind it on the stop line of the eastern sector. The western sector had eleven strongpoints in the main line, backed by seven more in the stop line. An infantry position was dug into the rock of the Matmata heights at Ksar-el-Hallouf. Beyond it, in the Dahar, stood the strongpoint of Bir Soltane, which included two 75-mm gun turrets removed from one of the ten Char 2C tanks built in 1918.[10] German documents confirm the existence of two turrets for 75-mm guns and mentioned four smaller turrets (*Das Franzoische ubergangsheer im Fruhjaha*, 1942, map of Tunisia). The advanced position of Ben Gardane formed a square redoubt surrounded by an AT ditch with flanking casemates and concrete abris for the troops. There, small triangular positions at each corner of the redoubt that served as strongpoints were surrounded by AT rails that continued around the entire position. Another advanced position located on the Matmata heights consisted of two groups of casemates cut into the terrain. A line of *avant-postes* was set up about ten kilometers south of the main line, on the heights of Aram early in the war (Dailler, *Terre d'Affrontements*, pp. 44–47, 66).

Since Tunisia was low on the priority list for weapons as well, its fortifications were armed with older 75-mm naval guns that served as AT weapons. Some casemates and open positions mounted older 47-mm naval guns or the new 25-mm guns for AT use. Most positions relied on machine guns and automatic rifles. About eight artillery casemates for 75-mm guns and most of the blockhouses and casemates had embrasures for light automatic weapons. The command posts represented some of the largest structures built on the Mareth Line. In 1938, so much work was done on the Mareth Line that construction on the coastal defenses in Tunisia had to be halted (Moullins, *Bizerte*, p. 56). The curators of the present-day museum at Mareth claim that there were eight artillery casemates, forty casemates or blockhouses for infantry, and fifteen command posts. In 1939, colonial divisions and some native units took up position in the Mareth Line.

Final Costs for the Maginot Line

By the time the last government credits were spent in 1940, the Maginot Line's fortifications included fifty-five GOs (twenty-two on the Northeast Front and twenty-three on the Southeast Front) and 68 POs (thirty-five on the Northeast Front and thirty-five on the Southeast Front). These forts mounted 344 pieces of artillery (75 mm, 135 mm, and 81 mm), over 150 turrets, and 1,500 cloches. Over 100 kilometers of galleries for the *ouvrages* had been excavated, over 1.5 million cubic meters of concrete poured, and 150,000 tons of steel used.

The average cost of the *ouvrages* is not known because the numbers quoted by the various sources vary, but it is estimated that the largest forts cost between 100 million and 130 million francs. However, Hackenberg cost 172 million francs and Hochwald over 150 million francs. The expenditures would have been much higher if the *Réduit* at Hochwald and other positions had been completed. Other GOs ranged between 50 and 90 million francs; the POs ranged between 8 and 24 million francs. The more economical *ouvrages* of the New Fronts cost about 36 million francs per GO and between 6 and 20 million francs per PO.

The expenditure on the *ouvrages* in the Alps was almost half of those in the Northeast Front because they were much smaller. Monte Grosso, the largest GO in the Alps, cost 40.4 million francs, whereas St. Agnès, which included the largest of all Maginot casemate blocks, was built for 16.8 million francs. The Alpine forts further removed from the Mediterranean coast cost more because the climate and altitude restricted construction time to the fair seasons only. However, the average GO in the Alps was in the 20 million franc range. The interval casemates and observatories had a price tag of from 1.4 to 2.2 million francs. The total amount spent on the Northeast Front alone was about 5,000 million francs, almost twice the amount allotted by Parliament in 1930.

Only 10% of the funds appropriated for the construction of the Maginot fortifications went to the Southeast Fronts. Although this percentage seems too small since the total number of *gros ouvrages* was about the same as in the Northeast, one must take into account that the *ouvrages* were smaller in the Alps, and major lines of obstacles were unneeded. The Mareth Line in Tunisia was the cheapest, at less than 20 million francs (Claudel, *Ligne Maginot*, p. 38; Mary, *Maginot*, p. 34; Mary, *Maginot*, Vol. 1, pp. 52, 57; Truttmann, *La Muraille*, 1992, pp. 511–512; Vermeullen and Vermeulen, *Atlas CORF*).

Maginot Fort Garrisons

The garrisons of the *ouvrages* were set up like the crews of a naval warship since this was considered the most effective way to operate the new forts. The crews that manned the combat blocks consisted of four teams. One team would remain in the *caserne* for an entire day to rest, including time outside the fort. The next day, the team rotated back to its block, replacing one of the other four teams. The three teams in the block changed their assignment shifts every eight hours. One team stood watch, manning the weapons and communications system of the cloche and block; another team performed general duties in the block; and the third team rested the residential area of the block. During an alert, the two teams not resting alternated every four hours. When the alert called the garrison to battle stations, the team in the *caserne* moved up to the block, and all four teams prepared for action.

In some *ouvrages*, the artillery blocks only had three teams that alternated their duties, while in others there were four. The watch team consisted of enough men to operate the turret (Table 3.1). A fully manned 75-mm gun turret block required twelve men on duty, four of whom were in the turret. The 135-mm *lance-bombe* turret needed fourteen men on duty, two of whom manned the turret. In the 81-mm mortar turret block, there were nine men on duty, but only one of the normal two-man crews was inside the turret. In all cases, the team on watch manned the cloches and the telephone, ready to communicate with the command post, like in the infantry block. When there were only three teams, one was in the *caserne* for a full day, while the other two alternated watches.

The size of a crew varied according to the type of block it had to serve and the type of turret the block mounted. The number of cloches also affected the total number of men. A typical three-gun artillery casemate needed a platoon of about thirty men, half of whom had to be on duty during a watch period so that two of the

TABLE 3-1. Turret personnel in Maginot turrets

Turret Block	Men in Turret	Men at Control Level	Men at Lower Level
75-mm watch duty	4	7	1
75-mm battle stations	4	Turret chief plus 18	3
81-mm watch duty	1	6	1
81-mm battle stations	2	Turret chief plus 19	3
135-mm watch duty	2	11	1
135-mm battle stations	2	Turret chief plus 15	3
MG turret watch duty	1	2	1
MG turret battle station	Turret chief plus 1	1	3
AM turret watch duty	1	2	1
AM turret battle station	6	Turret chief plus 4	6
AM cloche	3	2	
JM cloche	2	3	
GFM cloche	1	1	

AM, mixed arms turret; MG, machine gun.

guns could be ready for operations at all times. A casemate with two mortars required a platoon of about twenty men, half of whom were involved in one capacity or another in the operation of the weapon. The platoon for a 135-mm *lance-bombe* block only numbered about ten men, five of whom stayed on watch to keep the weapon ready. Infantry casemate crews varied in size from sixteen to thirty men. Roughly the same number was required for the CORF interval casemates (Koch, "La Tourelle Mitrailleuse Model 1935 (2)," *39–45 Magazine*, pp. 58–59; LTC Ph. Truttmann, correspondence; Mary, *Maginot*, Vol. 3, pp. 10–15).

CHAPTER 4

SEA AND AIR DEFENSES

THE FRENCH NAVY AND COASTAL DEFENSES

Although the Treaty of Versailles neutralized the German navy in the 1920s, new threats loomed on the horizon not only from France's traditional enemies, but also from nations, like the Soviet Union, pushing their ideologies. However, the Baltic and Black Seas virtually locked in the Soviet navy, preventing it from being a serious threat. While the French army, despite the Treaty of Versailles, planned to defend itself against a resurgent Germany, Italy fell under the control of fascism in the early 1920s. This highly nationalistic ideology revived old territorial disputes between Italy and France both in Africa and in southeast France. Benito Mussolini, proclaiming the Mediterranean as *Mare Nostrum* (Our Sea), challenged British and French naval dominance in the area by expanding his fleet. Soon, Italy's growing navy jeopardized the lines of communication between France and its North African colonies.

The Washington Conference of 1921/1922 resulted in a naval treaty that set the number of capital ships that each of the five great naval powers (Great Britain, United States, Japan, France, and Italy) could build at a fixed ratio between them. The treaty also set restrictions on the displacement tonnage of battleships at 35,000 tons, cruisers at 10,000 tons, and aircraft carriers at 27,000 tons. France and Italy were allotted an equal number of capital ships, but their ratio was lower than that of the other three nations. Although the treaty allowed for special exceptions, Japan and Italy disregarded its restrictions outright. Great Britain and the United States, on the other hand, respected them until the treaty was abandoned in 1936.

France's dilemma was that its fleet had to maintain a presence in the Atlantic as well as Mediterranean since it had coastlines on both bodies of water. In addition, France had colonies in America and the Orient, whereas Italy's overseas possessions consisted of Libya on the Mediterranean coast of Africa and Somalia and Eritrea in East Africa. Thus, the treaty in fact gave the upper hand to Italy since its fleet was tied to the Mediterranean.

It is not surprising, therefore, that France and Great Britain refused to sign a new treaty after the London Conference of 1930—which restricted new battleships to 25,000 tons and 12-inch guns and put further limits on cruisers, destroyers, and submarines—on the grounds that it was too unrealistic. The next London Conference in 1936, which attempted to impose additional restrictions, failed, ending all attempts to control the world's fleets (Worth, *Fleets of World War II*, pp. ix–x). In addition, the Anglo-German agreement of 1935 lifted the Versailles restrictions on the German navy, allowing it to become a new naval power.

In the 1920s, the French navy's capital ships consisted of three battleships of the *Bretagne* class built in 1913 and mounting ten 13.4-inch (340-mm) guns in five turrets and three older battleships of the *Courbet* class of 1911, mounting twelve 12-inch (305-mm) guns in six turrets. It also included three obsolete battleships from 1909, mounting four 12-inch guns (two turrets) and twelve 9.4-inch (240-mm) guns (six turrets). Several older battleships were broken up by 1921. The cruisers were all outdated armored ships, but a new modern 8-inch cruiser was on the drawing board. Three new 6.1-inch gun light cruisers were already being completed and going into service by 1924. Five German light cruisers, more modern than the older French ships that had been taken as reparations, were also pressed into service. Some of the smaller destroyers and warships were less than fifteen years old. In 1920, the *Normandie* class battleship *Béarn* was redesigned as an aircraft carrier during construction to extend the range of the French fleet. It was eventually finished as an aircraft carrier in 1926. When many of the old and outdated French ships were decommissioned, their armament was transferred to coastal and land defenses.

Georges Leygues, Minister of the Navy

French politician Georges Leygues, who served in various ministries, is best known for his role as president of the Council. He served as minister of the navy during four terms (1917–1920, 1925–1926, 1926–1930, and 1932) before he died in 1933. Leygues was to the French fleet what André Maginot was to France's Great Wall. After his first term as minister of the navy, he strove to revamp the French fleet. Thanks to his efforts, the French navy was on the way to becoming one of the world's major naval forces by the time of his death, surpassed only by the British, American, and Japanese navies. When the war began, the French fleet had no major warships older than eighteen years, with the exception of six older battleships that were being removed from first-line duty.

On paper, the Italian navy appears to have been at an advantage in the 1920s. It included two battleships of the *Duillo* or *Andrea Doria* class built in 1913 that mounted thirteen 12-inch guns in five turrets. It also had two 1911 battleships of the *Ceasare* or *Cavour* class with the same type of armament. The *Dante Alighieri*, completed in 1913 and mounting twelve 12-inch guns in four turrets, was scrapped at the end of the 1920s. Two pre-dreadnaught battleships, dating from the turn of the century and mounting two 12-inch guns in two turrets and twelve 8-inch guns in six turrets, were used for coastal defense. Three armored cruisers built early in the century joined two newer 8-inch gun cruisers laid down in 1924. One 6-inch gun cruiser built in 1914, four German light cruisers taken as reparations, three new *Leone* class flotilla leaders, six new destroyers of the *Generali* class, four of the *Curtatone* class, and four from the *Palestro* class built between 1919 and 1923 joined the fleet in 1923. A number of older destroyers built during the war were also in service (Parkes and McMurtrie, *Jane's Fighting Ships 1924*, pp. 209–235).

Both navies in 1923 established the life of a battleship at twenty years, but the French put cruisers at seventeen years, and the Italians put them at fifteen years. Most of the other warships were given a fifteen-year service life (Parkes and McMurtrie, *Jane's Fighting Ships 1924*, pp. 145, 208). Thus, by 1939, most of Italian and French warships were obsolete by their own standards. However, both nations had built new warships of all types during the 1930s, although several capital ships remained on the stocks when the war began.

The French Navy was unable to lay down a new battleship until 1932 because of the naval treaty limitations of 35,000 tons. The new *Dunkerque* class ships, the *Dunkerque* and *Strasbourg*, reached about 26,500 tons and were armed with eight 13-inch guns in two quadruple turrets, similar to the turrets of the British *Nelson* class of 1922. These ships were followed by two of the *Richelieu* class: the *Richelieu* and the *Jean Bart*, of 38,500 tons with eight 15-inch guns in two quadruple turrets.

The construction of the two *Dunkerque* class battleships sparked a naval race with the Germans, who no longer obeyed treaty restrictions, and the Italians, who produced the *Scharnhorst* and *Vittorio Veneto* classes, respectively. The Italians, like the French, had to modernize their capital ships. Thus, between 1933 and 1937, *Cavour* class battleships were laid up and almost totally rebuilt. The French completed the new *contre-torpilleur* of the *Fantasque* class, usually considered a cross between a light cruiser and destroyer. This warship attained speeds of thirty-seven to forty-five knots, mounted 5.5-inch guns, and had a highly efficient fire control system. Italy's response was the *Capitani Romani* class, a light cruiser with a speed of over 43 knots armed with 5.3-inch guns. The Italians, under even more stringent budget restraints than the French, did not even complete the first of these until after the fall of France in 1940 (Worth, *Fleets*, pp. 32, 149).

In the 1920s, the Italian navy did not have enough credits from the government to reach the treaty limits. It was not until 1932 that it laid down two new battleships of the *Vittorio Veneto* class. The new warships displaced over 41,000 tons and carried nine 15-inch guns in three turrets. The *Vittorio Veneto* and *Littorio* were ready by 1940. The *Roma* and *Impero*, laid down in 1938, were still under construction during the war. At the same time, the two *Doria* class battleships went out of service between 1937 and 1940 to be modernized.

During the 1920s, few capital ships were built. Between 1919 and 1920, the French modernized the old *Bretagne* class. However, by 1932, they had to refurbish these ships again, a process that took three years and drained additional funds from the navy budget during the depression. The *Courbet* class had to be overhauled between 1926 and 1929 and from 1936 to 1939 was relegated to harbor duties.[1] It was replaced by the *Dunkerque* class. The navy was awaiting the delivery of the new *Richelieu* class battleships with 15-inch guns when the war began.

When the war finally broke out, Italy, France's main naval antagonist, did not join the conflict until almost ten months after the onset of hostilities. The British took the main responsibility for containing the German fleet. The British, French, and Italian navies suffered from a lack of effective antiaircraft protection and fire control. However, the British were developing radar for fire control. This left the French and Italians on almost equal footing in the Mediterranean, making their island possessions even more important, especially with the addition of airpower (Tables 4.1–4.4).

TABLE 4-1. French warships 1939–1940

Warships	No. of Ships	Displacement (tons)	Main Armament	Speed (knots)	Crew
Battleships	8 + 2				
1940 *Richelieu* class	(2)	35,000	8 × 15 inches	32	2,000
Richelieu[a]		95% complete	By July 1940	30	1,670
Jean Bart[a]		75% complete	By July 1940		
1937 *Dunkerque* class	(2)	26,500	8 × 13 inches	29.5	1,430
Dunkerque					
Strasbourg					
1915 *Bretagne* class	(3)	22,200	10 × 13.4 inches	22.4	1,030
Bretagne					
Province					
Lorraine					
1913 *Courbet* class	(3)	22,189	12 × 12 inches	21	1,060
Courbet					
Paris					
Ocean					
Aircraft carriers	2 + 1				
Joffre[a] (begun 1938)		18,000	40 aircraft	33	1,250
1926 *Bearn*		22,156	40 aircraft	21.5	875
1932 *Commandant Teste*		10,000	26 sea-planes	20.5	686
Heavy cruisers	7				
1934 *Algerie* class	(1)	10,000	8 × 8 inches	34	616
1930 *Suffren* class	(4)	11,000	8 × 8 inches	31.3	605
1928 *Dusquesne* class	(2)	10,000	9 × 8 inches	33.7	605
Light crusiers	9				
1936 *Galissoniere* class	(6)	7,600	9 × 6 inches	36.1	540
1926 *Duguay* class	(3)	7,250	8 × 6.1 inches	33	580
Destroyers: 9 classes	78	1,290 to 2,436	5.1 or 5.5 inches	33–40	250
Submarines	75				

Total number of ships in each class in parentheses; for instance, (5) means five ships of this class. A number following a plus sign indicates number of ships under construction; for example 2+1 means total of 2 ships, plus 1 under construction.
[a]Not completed by 1940.

TABLE 4-2. Italian warships 1939–1940

Warships	No. of Ships	Displacement (tons)	Main Armament	Speed (knots)	Crew
Battleships	6				
Littorio class	(2)	40,700	9 × 15 inches	30	1,600
Doria class	(2)	26,100	10 × 12.6 inches	27	1,200
Cavour class	(2)	25,900	10 × 12.6 inches	28	1,200
Heavy cruisers	7				
Zara class	(4)	11,700	8 × 8 inches	32	800
Trento class	(3)	10,340	8 × 8 inches	35	800
Light cruisers	12	5,300 to 9,500	8 to 10 × 5.3 or 6 inches	33–36	650
Destroyers	54	1,000 to 2,000	4 or 4.7 inches	31–38	250
Light destroyer	63				
Submarines	117	*Note:* Several older ships not included.			

TABLE 4-3. British warships 1939–1940

Warships	No. of Ships	Displacement (tons)	Main Armament	Speed (knots)	Crew
Battleships (20)	20				
1940 *King George V* class	(5)	37,000	10 × 4 inches	28	1,500
1927 *Nelson* class	(2)	33,900	9 × 16 inches	23	1,360
1920 *Hood*	(1)	42,100	8 × 15 inches	31	
1916 *Renown* class	(2)	32,000	6 × 15 inches	29	1,200
1915 *Queen Elizabeth* class	(5)	30,600	8 × 15 inches	24	1,180
1915 *R* class	(5)	29,150	8 × 15 inches	21.5	1,150
Aircraft carriers	6	11,000–23,000	33–70 aircraft	24–31	1,200–1,600
Heavy cruisers	15				
1930 *Exeter* class	(2)	8,250	6 × 8 inches	32.3	750
1928 *County* class	(13)	9,830–10,000	8 × 8 inches	30–33	750
Light cruisers	40	5,000–7,000	6 inches	30–33	500–680
1927–1939 **Destroyers**	113				
1916–1924 **Old destroyers**	68				
Submarines	47				

FRANCE'S BACKDOOR: COASTAL DEFENSES

The defense of the French coastline was always important, even before the Napoleonic era. The danger diminished when Great Britain, France's main rival, eventually became an ally after the Napoleonic wars. However, the emergence of Germany and Italy as naval powers late in the nineteenth century put the French coastline at risk once again. By that time, the advent of the all-steel warship forced all sea powers to rebuild their navies with these new warships. Germany was able to take the lead over France and Italy, despite their long maritime heritage, because it was able to surpass them both in steel production, particularly after the Franco-Prussian war, when much of the French iron ore resources of Lorraine fell in its hands.

After World War I, Italy's territorial disputes with France over the Mediterranean coast of Africa and Europe became exacerbated under Mussolini. During the 1920s, France, increasingly concerned with the possibility of raids or major assaults against its naval bases and ports, began improving its coastal defenses. In addition, it was forced to maintain a first-rate navy to dominate the western Mediterranean and defend its southern coastline, Corsica, and its shipping lines to the territories it held in northwest Africa.

During the Great War, aircraft and dirigibles emerged as important weapons, capable of striking well beyond the front lines. Nonetheless, the French military concluded their Maginot Line fortifications did not require antiaircraft defenses because they were largely bombproof. However, in the ports, where largely unprotected civilian and industrial centers as well as ships lay exposed, the necessity of integrating antiaircraft positions into the defensive system was obvious. Thus, the key ports of France received antiaircraft defenses. In addition, coastal artillery positions were expanded or upgraded wherever possible. To this purpose, a variety of 75-mm to over 200-mm guns, old and new, many taken from old warships or surplus, were installed in the defended ports. During the 1920s and 1930s, further improvements included plans for construction of

TABLE 4-4. Main armament of warships (secondary weapons not included)[a]

Gun	Range (meters)	Warship Class	Nation
16 inches	**41,700**	*Richelieu*	**France**
13.4 inches	**26,915**	*Bretagne*	**France**
13 inches	**41,700**	*Dunkerque*	**France**
12 inches	**23,000**	*Courbet*	**France**
8 inches	30,000	Cruisers	France
6.1 inches	26,100	Cruisers	France
6 inches	26,475	Cruisers	France
5.5 inches	20,000	*Fantasques*	France
16 inches	**36,375**	*Nelson*	**UK**
15 inches	**27,600**	R	**UK**
14 inches	**35,260**	*George V*	**UK**
8 inches	28,030	Cruisers	UK
6 inches	23,300	Cruisers	UK
5.25 inches	22,010	*Didos*	UK
4.7 inches	15,520	Destroyers	UK
15 inches	**42,260**	*Littorio*	**Italy**
12.6 inches	**28,605**	**Battleships**	**Italy**
8 inches	31,565	*Zara*	Italy
8 inches	28,000	*Trento*	Italy
6 inches	22,600	Cruisers	Italy
5.3 inches	19,600	*Capt Romani*	Italy
4.7 inches	19,200	Destroyers	Italy
4 inches	11,830	Destroyer	Italy
15 inches	**35,550**	*Bismarck*	**Germany**
11.1 inches	**40,930**	*Scharnhorst*	**Germany**
11.1 inches	**36,475**	*Deutschland*	**Germany**
11.1 inches	**25,640**	*Schlesien*	**Germany**
8 inches	33,540	Cruisers	Germany
5.9 inches	25,700	Cruisers	Germany
5.9 inches	17,400	Destroyers	Germany

Note: Battleship guns in bold.
Capitani Romani class begun in 1940.
[a]Not all destroyer and cruiser guns listed.

large naval turrets mounting surplus 340-mm cannons.[2] One of the first of these major projects involved Battery Cépet at Toulon in 1924.

The French minister of the navy and officers from the naval high command worked out plans for coastal protection while their counterparts at the War Ministry designed the Maginot Line. However, in the final contest for funding from Parliament, the army came out ahead because Germany was considered the primary threat. In 1926, George Leygues, the minister of the navy, and Vice Admiral Henri Salaun, the navy's chief of staff, devoted their efforts to rebuilding the fleet and coastal defenses. They urged the government to acquire twenty 340-mm guns instead of 305-mm cannons, fifty-four of the newer 240-mm Mle 1902/06, fifty-two 240-mm G, and four 194-mm guns. Their plan also called for a battery of four 340-mm rail guns for Zuidcotte near Dunkirk. The other 340-mm guns, mounted in twin gun turrets, were designated for two turrets at Cherboug, two at Brest, and one, with the possibility of a second, at Bizerte. At the time,

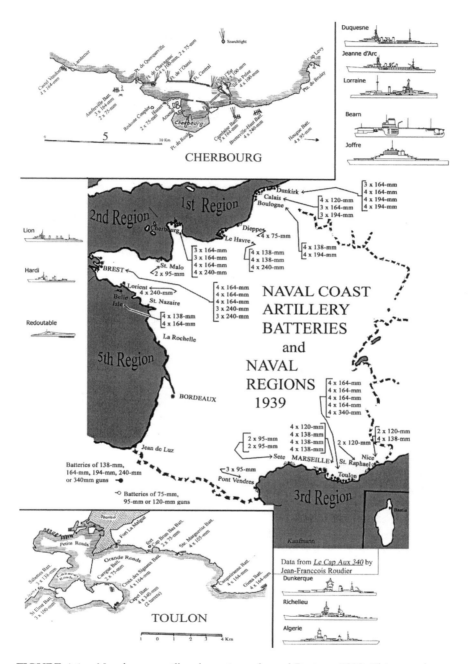

FIGURE 4-1.   Naval coast artillery batteries and naval Regions, 1939. This map shows the location of coast defense batteries and includes detailed maps of Toulon and Cherbourg plus drawings of major types of French warships. [Joseph Kaufmann]

work had already begun on the two-turret battery at Cépet, Toulon, where the bulk of the heavy construction work took place between 1928 and 1931. Due to the great expense involved in building the subterranean works for these large turret batteries and manufacturing the turrets, the project for Brest was dropped, and work on the other two sites was delayed (Roudier, *Le Cap Aux 340*, Vol. 1, pp. 31–32).

In 1933, when Legyues died in office and Admiral Hector Violette, Salaun's successor as chief of staff, retired, the navy lost its most ardent supporters in the government. Although it continued to receive appropriate funding for the fleet thanks to Legyues' past efforts, funds for coastal defenses were cut back, especially those earmarked for the huge turret batteries, which were quite expensive (Hood, *Royal Republicans*, pp. 130–131).

Only two batteries of turrets (with two guns per turret) at Toulon and Bizerte were actually completed. The turrets at Toulon were mounted and operational by the mid-1930s, but the tightening budget almost prevented the completion of the battery at Bizerte, which had a higher priority than Cherbourg due to the Italian naval threat. The Bizerte project was at the organizational stage in 1931, and the guns for the turrets were delivered at the port in 1933. However, the battery's completion date of 1934 was not met because construction had been delayed, and the site for the turret had not even been selected at that time. It was not until early 1935 that the French navy picked a contractor and work began.

The subterranean works at Bizerte were tunneled because, in contrast to Toulon, they had to be deeper underground. In July 1936, the government approved the addition of a second turret, but it was not until 1939, just before the war, that the first 340-mm turret at Bizerte was test fired. Thus, the battery was not completed by March 1940, as scheduled (Roudier, *Le Cap Aux 340*, Vol. 2, pp. 92–94). At Cherbourg, only part of the underground gallery and two turret-block positions were excavated and under construction in 1940. The position was far from ready to receive its two turrets when the war began.

During the 1920s, planning commissions carried out studies and made recommendations for the establishment of coastal defenses. In 1921, the navy authorized the implementation of those plans; in April 1927, a decree established the four maritime frontiers. In June 1932, the navy further divided the maritime frontiers into defensive sectors and coastal subsectors called *fronts de mer* (Roudier, *Le Cap Aux 340*, Vol. 1, p. 29). Thus, the First Maritime Frontier ran from Cherbourg to Dunkirk; the Second Maritime Frontier went from St. Malô to Brest and along the Bay of Biscay; the Third Maritime Frontier covered the south coast of France; and the Fourth Maritime Frontier covered the coast of French North Africa along the Mediterranean.[3] In 1939, the Second Maritime Frontier was divided into two parts, and the section along the Bay of Biscay became the Fifth Maritime Frontier. Special naval battalions were formed to man the battery positions and defend the key ports of each frontier.

The sectors within these maritime frontiers did not consist of entire stretches of coastline covered with defended positions. They were subdivided into *fronts de mer* centered on one of the ports in the defensive sector. For instance, the Dunkirk defensive sector included the sea fronts of Dunkirk, Calais, and Boulogne. At the time, it was believed that an invasion from the sea must take place near a port that could be quickly captured to allow the unloading of logistical support.

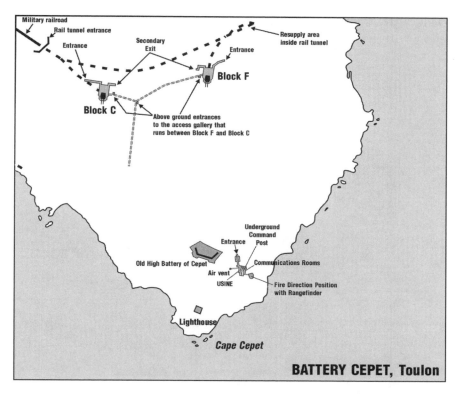

FIGURE 4-2.   Battery Cepet near Toulon. [© Tomasz Idzikowski]

The army contributed to the defense of the coasts in 1939 when it mobilized fifteen Series B coastal defense infantry battalions that joined nine coastal defense brigades early in the war. These brigades were headquartered in Dunkirk (Brigade A), Le Havre (Brigade B), Cherbourg (Brigade C), Brest (Brigade D), Lorient (Brigade E), Rochefort (Brigade F), Marseilles (Brigade G), Toulon (Brigade H), and Nice (Brigade I). The army organization fluctuated and changed after the war began (Sharp, *French Army*, Vol. 3, pp. 122–123). On the Southeast Front, the *ouvrages* of the Little Maginot Line covered the coastline from the Italian border to Cap Martin (the Menton sector). The 75-mm guns of the *gros ouvrage* (GO) of St. Agnès covered the invasion beaches of Menton to Cap Martin. The GO of Roquebrune defended Cap Martin. These GOs, including the GO of Mont Agel, although unable to engage an enemy fleet like the coast artillery, were capable of deterring a landing force. On the North Sea, it was the navy that held sway with positions such as Battery Zuydcoote near the Belgian border, which occupied a position from the 1880s and consisted of four 194-mm Mle 1902 guns in gun houses. Further down the coast, at Calais, the navy manned Fort Lapin with a battery of old 95-mm guns, even older 190-mm guns, and newer 164.7-mm Mle 93/96 guns.

The ports that were thought to require fortifications urgently included Cherbourg, Marseilles, Toulon, and Bizerte. Corsica had no major ports, but was on the high-priority list for coastal defense because of its strategic position. The naval coastal gun batteries of 100-mm and greater caliber generally consisted of either three or four guns. In many cases, they were mounted en barbette and generally included a gun shield or

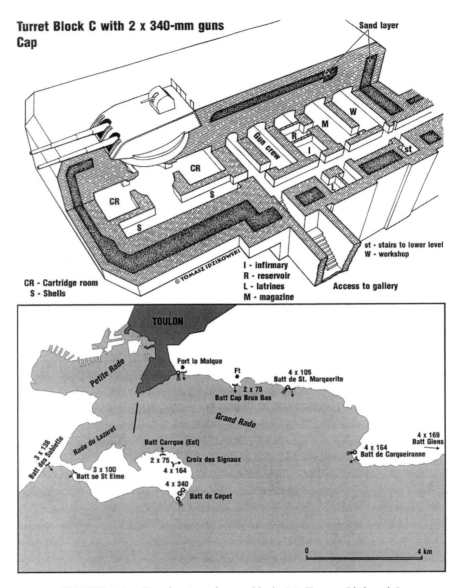

FIGURE 4-3. Top drawing of turret block. [© Tomasz Idzikowski]

gun house. All four of these key ports were designated to receive or actually received gun turret batteries, but only Toulon and Bizerte got 340-mm gun turrets (Table 4.5).

Toulon, the main naval base on the Mediterranean in addition to Battery Cépet, received twelve batteries of artillery of 100-mm caliber, four batteries of 164-mm guns, and three of 138-mm guns between World War I and World War II. Four batteries of 90-mm antiaircraft guns had not yet been emplaced in January 1940. Later, many of these naval antiaircraft weapons were diverted north to defend Paris.

The impressive battery of two 340-mm turret guns further protected Toulon from Cape Cépet. An underground gallery linked the subterranean works of the battery

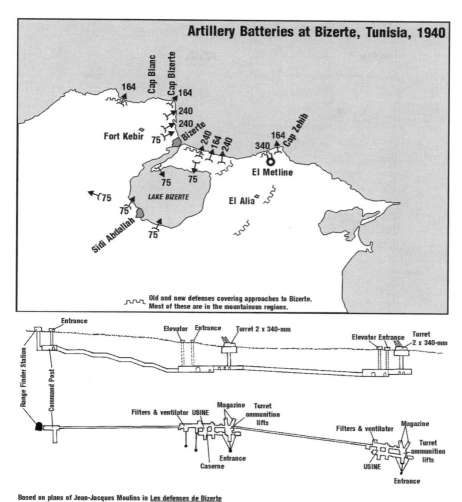

FIGURE 4-4. Batteries defending Bizerte, Tunisia. Plan of Battery Metline at Bizerte.
[© Tomasz Idzikowski]

blocks. Armored plates covered with concrete formed the forward armor that protected the base of the turret, like the frontal armor of the turrets of the Maginot Line and other forts. The big guns could be elevated 50° for maximum range and operated like shipboard guns. Battery Cépet stood at the end of a peninsula, and combined with the nearby battery of Croix des Signaux with four 164-mm guns, it covered the seven-kilometer wide entrance to the *Grande Rade* (Outer Roads), which in turn led to the *Petite Rade* (Inner Roads) and the harbor of Toulon. Battery Carqueiranne, with four 164-mm guns, stood across the entrance from Battery Cépet.

Since the subterranean facilities were not deep underground, the open excavation method was used to build the positions and blocks of Battery Cépet.[4] The concrete for the blocks was poured in the open and covered with the excavated earth, making the position look like a small hill. Standard tunneling methods employed in the Maginot

TABLE 4-5. Naval guns for ships and coastal defense

Gun	Model	Range (meters)	Uses
380 mm (14.9 inches)	1935	41,700	S
340 mm (13.4 inches)	1912	26,600	S, CD
330 mm (13 inches)	1931	41,700	S
305 mm (12 inches)	1906/10	34,000	(S), RR
240 mm (9.5 inches)	1893/96	23,810	CD
203 mm (8 inches)	1924	30,000	S
203 mm (8 inches)	1931	31,000	S
194 mm (7.6 inches)	1902	25,960	(S), CD
164 mm (6.6 inches)	1893–96	17,500	(S), CD
155 mm (6.1 inches)	1920	26,100	S
152.4 mm (6 inches)	1930	26,474	S
138.6 mm (5.5 inches)	1929	20,000	S
138.6 mm (5.5 inches)	1927	16,600	S
138.6 mm (5.5 inches)	1923	18,200	S
138.6 mm (5.5 inches)	1910	16,100	S, CD
130 mm (5.1 inches)	1932/35	20,870	S
130 mm (5.1 inches)	1924	18,700	S
100 mm (3.9 inches)	1933	—	S-AA
100 mm (3.9 inches)	1932	15,000	S
100 mm (3.9 inches)	1930	15,000	S-AA
90 mm (3.5 inches)	1926	15,440	S-AA
75 mm (3 inches)	1922/24/27	14,100	S-AA

Sources: J. Campbell, *Naval Weapons of World War II* and *France 1940;* Ferrard, *L'Armement Terrestre.*

Note: This is not a complete listing of all naval weapons used on ships or for coastal defense.

S, ship; (S), older ship; CD, coast defense; S-AA, ship antiaircraft (dual purpose of range given).

Line were also used to excavate the railroad tunnel, with spurs leading to the two blocks of Battery Cépet. Most of the heavy construction in the first block was completed by early 1929. The subterranean chambers of the block below the turrets contained cartridge and shell rooms, two elevators, a stairway, positions for the block crew, a first aid room, a radio room, a filter room, and a ventilation room. The lower level of the block included a *usine* and access to the gallery linking the two turret blocks, which were about three hundred meters apart. The main and secondary entrances for each block were located on the upper level.

The turret blocks were surrounded with a 2-meter thick layer of sand sandwiched between two 1.5-meters thick concrete walls that formed a burster layer beginning just below the roof level of the upper level of the block. The roof over the section of the block not covered by the turret consisted of a 2-meter thick layer of concrete surmounted by a 1.5-meter layer of sand and a 1.5-meter layer of concrete, forming a conventional overhead burster layer. The wall of the section of the block with the turret consisted of a 1.5-meter thick layer of concrete, 2 meters of sand, and 2 meters of concrete forming the inner wall at the magazine level. The turret and the magazine level were separated by a concrete layer over 7-meters thick. Large plates of frontal armor surrounded the turret. By Commission for Organizing the Fortified Regions (CORF; *Commission d'Organisation des Région Fortifiées*) standards, these blocks (identified as Ouvrage C and F) were impressive: *Ouvrage F* was over 50 meters by 35 meters, and Ouvrage C was about 50 meters by 30 meters.[5]

The first turret was installed in February and the second in the fall of 1931. The gallery that connected the blocks was accessed through northern and southern entrances and was 370 meters long. It sheltered a military railway with underground spurs to each block. A range-finding position and a command post were located near the end of the cape, about 800 meters in front of the battery. They were linked to the battery solely by radio and telephone. The range-finding position included a turret-mounted rangefinder and an observation room located near the cliffs. A staircase led to the subterranean facilities, which included the battery command post and all the equipment needed to operate it, including a *usine*. The battery blocks and the command post were fully equipped to function independently under combat conditions. However, for maximum effectiveness the communications links had to function. A number of *abris* in the area provided shelter for the garrison of about 220 men. Some of the facilities of nearby older battery positions were also used. Battery Cépet was the first of the 340-mm turret batteries to be finished. Its completion coincided with the conclusion of the construction of the first *ouvrages* of the Maginot Line.

The second major defended port that received a heavy 340-mm turret battery was Bizerte, Tunisia. This port had been heavily fortified since the 1880s, and like Cherbourg and several other major sites, had received the large 240-mm Mle 1884 coastal defense guns mounted en barbette. Eight batteries of these guns had defended the port and coastline between Cape Bizerte to Cape Zébib. Like those on the coast of France, the Bizerte batteries included concrete firing positions; in most cases, they were built like forts with *fossés*, caponiers, and other facilities. Most of the batteries at Bizerte were newer than the positions in metropolitan France.

Due to its unique position between the sea and two large lakes, Bizerte also received landward defenses that, by 1914, included Fort Kébir on a hilltop northwest of the city. This fort mounted two eclipsing machine gun turrets and a battery of four 120-mm guns. Other battery positions defended the landward front. There were plans to build another fort a few kilometers south of Lake Bizerte that would have included eclipsing turrets for 75-mm guns, 155-mm guns, and machine guns. It would have been similar in many ways to Fort Douaumont. The existing fortifications and the plans for new ones underscore the importance of fortress Bizerte prior to World War I.[6]

After World War I, more plans were proposed for the improvement of the defenses of Bizerte. Thus, several batteries of 75-mm antiaircraft guns, an airbase, and a naval airbase were added. The coastal batteries, which included subterranean magazines, *abris*, a *usine*, a range-finding position, and a command post, covered the approaches to the port of Bizerte. The positions between Cape Bizerte and Cape Zébib mounted the old 240-mm guns with a range of 17,500 meters. New batteries of 164-mm guns were placed at Cape Bizerte, at Soumeur, to the west, at Ain Bittar, to the east, and at Cape Zébib. The last was to be the most modern of the battery positions. The 164-mm Mle 1893–96 guns, salvaged from old warships, obtained a range of about 17,200 to 19,200 meters. A newer postwar mount used at the batteries of Soumeur and Cape Zébib—both on the extreme flanks—increased their range to 20,100 meters.

Finally, a 340-mm battery known as Battery El Metline was built a few kilometers behind Cape Zébib. Outwardly, it resembled the Cépet Battery at Toulon, but its subterranean works were organized differently. Instead of forming a blocklike position, the chambers below the turret consisted of a large central chamber from where the shells and powder charges were hoisted to the turret. This large room was linked to four large chambers, each separated from the other by concrete and earth. Two galleries led off to a caserne, *usine*, and the ventilation rooms, connected by lateral galleries. The ceilings of the subterranean works were 1 meter thick. The gallery level was about 16 meters below the surface. The roof of the block on which the turret rested was up to 6 meters thick in some sections. In addition, a layer of sand was sandwiched between the inner wall and an outer wall of the block, creating a burster layer. The whole was further surrounded with rock work for a width of 5 meters and a depth of about 3.5 meters. This battery was even more impressive in size and scope than the Battery Cépet at Toulon. Unfortunately, the planning and work did not begin until early in the 1930s, deadlines were not met, and priorities changed. The battery project, which began as a single turret position, changed to a two-turret battery in the mid-1930s. As a result, the two turrets were not installed and ready for test firing until 1940, but according to some sources, the battery was not fully operational before the surrender in 1940.

Some improvements, such as new casemates for machine guns, command posts, *abris*, and concrete firing positions for 47- and 75-mm guns, were added to the land defenses of the Bizerte fortified area. These structures were distributed among six groups, each of which numbered between seven and twelve casemates. Some of these groups comprised observatories and command posts. According to Moulins, the group that covered the road from Bizerte to Tunis consisted of three small works similar to the small Italian forts of the *Vallo Alpino*, Italy's fortifications in the Alps. Two of the groups included a few blockhouses, an observatory, and a command post linked by an underground gallery 140 to 170 meters long. The groups near the beaches had a steel cupola for frontal machine gun fire, but it was only 10 mm thick (Moulins, *Les Défenses de Bizerte*, p. 58).

The concrete protection for most casemates and blockhouses only equaled Protection 1 or less of the Maginot Line. The best-protected positions were not intended to resist guns heavier than of 155 mm. Many of the casemates included armored embrasures for automatic rifles and Hotchkiss machine guns.[7] These positions included periscopes for observation, ventilators with air filters, and a supply of water. The casemates were designed, like those in France, for flanking fire.

The communication system was also similar, including aerial cable that went underground 250 meters before arriving at the site (Moulins, *Les Défenses de Bizerte*, pp. 34–101). The fortified zone remained a firm anchor at the end of the French navy's line of communications across the Mediterranean. Along the eastern Tunisian coast, the navy installed the standard coastal artillery consisting of three- or four-gun batteries of 138-mm guns. There was one battery of 138-mm guns at Tunis, one of 100-mm guns at Sousse, two of 100-mm guns at Sfax and Gabès, and one of 155-mm guns at Gabès.

A variety of coastal defense batteries with 75- to 138-mm cannons protected the ports along the Algerian coast. Algiers and Oran received the bulk of the coastal defense positions. Algiers included two batteries of 194-mm guns and one of 120-mm guns. In addition, plans were drawn up for two four-gun batteries of 90-mm antiaircraft guns to protect the port area, but these weapons were never delivered. The port of Oran was partially protected by an old fort, the Canastel Battery, with three 240-mm guns and Battery Gambetta with four 120-mm guns. To the west of Oran, the fleet anchorage of Mers El Kébir was defended by three old forts, the most important of which, Fort Santon, mounted four 194-mm guns. Plans were made for the construction of two four-gun batteries of 90-mm antiaircraft guns to protect Mers El Kébir and Oran. The only other major coastal artillery units were located at a few ports of Morocco, the most notable of which were the batteries of 138-mm guns and a larger 194-mm gun battery at Casablanca.

Along the coast of metropolitan France, the main ports of the First Maritime Frontier between Dunkirk and Cherbourg included batteries with weapons no larger than 138-mm, 164-mm, 194-mm, and a few old 240-mm guns. Dunkirk, one of the most heavily protected ports because of its location, was allotted two batteries of 194 mm and two of 164 mm. At Cherbourg, there was a battery of 194 mm and three of 164 mm. Construction on the underground works for a battery of two 340-mm turrets was still under way. With three batteries of 164-mm guns and two of 240-mm guns, Brest was the most heavily defended port in the Second Maritime Frontier. The Fifth Maritime Frontier had a mixture of batteries, a number of which were concentrated at Belle Isle/Lorient and Rochefort/Re. In addition to Marseilles and Toulon, the Third Maritime Frontier had a similar assortment of batteries. On the island of Corsica, Bonifacio was the most heavily defended area, with two batteries of 164 mm and one of 138 mm. Ajaccio and Bastia had one battery of 138-mm guns apiece.

The main antiaircraft weapon was the French navy's dual-purpose 90-mm mobile gun. Although there were plans to install antiaircraft weapons, only a few were delivered by the factory by 1940.

COMMANDING THE SKIES

The Great War opened a new arena for military action when aircraft turned out to be an important factor in offense as well as defense. Long-range air raids by zeppelins and later bomber aircraft demonstrated the need for air defenses for soft targets behind the lines, including population centers. Air war theorists like the Italian Douchet and the American William "Billy" Mitchell made the world aware of the real threat aviation presented to civilians.

During World War I, the French developed the largest air force in Europe and used it to great effect under the leadership of such men as General Duval, who took part in massive air battles to help dominate the battlefield. In 1918, as commander of the aeronautics at General Headquarters, Duval used his air arm to break up an enemy offensive. In that operation, the pilot leading the assault was Major Joseph Vuillemin, who eventually assumed the command of the French *Armée de l'Air* (Air Force) in the 1930s. Vuillemin was a key figure in the growth of the French air arm during the 1920s and was admired for his daring exploits, which included long-range flights to West Africa (Christienne and Lissarrague, *French Military Aviation*, pp. 205–210).

At the end of the war, the French were left with a large surplus of aircraft, which they hoarded, the same as their artillery and tanks. As was to be expected, the aircraft quickly became obsolete. In the meantime, French aviators acquired more combat experience during operations of the Riff War and the insurrection in Syria. However, the French aircraft had little impact on the outcome of these conflicts other than spreading shock among the enemy troops.

The Air Ministry, founded in 1928, led to the creation of the *Armée de l'Air* in 1933. At this time, most of the government credits appropriated for the military had been funneled to the construction of fortifications and on the maintenance of the army and the air force, and the navy had to vie for the remaining crumbs. However, since Legyues was so successful in advancing the cause of the navy, the new air force was left practically destitute. Throughout the 1920s, the development and acquisition of modern aircraft was enmeshed in bureaucratic procedures so convoluted that by the time the new aircraft rolled off the production line, they were obsolete. In the early 1930s, Air Minister Pierre Cot and Victor Dénian, the first chief of staff of the new air force (officially established in 1933) and later air minister, tried to correct this policy. In 1936, the government began the nationalization of large segments of the aviation industry, providing a partial remedy to the problems plaguing the air force. However, these actions provoked chaos, unrest, and even sabotage.

In 1934, Dénian began to rebuild the air force, and fearing a resurgent Germany, the government rushed forward his three-year building plan to create a thousand-plane air force in only two years. This action actually hindered the development of more modern aircraft by not allowing the gradual replenishment of the air force, but it gave France a slight edge, one it did not use against the German *Luftwaffe* in 1936.

When Cot returned to head the air ministry in 1936, after nationalization of the aircraft industry, he proposed a five-year plan to rebuild the French air force. Unfortunately, the only aircraft he could order were models listed on Plan I, which were reaching obsolescence by that time. Plan II replaced Plan I in September 1936, increasing the air force to 2,795 aircraft by the end of 1939. However, new models of aircraft were not ordered until 1937. The situation did not change until Guy La Chambre, who became air minister in early 1938, tried to reform and modernize the system with Plan V and new, more modern aircraft. Fighters, 41% of the new force, received priority. Due to production problems, the 4,739 aircraft were not slated for completion until March 1941 (Christienne and Lissarrague, *French Military Aviation*, pp. 266–272, 294–296). Even that date may not have been realistic because the French aviation industry was able to produce less than half (in many cases, less than a third) of the monthly requirements. The new aircraft actually built were finally on the way by the time the war broke out, but it was too little, too late.

Under La Chambre, General Joseph Vuillemin became the commander in chief of air forces, but he was still under the control of General Gamelin, who was in overall command. Since Vuillemin had little influence with his superior, the French air force remained insignificant, and its operations were left to the discretion of the army commanders. All the instructions for the army emphasized that the air element was to support the army by providing observation, reconnaissance, and attacks on enemy formations. The high command showed no interest in bombing strategic targets.

When General Vuillemin visited Germany in 1938, he was easily fooled into believing in German air superiority. His hosts from the *Luftwaffe* showed him production lines and some of their advanced aircraft not yet beyond the prototype stage. On his return to France, Vuillemin informed the political leaders of the woeful inadequacy of the French air force. His report may well have influenced the outcome of the events at the Munich Conference (Horne, *To Lose a Battle*, pp. 77–78). Although the great aviator had lost heart, he remained in command of the air force until the fall of France.

The French air force also had a problem with its BCR (bomber, combat, and reconnaissance) project, which was first mentioned in Plan I and called for aircraft that could undertake bombing, combat, and reconnaissance missions with long-range capability. In most cases, the aircraft built for this purpose were unable to perform these missions adequately. In addition, the inadequate radio equipment of French aircraft prevented efficient coordination with ground units. Furthermore, most French pursuit planes were outmatched by the faster German Me-109 fighters. Finally, the air force was understrength and lacked a sufficient number of junior flying officers. Many of its elderly pilots were not ready to meet the demands of modern aviation in the 1930s.

When some French aircraft took part in the Spanish Civil War, they generally performed poorly, disheartening the air ministry. The bomber force, largely obsolete, was too slow to effectively raid behind the lines. On the other hand, there were too many reconnaissance and observation aircraft, but most were slow and unable to operate during normal daylight hours. To make up for these shortcomings, La Chambre ordered aircraft from American manufacturers, including Curtis fighters and Douglas bombers. Between 1939 and 1940, the *armée de l'air* was the weakest of France's armed forces and largely without a mission.

Airbases and Air Units

Before the creation of the *armée de l'air*, French air units were organized into divisions, broken down into brigades, regiments, groups, and flights in descending order. In 1929, the 1st Air Division stationed at Metz had a brigade at Thionville and a bomber brigade at Nancy. The Second Air Division at Paris had a regiment at Le Bourget and a bomber regiment at Chartres. The 3rd Air Division at Tours had a brigade at Toulouse, one regiment at Tours, and one regiment at Chateauroux. Additional air regiments occupied airfields at Lyons and Mayence. A number of units were stationed in Africa and the Middle East. Thus, it is clear that the French air arm was mainly oriented toward a war with Germany.

In 1932, the Air Ministry redesignated some of its regiments as squadrons. In 1934, the new *armée de l'air* was organized into regional commands. The First Air Force Region included the 2nd Brigade at Dijon, the 8th Brigade and a demibrigade at Metz, and the 11th Brigade and a demibrigade at Nancy. Each brigade consisted of pursuit, observation, and reconnaissance squadrons. The Second Air Force Region included the 4th Brigade, 12th Brigade, and two demibrigades at Paris and a demibrigade at Compiègne. The 3rd Air Force Region headquartered at Tours comprised the 1st and 3rd Brigades and three demibrigades. The Fourth Air Force Region at Lyons included the 5th Air Brigade. Overseas, the Fifth Air Force Region, headquartered at Algiers, had a regiment at Rabat.

In addition, the air force set up five air bases located at Le Bourget, Nancy, Dijon, Lyon, and Pau where brigade headquarters with a training center, a mobilization center, and numerous other services were established.

During the war, the *armée de l'air* was under a different organization. General Vuillimen commanded the GQGA (General Headquarters of the Air Force), and under him was General Têtu in charge of the air units for ground support and

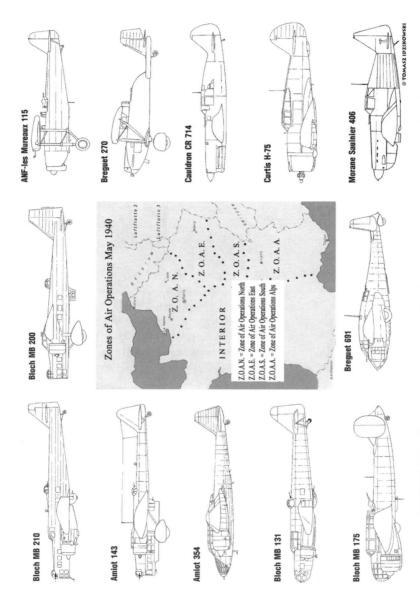

FIGURE 4-5. Drawings of various aircraft and map of air zones. [© Tomasz Idzikowski]

TABLE 4-6. Allied and axis fighter aircraft 1939–1940

Aircraft	Type	Machine Guns	Cannons	Range (kilometers)	Speed (kilometers/hour [kph])	Crew
Bloch 151, 152	Pursuit	4 or 2	0 or 2	600	520	1
D-520	Pursuit	4	1	1,240	530	1
D-501, 510[a]	Pursuit	2	1	820	350	1
MS-406	Pursuit	2	1	800	485	1
Me-109	German	4		700	570	1
Me-110	German	4	2	850	562	2
Fiat CR-42	Italian	2		775	430	1
Potez-631	Pursuit	2	2	1,000	440	2–3
Curtiss H-75	Pursuit	2		1,000	488	1
Hurricane	British	8		740	540	1
Spitfire	British	2	2	652	580	1

[a]Obsolete.

TABLE 4-7. Allied and axis bombers and reconnaissance aircraft 1939–1940

Aircraft	Type	Armament	Bombs (pounds)	Range (kilometers)	Speed (kilometers/hour [kph])	Crew
Amiot-143[a]	Bomber	4 MG	1,980	1,280	300	4–6
Amiot-350s	Bomber	3 MG, 1 cannon	1,760 to 2,600	2,480	480	4
He-111	German	7 MG, 1 cannon	4,400	1,200	400	4–5
SM 79	Italian	4 MG	2,200	2,000	434	4–5
Bloch-210[a]	Bomber	3 MG	3,520	1,100	210	5
Farman-222	Bomber	3 MG	9,240	2,000	320	5
Farman-223	Bomber	1 MG, 3 cannon	9,240	5,000	385	5–6
Poetz-540[a]	Bomber	3 MG	2,000	1,000	330	5
Poetz-631/633	Bomber	2 MG, 2 cannon	880	1,000	440	3
LeO-451	Bomber	2 MG, 1 cannon	3,100	1,600	500	4
Breguet-693	AB	6 MG, 1 cannon	880	690	480	2
Douglas DB-7	AB	4 MG	2,400	1,000	630	4
Martin-167	Rec/B	6 MG	1,250	1,200	451	3
Whitley	British	5 MG	7,000	2,650	357	5
Bloch-174	Rec/AB	7MG	1,100	1,700	510	3
Bloch 131[a]	Rec	3 MG	1,760	800	340	5
Bloch-174	Rec/LB	7 MG	110	1,450	329	3
Poetz-63.11	Rec	10 MG	660	1,220	430	3
Mur-115/117[a]	Rec	2 MG, 1 cannon	660	710	330	2

AB, attack bomber; LB, light bomber; MG, machine gun; Rec, reconnaissance.
[a]Obsolete.

antiaircraft units assigned to the Northeast Front. The air force units served in several zones: ZOAN (*Zone d'Opérations Aériennes Nord* or Zone of Aerial Operations North), with headquarters at Chauny; ZOAE (*Zone d'Opérations Aériennes Est* or Zone of Aerial Operations East), with headquarters at Nancy; ZOAS (*Zone d'Opérations Aériennes Sud* or Zone of Aerial Operations South), with headquarters at Dole; and ZOAA (*Zone d'Opérations Aériennes des Alpes* or Zone of Aerial Operations of the Alps), with headquarters at Valence; and several squadrons assigned to French Northwest Africa (Christienne and Lissarrague, *French Military Aviation*, pp. 219–21, 252–54, 258, 323–24).

Early in the 1920s, the military established the Antiaircraft Defense Command (DCA; or *Défense Contre-Avion*) with headquarters at Chartres. This included five regiments, a training school, and a technical section for research and development. The air ministry's Plan III of the 1930s was devoted to the improvement of the antiaircraft forces. Although this appears to have been a good start, the plan was dropped, and the antiaircraft arm became an impotent entity by 1939 since it lacked smaller-caliber weapons to deal with enemy ground attack aircraft. In addition, the fact that each army was responsible for its own air protection further weakened the overall defensive system due to lack of coordination. Thus, the serious shortcomings in the quality and quantity of aircraft and guns prevented France's air defenses from playing a major role during the war (Tables 4.6 and 4.7).

CHAPTER 5

THE MARCH TO DEFEAT

In Europe, the French and their British allies formed the main bulwark against the advancing tide of fascism and communism between World Wars I and II. During this time, France had tried to build a new set of alliances. Thus, early in the 1920s France and Belgium occupied the industrial heart of the Rhineland when the Germans failed to meet the required reparations payments. In 1921, the French also backed the creation of the Little Entente in eastern Europe, which comprised Yugoslavia, Czechoslovakia, and Romania. This weak alliance lasted until the late 1930s, when pressure from fascist nations caused it to crumble. The Poles refused to join any alliance with Czechoslovakia after the Czechs had annexed Teschen while the Poles had been engaged in their struggle against the Red Army. The rise of Mussolini in Italy during the 1920s presented a threat to French security and tested their Little Entente as the Italians pursued claims against the Yugoslavs. This was why the first new postwar fort, Rimplas, was built on the Southeast Front during the 1920s.

Central and eastern Europe proved to be volatile areas, with fascist-type dictatorships dominating most countries. After he slipped into power in 1933 and concluded a nonaggression pact with Poland at the beginning of 1934, Hitler attempted to take over his native Austria in the summer of 1934. However, Austria had formed an alliance with Mussolini's Italy, which intervened to nip the German-sponsored revolt in the bud. The assassination of King Alexander of Yugoslavia and the French foreign minister at Marseilles in October of 1934 further complicated matters.[1] The new foreign minister, Pierre Laval, worked quickly to obtain a rapprochement with Mussolini to forge an alliance with Italy against German expansion. The Rome Agreement (or Laval-Mussolini Accords) of 1935 secured France's Southeast Front in theory, bringing to a halt for almost a year much of the defensive work taking place in the Alps and in Tunisia (facing Italian Libya). This agreement also enlisted Yugoslavia and Czechoslovakia in France and Italy's efforts to maintain Austria's independence. France formulated a new plan for an offensive operation known as the Foch Plan. It called for French, Italian, Yugoslav, and Czech forces to occupy Austria in the event of another German takeover attempt.[2] In exchange for Italian cooperation, Laval gave Mussolini a free hand in East Africa (Komjathy, *Crises*, pp. 101–103).

Mussolini's campaign in Ethiopia, which began in the fall of 1935, ended in early 1936, bringing a political realignment that terminated the Laval-Mussolini agreement. When Italy joined the Axis, the instability of the Little Entente increased. Meanwhile,

in 1935 a plebiscite returned the Saar to Germany, which triggered a defense buildup in
France's Sarre Gap, in the part of the Maginot Line facing the Saar. On 7 March 1936,
German troops marched into the Rhineland. Only three battalions actually crossed the
Rhine River, with orders to withdraw if any French forces appeared. Their mission was
mainly to fool the French into believing that the German force was greater than it
actually was.

The French army mobilized and took up position in the Maginot Line but did little
else. Only months earlier, Minister of War Maurin had verbalized France's reluctance to
take the offensive when he asked the Chamber of Deputies, "How can we still believe in
the offensive when we have spent milliards to establish a fortified barrier?" (Horne, *To
Lose a Battle*, p. 35). General Gamelin exaggerated the *Deuxième Bureau's* (French army
intelligence's) calculations and concluded that he was facing twenty-two German divisions in the Rhineland instead of the estimated seven (Duroselle, *France and the Nazi
Threat*, pp. 125–126). Thus, Hitler's bluff succeeded. Soon, he remilitarized the Rhineland and began the construction of the West Wall. In the meantime, the French lost
their Belgian ally when the new king declared the neutrality of his nation, leaving
France's left flank open.

The European situation further deteriorated with the outbreak of civil war in Spain
in July 1936. In July, the Italians and Germans helped to transport some of Francisco
Franco's Nationalist forces from Spanish Morocco into Spain. At the same time, the
Republican government appealed to the Soviets and the French for support. Pierre Cot
dispatched over four hundred aircraft to the Republicans in Spain. The Germans sent
the Condor Legion and the Italians sent an army to fight for the Nationalists. Volunteers from the west joined the communist-inspired International Brigades fighting
for the Republicans, who used weapons from various nonfascist nations. The war, which
lasted until the spring of 1939, became a testing ground for new weapons and tactics.
Thus, the Spanish Civil War was the prelude for a new world war.

In 1938, Hitler, with the consent of Mussolini, marched his army into Austria
unopposed and annexed that nation. France stood passively by, continuing to rely on its
Little Entente to further check fascist expansion. The next test came in late summer of
1938 when Hitler prepared for war with Czechoslovakia. Romania was already rea-
ligning with the fascists, leaving Yugoslavia isolated. The Yugoslavs were frantically
building the Rupnik Line, a line of defenses along the Italian and Hungarian borders.
These fortifications, partially inspired by the French, were to have armored components
provided by the Czechs. However, the work could not be completed when the Czech
supply was cut short by drastic events of 1938 and early 1939.

Although geographically isolated from allies, the Czechs had a modern army and air
force. They also were building heavy fortifications along their vulnerable flanks with
Austria and Germany. In addition, they relied heavily on the mountainous terrain of the
Sudetenland for their defense against a German invasion and fortified this area only
lightly. The Czech fortifications were very similar to those of the Maginot Line since
a group of French liaison officers had helped the Czechs design their forts in the
mid-1930s. When Hitler demanded the Sudetenland from Czechoslovakia, none of the
new forts was completed or fully operational. In some cases, the guns were placed in
front of the unfinished artillery casemates in preparation for war. Nonetheless, the
Czech army was large enough to stand up to the German military. In addition, for the

FIGURE 5-1. Map of French military regions showing the military regions with the divisions in them before mobilization. [Joseph Kaufmann]

Germans to launch an offensive, they had to leave the West Wall manned by a small number of reservist divisions.

Once again, the French army prepared to move into the Maginot Line but contemplated no offensive action. Joseph Vuillemin had just returned from Germany, overwhelmed by his visit to the *Luftwaffe* and discouraged by the state of the French air force and the performance of its aircraft in the Spanish Civil War. He conveyed this gloomy perspective to the government. During the crisis, General Louis Maurin, then minister of war, informed Pierre Flandin, head of the council, that the French army had been conceived for a purely defensive role and was unable to undertake a military intervention of the most limited scope (Goutard and Burgess, *Battle of France*, p. 46).

Nonetheless, Gamelin ordered General Prételat to draw up plans for an offensive into the Saar.

The forces for this offensive would come from the army group stationed on the Northeast Front. In the fall of 1938, at the Munich Conference, the British and French governments abandoned Czechoslovakia to the mercy of the Germans. British Prime Minister Neville Chamberlain returned to Britain declaring, "Peace in our time." The planning for the Saar offensive was shelved (Prételat, *Le Destin Tragique*, p. 19). Czechoslovakia, bereft of allies, was forced to give up the Sudetenland and virtually all of its new fortifications.

As the feeling that war was inescapable soon became widespread, France and Great Britain strove to overhaul their armed forces before it was too late. They also cemented an alliance with Poland that did little to replace the dissolution of the Little Entente. Poland now found itself in the same position as Czechoslovakia. The French air minister tried to rebuild and modernize the air force, while Gamelin forged ahead with the reinforcement of the remainder of the Northeast Front with defensive strong points to aid the army maneuvers (Prételat, *Le Destin Tragique*, pp. 11–12).

FRANCE AND THE ALLIES ON THE EVE

Although the New Fronts of the Maginot Line were nearing completion, a good deal of work had been canceled for economic reasons. Furthermore, despite efforts to develop and adequately equip the army and air force, the French war industry was too slow and inefficient to meet the added demands. For this reason, Vuillemin asked the French government to order Curtis Hawk-75 fighter aircraft from the United States. Many French tanks were also inadequate, having, among other defects, small one-man turrets. However, the heavy Char B-1, with a hull-mounted 75-mm gun, was one of the best-armed tanks of 1939. The new Somua medium tank was also a match for most of the German tanks, including the Panzer III (Table 5.1).[3] Unfortunately, the French army lacked a large, well-trained mobile force and a high command ready to fight a modern war. The best French units served in the Maginot Line, the Alps, and the few mechanized divisions. However, French military doctrine limited the ability of commanders to react to a situation without orders from above. General Gamelin, whose headquarters even lacked modern radio communication, was courting disaster.

When the Germans invaded Poland in September 1939, the French military fell back on the defensive doctrine developed with the creation of the Maginot Line, which was originally intended to cover the frontier provinces as the army mobilized and prepared to strike back. In 1939, the Maginot Line had become the main line of resistance. The high command intended to mobilize and train the army behind this shield while preparing to equip itself with modern offensive weapons that would make it possible to launch an assault against Germany in 1941. By November 1939, General Gamelin's staff produced two plans for French forces to advance: Plan E for Escaut and Plan D for Dyle. Neither plan involved an offensive operation; instead, they proposed a move into Belgium to shorten the line and take up new defensive positions. A third plan actually involved an offensive against Italy through the Alpine front, but Italy was not at war in 1939.

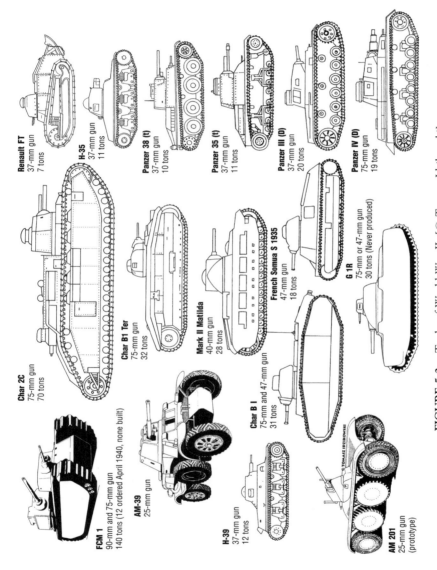

Renault FT
37-mm gun
7 tons

H-35
37-mm gun
11 tons

Panzer 38 (t)
37-mm gun
10 tons

Panzer 35 (t)
37-mm gun
11 tons

Panzer III (D)
37-mm gun
20 tons

Panzer IV (D)
75-mm gun
19 tons

Char 2C
75-mm gun
70 tons

Char B1 Ter
75-mm gun
32 tons

Mark II Matilda
40-mm gun
28 tons

French Somua S 1935
47-mm gun
18 tons

G 1R
75-mm or 47-mm gun
30 tons (Never produced)

FCM 1
90-mm and 75-mm gun
140 tons (12 ordered April 1940, none built)

AM-39
25-mm gun

Char B I
75-mm and 47-mm gun
31 tons

H-39
37-mm gun
12 tons

AM 201
25-mm gun
(prototype)

FIGURE 5-2. Tanks of World War II. [© Tomasz Idzikowski]

TABLE 5-1. Comparative Chart on Tanks

Tank	Total (1940)	Main Gun	Armor	Weight (tons)	Speed (kilometers/hour [kph])	Crew
Char 2C (Fr)	6	75 mm	45 mm	68	12	12
Char B1bis (Fr)	321	75 mm and 47 mm	60 mm	32	28	4
Somua S35 (Fr)	260	47 mm	55 mm	20	40	3
D-2 (Fr)	310	47 mm	40 mm	20	25	3
Inf Matilda A12 (Br)	75	40 mm	78 mm	26.5	24	4
PzKw IV (Ger)	278	75 mm	30 mm	17.3	29	5
D-1 (Fr)	150	47 mm	37 mm	13	20	3
FCM 36 (Fr)	90	37 mm	40 mm	12	34	2
Hotchkis H39 (Fr)	276	37 mm	45 mm	12	36	2
Hotchkis H35 (Fr)	545	37 mm	34 mm	12	34	2
Renault R40 (Fr)	90	37 mm	45 mm	12.5	20	2
Vickers A-10 (Br)	126	40 mm	30 mm	14	26	5
Vickers A-13 (Br)	30	40 mm	14 mm	14	48	4
Inf Matilda A-11 (Br)	100	MG	60 mm	11	12	2
PzKw 35t (Czech-Gr)	135	40 mm	35 mm	10.5	40	4
PzKw 38t (Czech-Gr)	410	37 mm	25 mm	9.7	41	4
PzKw III (Gr)	388	50 mm	30 mm	20	40	5
Renault R35 (Fr)	855	37 mm	40 mm	9.8	20	2
Renault AMC (Fr)	180	25 mm	25 mm	10.8	40	3
T-15 (British 1934) (Bel)	42	MG	9 mm	9	64	2
PzKw II (Gr)	1095	20 mm	30 mm	9	26	3
Renault FT (Fr)	534	MG or 37 mm	22 mm	7	7	2
Renault AMR 35 (Fr)	380	MG or 25 mm	13 mm	6	50	2
Mark VI (Br)	402	MG	15 mm	5.2	55	3
PzKw I (Gr)	1,045	MG	13 mm	5.8	40	2

MG, machine gun; Bel, Belgian; Br, British; Fr, French; Gr, German; Czech-Ger, Czech tanks used by German army.

The informed public of the day was not blind to the potential problems of the day as *Defence of Britain*, a book written by military historian Liddell Hart before the war, demonstrated. France, Hart argued, was at the center of the allied position, but its strength left much to be desired. The efficiency of its navy was in doubt not only in technical respects but also because the completion of many ships was far past the planned date. In addition, Hart claimed, the Italian navy had grown so rapidly—especially in the category of small, fast craft—that France's lines of communications with Africa were in jeopardy. However, the British navy was there to back up its ally. "Still more depressing," wrote Hart, "was the effect of revelations as to the efficiency of the French Air Force and aircraft industry." (Hart, pp. 197–98) He also pointed out correctly that France had begun to expand its first-line aircraft strength only early in 1938. At the time of the Munich Crisis, the French air force may have numbered as few as seven hundred modern aircraft. Plan V of 1938 was an attempt to correct those shortcomings. The main problem, Hart bemoaned, was the "eye-on-the-ground habit of subordinating the needs of the air to those of the Army" because "the French have pinned their faith to the strength and solidity of the army," which still relied a good deal on outdated equipment. In 1939, Hart said, the French army was "pedestrian rather than athletic in nature, solid rather than brilliant in performance." However, Hart mistakenly believed that the French army was better trained than the newly expanding Germany army was.

As for the tank force, Hart and his contemporaries realized that France had more and better-armored tanks than Germany, but that the majority were under the control of the infantry (Hart, *Defence of Britain*, p. 199).[4]

On the subject of the French fortifications, Hart wrote that they consisted of a chain of forts and blockhouses extending from Longuyon to the Swiss frontier, skirting the Rhine. He also noted new construction along the Belgian frontier to Lille and concrete defenses on the Southeast Front. Along the German frontier, he observed, "the strength of the fortifications" makes it "not easy to imagine that any assault upon it could have much chance of success." Realizing that Poland might be attacked by Germany, Hart also opined that the French could not offer direct help or reinforce the Polish position, but that they might feel compelled to launch an offensive for their ally's sake, despite the fact they were unprepared for such action (Hart, *Defence of Britain*, pp. 206–210).

Nonetheless, Hart believed that the center (the French front with Germany) was secure. The Ardennes sector on the left flank, Hart felt, could be yielded to the Germans to create a trap in which to crush their forces if they were stopped at the Meuse, which he called "Belgium's Moat." The main problem for the Belgian army, he felt, was to protect against a surprise attack (Hart, *Defence of Britain*, pp. 216, 229). Between the wars, the Belgians had rebuilt their defenses but decided to protect the Ardennes only lightly and abandon the area in case of a major enemy thrust. Belgium's main fortifications consisted of three renovated fortress rings at Liège, Namur, and Antwerp. The first two served as bridgeheads on the Meuse. Old forts in these rings were refurbished and somewhat modernized. However, at Liège, beyond the old forts, a new line of four modern forts was built. The most spectacular of these new forts was the Ében Émael, which anchored the line and went into operation in the 1930s. Two of the new Liège forts mounted 120-mm turret guns. The rest of the armament was similar to that of the Maginot Line. The design of the Belgian forts, however, was quite different from that of the French.

The Meuse offered a defensive barrier between the new forts and other light fortifications that formed additional defensive lines. Furthermore, before the war, the Belgians extended a line of fortifications from the Antwerp ring to the Dyle River (the KW Line) in front of Brussels. They also strove to close the gap between Brussels and the Meuse with a line of antitank (AT) obstacles made of "Belgian Gates."

The Achilles' heel of the Belgian defense system was the Dutch Maastricht Appendage, which covered a large section of Belgium's frontier. Indeed, a German invasion of the Netherlands could leave this front wide open because the Dutch had built only light frontier fortifications in the Peel-Raam Line. In 1939, when General Izaak Reynders stepped down as commander in chief, the Netherlands switched from defending its frontiers to concentrating on the defense of Fortress Holland. Fortress Holland was the section of the Netherlands between river barriers of the Lek, Waal, and Maas on the south, and the Zuider Zee on the north with fortified lines on the west protecting the area between Rotterdam, Utrecht, and Amsterdam. When Belgium returned to neutrality in 1936, the likelihood of the French troops coming to the rescue of the line of the Meuse at Liège melted away. In addition, since France no longer had an alliance with Belgium, it scrapped the plans to enter the territories of its erstwhile ally, even after a violation of its neutrality on the part of Germany. Therefore, in November 1939, the French army quickly formulated Plan E and Plan D, which called for the occupation of Belgian positions that could be reached rapidly after a German invasion was launched.

The Right Flank of the front with Germany was formed by Switzerland, but an invasion of this country offered too many negatives. It was possible, nonetheless, for the Germans to overwhelm the Swiss along the Rhine border and move quickly toward the French border and the Belfort Gap. This move, however, meant that several of the key transportation routes between Germany and Italy could be barred. To secure these lines, the Germans would have to deal with the Swiss line of border forts and with the National Redoubt, whose Alpine forts guarded those key transportation routes. The Swiss border forts and even those of the National Redoubt were somewhat similar to the Maginot forts, but smaller. Their armament consisted mainly of 75-mm guns.[5]

The French high command was well aware of the likely direction of the German assault. The main thrust would have to come through Belgium to avoid the French fortifications. Nonetheless, an assault through the borderlands of Switzerland outflanking the French position on the Rhine was also considered a possibility. For this reason, a number of French divisions would be stationed near Belfort. The wild card remained Italy since its entry into the war would throw the allies off balance and open a front along the Mediterranean and in Africa.

Although the *Deuxième Bureau* was criticized for providing inflated numbers and poor estimates of the enemy situation, recent studies indicated that it reported accurately on German intentions and plans as well as the development of armored divisions and new weapons. Colonel Louis Rivet, chief of the *Services Spéciaux* (covert intelligence agency), claimed that the success of the German *blitzkrieg* against Poland "had come as no surprise to anyone but the Poles and 'our General Staff' " (May, *Knowing One's Enemies*, pp. 307–308). Indeed, Gamelin and his staff believed the Germans might launch an assault against the Maginot Line and assigned a larger-than-needed number of infantry divisions to support it. Army intelligence had a different view.

After May 1939, French intelligence found that the German *Abwehr* had stopped sending agents to report on the Maginot Line. Colonel Paul Paillole attributed this to the fact that they found in Czechoslovakia technical plans related to the Maginot Line supplied by the French before the German takeover. In addition, the Germans had occupied many of the Czech fortifications since late 1938 and had months to inspect them and test their weapons against them. Paillole related that Major Guy Schelesser, who "entered a fortress near Thionville," picked up electrical blueprints left on a table, and left the site after convincing the guard he was a civilian engineer and had come to pick up his briefcase (Paillole, *Fighting the Nazis*, pp. 60, 81).

Although the Germans may have obtained intelligence after their takeover of Czechoslovakia, they had detailed information about the Maginot Line since 1937. Two German reports dated 1936 included some maps and general information on the Maginot Line, and the next year's report contained even more details as well as plans that included accurate blueprints of an interval casemate, an *abri*, a blockhouse on the Rhine, and Maginot *ouvrages*. Thus, the report included a map identifying the location of the blocks and entrances to the *gros ouvrage* (GO) of Hochwald. One of the plans showed a casemate for 75-mm guns at Métrich. Another plan depicted a cross section and plan of a block at the *petit ouvrage* (PO) of Coume with a 75-mm gun turret instead of the machine gun turret it actually has. Yet another blueprint represented the PO of Mottenberg as a GO and revealed the original plans for the fort before budget limitations prevented the construction of the artillery blocks. Most important, there was an accurate plan of the GO of Simserhof that included detailed plans of the fort's *entrée des munitions* (munitions entrance, EM) and Block 3 (81-mm mortar turret). There were also cross sections of embrasure positions and the galleries, all with measurements. However, not all the details were accurate. For instance, the 47-mm AT gun of the EM does not appear. In addition, although the type of weapons for each of the block was identified, for some reason the Germans did not seem to realize that the turrets mounted pairs of weapons rather than single weapons.

By 1939, the Germans had acquired more information on the Maginot Line. In August of that year, air reconnaissance flew over several of the forts, bringing back photographs that enabled interpreters to identify many of the turrets and cloches and the general outline of the *ouvrages* based on their lines of obstacles. On one of these flights, the Germans photographed the old fort of Guenterange at Thionville, where two blocks of four single-gun turrets had been armed with new long-range 105-mm guns and put back into operation. However, the photo interpreter was able to identify only one of these blocks of four turrets. German reconnaissance aircraft were able to fly over the Maginot forts with impunity because the flight took only ten to fifteen minutes, and by the time they were spotted, they were already on their way back to their home field. The French were also hampered by their reliance on observers using the national telephone system, which further delayed the French fighters' response time. Although the French were working on a radar station, there was no chain of stations that would have sounded the alert more efficiently (Ellis, *The War in France and Flanders*, p. 25).

French mobilization began in late August 1939 as the Danzig crisis continued to move toward a violent conclusion. The French high command organized a covering force to move along the frontier, mainly on the Belgian front. The *Garde Républicaine Mobile* (Mobile Republican Guard or GRM) consisted of *gendarmes* whose mission was to occupy the fortified houses and blockhouses along the frontier, give advanced warning, and delay an enemy attack. The men of the GRM were recruited from former soldiers and were organized into eight legions that consisted of two to six groups (battalions), each of which included two to four companies. The 7th Legion covered the *Région Fortifiée* (RF) of Metz, and the 4th Legion of GRM covered the RF of Lauter.

At mobilization, the battalions of the existing fortress infantry regiments defending the Maginot Line served as the nucleus for new fortress infantry regiments being formed (Tables 5.2–5.4). Likewise, the battalions from the sixty-four regular army regiments— including twenty-four in infantry divisions, twenty in motorized divisions, and eight in

TABLE 5-2. Fortified sectors and fortress infantry regiments

Regions and Sectors 1939	Infantry and Fortress Infantry Composition		Army 1939	1940 Converts to	Army May 1940
	Before Mobilization	Aug/Sep 1939 on Mobilization			
SD Flanders		137 RIF	1st	SF Flanders 1	7th
SD Lille	Bn of 43 RI	100 RI	1st	SF Lille 1	1st
SF Escuat	2 Bn of 1 RI, 84 RIF	54 RIF	1st		1st
SF Maubeuge		84 RIF, 87RIF, 13 RRP	1st	101st Fortress Division 3	1st
SD Ardennes	Bn of 91 RI	148 RIF	DAA	LXI Fortress Corps 1 / 102nd Fortress Division	9th
SF Montmedy	155 RIF	136 RIF, 147 RIF, 155 RIF		LXI Fortress Corps 1 / Grp Burtaire 5	2nd
RF Metz					
SF Crusnes	149 RIF	128 RIF, 132 RIF, 139 RIF, 149 RIF	3rd	XLII Fortress Corps 3	3rd
SF Thionville	168 RIF	167 RIF, 168 RIF, 169 RIF	3rd	XLII Fortress Corps 3	3rd
SF Boulay	162 RIF	161 RIF, 162 RIF, 164 RIF	3rd	Division March Poisot 6	3rd
SF Faulquemont	146 RIF	146 RIF, 156 RIF, 160 RIF	3rd	Division March Besse 6	3rd
SD Sarre	69 RIF	69 RIF, 82 RIF,174 RIF, 41 Col MGR, 51 Col MGR (joins 1940)	4th	Group Girval 6 / SF Sarre (69 and 82 RIF detached) 3 / Becomes Group Dagan 6	4th

Unit			1940 Converts to		
RF Lauter					
RF Rohrbach	153 RIF	5th	*133 RIF, 153 RIF, 166 RIF*	XLIII Fortress Corps 3	5th
				Division March Chastanet 6	5th
SF Vosges	37 RIF	5th	*37 RIF, 154 RIF, 165 RIF*	XLIII Fortress Corps 3	5th
SF Haguenau	23 RIF	5th	*22 RIF, 23 RIF, 68 RIF, 79 RIF*	Division March Regard 6	5th
SF Bas Rhin	172 RIF	5th	*34 RIF, 70 RIF 172 RIF, 226 RI*	103rd Fortress Division 3	5th
RF Belfort					
SF Colmar	42 RIF	8th	28 RIF, 42 RIF	XLIV Corps 3	8th
SF Mulhouse	171 RIF	8th	10 RIF	104th Fortress Division 3	8th
SD Altkirch		8th	12 RIF, 171 RIF	105th Fortress Division 3	8th
Belfort Defenses		8th	371 RI (until March 1940)	SF Altkirch 1	8th
SD Montbeliard	(Elements of 60 RI)	8th	(2 battalions of *chaussers*)	SF Montbeliard 3	8th
SF Jura	1 DB Pyrennes		1 DB Pyrennes		

Note: In the column "1940 Converts to," the 1, 3, or 6 refers to the month the unit converted (January, March, or June, respectively). Bn, battalion; ColMGR, colonial machine gun regiment; DAA, army detachment ardennes; DB, demibrigade; RI, infantry regiment; RIF, fortress infantry regiment.

TABLE 5-3. Mobilization of fortress infantry regiments and new fortress infantry regiments from premobilization fortress infantry regiments

Before Mobilization	New RIF[a]	Sectors Sept 1939
43rd RI	*100th RI*	SD Lille
84th RIF[b]	*54th RIF*	SF Escuat
	84th RIF	SF Maubeuge
	87th RIF	
91st RI	*91st RIF*	SD Ardennes
	148th RI	
155th RIF	*136th RIF*	
	147th RIF	SF Montmedy
	155th RIF	
149th RIF	*128th RIF*	
	132nd RIF	
	139th RIF	SF Crusnes
	149th RIF	
168th RIF	*167th RIF*	
	168th RIF	SF Thionville
	169th RIF	
162nd RIF	*161st RIF*	
	162nd RIF	SF Boulay
	164th RIF	
146th RIF	146th RIF	
	156th RIF	SF Faulquemont
	160th RIF	
69th RIF	69th RIF	
	82nd RIF	SD Sarre
	174th RIF	
153rd RIF	*133rd RIF*	
	153rd RIF	SF Rohrbach
	166th RIF	
37th RIF	37th RIF	
	154th RIF	SF Vosges
	165th RIF	
23rd RIF	*22nd RIF*	
	23rd RIF	
	68th RIF	SF Haguenau
	79th RIF	
172nd RIF	*34th RIF*	
	70th RIF	SF Bas Rhin
	172nd RIF	
42nd RIF	*28th RIF*	SF Colmar
	42nd RIF	
171st RIF	*10th RIF*	SF Mulhouse
	12th RIF	
	171st RIF	SD Altkirch

[a]This column shows each regiment formed from a battalion of the pre-August 1939 RIF (fortress infantry regiment) or RI (infantry regiment) including the old regiment. Two reserve battalions were added to each of these regiments.

[b]Created in April 1939.

TABLE 5-4. Mobilization on the southeast front

Premobilization: Active DBAF and Active BAF	New DBAF Formed with Active BAF on Mobilization	Sectors Sept 1939
	230th DBAF	SD Rhone
	179th BAF	
	189th BAF	
	199th BCHM	
30th DBAF	16th DBAF	SF Savoy
	6th BM	
70th BAF	**70th BAF**	
	80th BAF	
	30th DBAF	SF Savoy
71st BAF	**71st BAF**	
	81st BAF	
	91st BAF	
157th DBAF	75th DBAF	SF Dauphine
	82nd BAF	
	92nd BAF	
	102nd BAF	
72nd BAF	**72nd BAF**	
	157th DBAF	SF Dauphine
	72nd BAF[a]	
73rd BAF	**73rd BAF**	
	83rd BAF	
58th DBAF	61st DBAF	SF Maritime Alps
74th BAF	**74th BAF**	
	84th BAF	
	94th BAF	
	40th DBAF	SF Maritime Alps
75th BAF	**75th BAF**	
	85th BAF	
	95th BAF	
	58th DBAF	SF Maritime Alps
76th BAF	**76th BAF**	
	86th BAF	
	96th BAF	

BAF, alpine fortress battalion; BM, machine gun battalion; DBAF, alpine fortress demibrigade.

[a]72nd BAF was used to form the 75th DBAF on mobilization and then moved back to the 157th BAF.

mountain divisions—formed new regiments and divisions for the field army. The peacetime army also included three demibrigades (equal to a reinforced regiment), eleven *chausseurs*, and twelve *chausseurs Alpins* battalions that joined other formations moving into the defensive positions (Sumner, *The French Army*, pp. 6–11).

The artillery also had to expand at mobilization. The *régiment d'Artillerie de Position* (RAP; nonmobile or static artillery regiment); the *régiment d'artillerie mixte de forteresse* (RAMF; mixed fortress artillery regiment); and the *régiment d'artillerie de région fortifiée*

(RARF; artillery regiment of a fortified region) served the fortified areas. The *régiment d'artillerie lourde* (RAL; heavy artillery regiment) and the *artillerie lourde sur voie ferrée* (ALVF; heavy rail artillery) provided long-range support. The RAPs provided the companies that manned the artillery of the *ouvrages*, the intervals, and the support areas, including the old forts at Metz, Thionville, Verdun, and Belfort. The RAMF and RARF were a little more mobile, whereas the rail artillery and heavy artillery regiments provided the long-range firepower. The main units on the fortified Northeast Front were the 151st, 155th, 159th, and 163rd RAP and the three RARFs during the 1930s. The groups (battalions) of these four RAPs split to form twelve RAPs at mobilization. Although these units had a variety of weapons that ranged from 75 mm to 240 mm, several models of 155-mm guns and 75-mm guns predominated.

The troops of the fortress infantry regiments (RIFs) and their mobilized reserves were among the best in the French army (Tables 5.5 and 5.6). In mid-1935, the regular infantry regiments serving in the RFs of the Maginot Line became RIFs. Normally numbering three battalions, each of these RIFs was intended to expand into two additional RIFs on mobilization. At about the time these plans were made, security *casernes* were built near the *ouvrages* to allow faster reaction time. General Prételat warned Gamelin that the RIF battalions were only suited for static operations because they were similar to the machine gun battalions; the contingent of these battalions carried mainly heavy infantry weapons, and only 25% was composed of riflemen. Only a minority, about 25%, of these troops consisted of *frontaliers*, native to the fortified border regions, who were generally well motivated and skilled in their duties. Of the remainder, 50% to 55% came from the heavily populated regions of Paris and the north of France and required four to six days to reach their units on mobilization.

The cadre for each mobilized regiment included about 25% active duty troops (23% officers, 31% noncommissioned officers, 20% enlisted men). Shortly before completing their active duty training, a number of reservists were assigned to a position on the Maginot Line, which became their reserve duty assignment. On mobilization, the local reservists reinforced the active companies serving in the *ouvrages*. Unfortunately, since the number of skilled reservists on fortress duty was insufficient, a second group of reservists assigned to fortress units and intended for interval duty went into the forts as well (Mary, *Maginot*, Vol. 1, p. 78; Prételat, *Le Destin Tragique*, pp. 22–28). The Alpine troops and the fortress troops, considered a specialized elite group, wore a distinctive khaki beret with Maginot insignia. The high morale among the well-trained specialized troops set them apart from most reservists.

Many of the new Series A divisions were formed around reservists and some regulars. The cadres of regulars in the regiments thus formed included 19 of 81 officers (23%), 76 of 342 noncommissioned officers (17%), and 53 of 2,667 troops (2%). These divisions were given number designations below 50 not already assigned to active divisions. Older reservists formed divisions numbered 50 through 71. Their units included very few regulars, mostly officers in higher command positions; usually lacked an AT company; and were short of artillery. Despite these shortcomings, some Series B divisions performed well, but many were ill equipped for the rigors of modern warfare.

In 1934, General Prételat, who evaluated a test mobilization of the 41st Division (Series A), reported many deficiencies that continued to plague the French army until the outbreak of war to such an extent that all the reservists in the Series A and B divisions

TABLE 5-5. Mobilization of Artillery Units on the Fortified Fronts

Regions and Sectors 1939	Artillery Regiments: Composition		1940 Converts to
	Mobilization	Number of Batteries and Type of Guns 1939–1940	
SD Flanders	I/161st RAP	2 (12×75 mm, 6×37 mm)	SF Flanders
SD Lille			SF Lille 1
SF Escuat	I/161st RAP	3 (8×155 mm, 8×120 mm, 4×105 mm, 8×75 mm)	
SF Maubeuge	I & II/161st RAP	6 (16×155 mm, 16×120 mm, 8×105 mm, 16×75 mm)	101st Fortress Division 3
SD Ardennes	II/III 160th RAP[a]	4 (12×155 mm, 12×75 mm)	LXI Fortress Corps
			102nd Fortress Division 1
SF Montmedy	99th RAMF	6 (24×75 mm)	LXI Fortress Corps 1
	I/169th RAP	9 (8×155 mm, 4×120 mm, 24×105 mm)	
RF Metz			
SF Crusnes	152nd RAP	4 (16×155 mm) plus *ouvrages* of Fermont, Latiremont and Brehain)	XLII Fortress Corps 3
	46th RARF	9 (12×155 mm, 24×75 mm)	XLII Fortress Corps 3
SF Thionville	151st RAP	9 (2×240 mm, 2×220 mm, 20×155 mm, 8×120 mm) plus 100 mm guns of Ft. Konigsmacker and Guentrange and *ouvrages* of Rochonvillers, Molvange, Immerhof, Soetrich, Kobenbusch, Gagenberg, Metrich, and Billig.	Division March Poisot 6
	70th RARF	9 (12×155 mm, 24×75 mm)	
SF Boulay	153rd RAP	15 (4×240 mm, 20×155 mm, 8×105 mm, 40×75 mm) plus *ouvrages* of Hackenberg, Mont Welches, Michelsberg, and Anzeling.	Division March Besse 6
	23 RARF	9 (12×155 mm, 24×75 mm)	
SF Faulquemont	III/153rd RAP	3 (12×155 mm)	Group Girval 6
	163 RAP	18 (36×155 mm, 22×75 mm)	
	II/166[b] RAP[c]	3 (8×155 mm, 16×75 mm)	
	39th RARF	9 (12×155 mm, 24×75 mm)	
SD Sarre	166th RAP[d]	9 (2×280 mm, 2×220 mm, 36×155 mm, 12×120 mm, 28×75 mm)	SF Sarre 3
	166th RAP[c]	6 (40×155 mm, 12×105 mm, 8×75 mm)	
	49th RARF	9 (12×155 mm, 24×75 mm)	

(Continued)

TABLE 5-5. (Contd.)

Regions and Sectors 1939	Artillery Regiments: Composition		
	Mobilization	Number of Batteries and Type of Guns 1939–1940	1940 Converts to
RF Lauter			
SF Rohrbach	150th RAP	6 (32×150 mm, 8×145 mm, 8×120 mm) plus *ouvrages* of Simserhof, Schiesseck, Otterbiel	XLIII Fortress Corps 3 Division March Chastanet 6
	59th RARF	9 (12×155 mm, 24×75 mm)	
SF Vosges	168th RAP	6 (40×155 mm, 16×75 mm) plus the *ouvrages* of Grand Hohekirkel and Four Chaux	XLIII Fortress Corps 3
	60th RARF	9 (12×155 mm, 24×75 mm)	
SF Haguenau	156th RAP	5 (24×155 mm, 4×145 mm, 4×75 mm) plus the *ouvrages* of Hochwald and Schoenenbourg	Division March Regard 6
	69th RARF	9 (12×155 mm, 24×75 mm)	
SF Bas Rhin	155th RAP	8 (12×155 mm, 8×150 mm, 8×145 mm, 24×75 mm)	103rd Fortress Division 3
RF Belfort			XLIV Corps 3
SF Colmar	I/170th RAP	2 (8×155 mm, 4×120 mm, 12×75 mm)	104th Fortress Division 3
SF Mulhouse	II/159th RAP	1 (4×155 mm, 6×150 mm, 8×75 mm)	105th Fortress Division 3
SD Altkirch	III, IV/159th RAP	4 (16×155 mm, 22×75 mm)	SF Altkirch 1
Belfort Defense	V, VI/159th RAP	6 (4×240 mm, 8×155 mm) plus the old forts of Belfort	
SD Montbeliard	VII/159th RAP	2 (8×155 mm, 4×120 mm, 8×105 mm, 4×75 mm)	SF Montbeliard 3
SF Jura	II/170th RAP	4 (22×155 mm, 4×90 mm, 10×75 mm)	

Note: Some *Groupements* of artillery regiments had batteries of two, four, and eight guns. The 150th RAP, 155th RAP, 166th RAP, 168th RAP, and 170th RAP had eight-gun batteries, while most other regiments, like the 161st RAP, had mostly four-gun batteries. The 155th RAP had both four- and eight-gun batteries, and others like the 159th RAP and 165th RAP had batteries that varied.

[a] Assigned in January 1940 (160th RAP was located at the old forts of Verdun and Metz).
[b] Becomes part of III/163rd RAP.
[c] Reorganized after March 1940.
[d] Until March 1940.

TABLE 5-6. Artillery on the Southeast Front

Sector 1939	Artillery Regiments Composition: Regiments-Batteries		Assigned Army in May 1940
SD Rhone	I/164th RAP	1	Alps
SF Savoy	164th RAP	7	Alps
SF Dauphine	154th RAP	7	
	162nd RAP	5	Alps
SF Maritime Alps	157th RAP	6	Alps
	158th RAP	6	
	167th RAP	7	

required considerable training before they could operate effectively. This exercise also found reserve infantry officers lacked spirit and self-assurance and failed to take the initiative. However, it must be admitted that army regulations did not allow much freedom. In addition to lacking basic military knowledge, reported Prételat, the non-commissioned officers appeared to have forgotten most of what they had learned on active duty.

Although further instruction and training were needed, little changed after Prételat's scathing report. By 1939, only a third of reserve officers and a tenth of reserve NCOs had taken the necessary courses until they became mandatory in March 1939, but by then it was too late. At the time of the mobilization, entire divisions needed additional training before they could be committed to action. However, some of these units were actually assigned to labor projects to strengthen the defenses instead of receiving the proper preparation (Prételat, *Le Destin Tragique*, p. 33).

Except for the officers, the French soldier presented a sorry figure in the poorly tailored uniforms of the 1930s, which further depressed morale. In addition, the infantryman was poorly armed due to a shortage of the new MAS 36 rifles, one of the last bolt-action rifles designed for a major army. Many of the troops had to make do with older rifles, and a few units even had to use the aged Lebel rifles, which made good parade ground pieces with their long bayonets. The average French soldier, like much of the public, may have well believed that the Germans would be stopped in their tracks by the Maginot Line, and that all he had to do was hold on. This attitude, known as the *Maginot mentality*, may have affected the average trooper and lowered his morale in adverse conditions. However, troop morale among German infantrymen was not much higher either at the time. It was up to the generals on both sides to make the command decisions that would influence the quality of the performance of these soldiers and decide the outcome of the campaign in the West.

When the war was finally declared after the German invasion of Poland on 1 September 1939, the French, who had already begun mobilizing their forces, moved into position and simply waited for events to unfold. The fortress units had reached their wartime strength during the last ten days of August. Unfortunately, the massive mobilization crippled the French war industries because too many men left the factories when they were called to duty. In the meantime, communist-inspired acts of sabotage also caused a drop in production of certain weapons and war materials during the months that followed. As a result, the government had to release a number of skilled soldiers to the industrial sector to increase output later in the year.

Facing the French army was the hastily built West Wall, better known as the Siegfried Line. Begun in 1936, it had become a formidable obstacle between 1938 and 1939. Based on the principle of defense in depth, the West Wall was studded with numerous bunkers, barriers of antipersonnel (AP) minefields[6] and the famous lines of dragon's teeth. However, despite the Herculean efforts of their famous Todt Labor Organization, the Germans never completed the great forts of the West Wall and in most cases did not even begin building them. The Germans relied on bunkers for machine guns and AT guns, most of which were able to shelter no more than a squad. Unlike the French, the Germans designed the fortifications of the West Wall so they would not require specialized troops. Any infantry unit could occupy its positions since all the equipment in the bunkers from ventilators to weapons positions (the troops brought their own weapons) required no special skills. The soldiers could also read instructions painted on the walls. Minefields were planted and marked, and the location of the mines was duly recorded. Although the West Wall had the depth the Maginot Line lacked, it never reached the proportions indicated on German wartime propaganda maps.

The Germans kept only thirty low-quality reserve divisions, backed by eleven regular army divisions, to garrison the West Wall during the first *blitzkrieg* campaign of the war against Poland (Table 5.7). The German western front was as vulnerable as it had been during the Munich Crisis.

The French military had prepared no offensive plans in spite of the fact that officers like General Henri Giraud had claimed for many years that the mission of the Maginot Line was to guard the flanks as the French army launched an offensive through the Sarre Gap. In May 1939, Gamelin proposed to mobilize three-quarters of the army on the frontier and use half of that force (fewer than forty divisions) to launch an offensive with limited objectives on the third day of the war and a major offensive on the fifteenth day (Goutard and Burgess, *Battle of France*, p. 65). In June 1940, he ordered Prételat once again to work out plans for an operation against the Saar. However, during the planning of the operation, Prételat discovered that the fortress troops were not adequate for his purposes, and that there were problems with air support (Prételat, *Le Destin Tragique*, p. 19). General Alphonse Georges approved and signed the plan on 14 July 1939.

Gamelin, who believed that honor required a token effort in support for the Poles, launched the offensive through the Sarre Gap. Thus, Operation Saar began when advanced elements of General Gaston Prételat's Army Group[7] crossed the border on the night of 6/7 September and not on 5 September, as was reported by the press. On 9 September, at dawn, this force was followed by the main body of the expeditionary body of seven regular divisions. The French Fourth Army advanced with three divisions, one of which was mechanized, and a battalion of R-35 tanks to be followed by two other divisions, one mechanized. The VIII Corps of the Fifth Army with two divisions (one mechanized) and a battalion of tanks from the left flank of the RF of Lauter advanced on its right. Two more divisions of the Third Army later joined the effort on the Fourth Army's left flank.

TABLE 5-7. Mobilization 1939–1940

1935–1936 Estimate[a] to Sept 1939	Field Army	Others Available	Total Divisions	Types of Divisions					
				Active	Infantry	Armor	Light	Motor	Cavalry
1935–1936				Reservist divisions not calculated in estimate					
German	480,000		32	32					
French	350,000		25	25	23	2			
1939				Includes reservist divisions					
German	2,758,000	996,000	103	52	89	5	4	4	1
French	2,776,000	2,224,000	99	45	94[b]	2[c]	2	4	3

May 1940	Total Divisions	Western Front	Types of Divisions				
			Infantry	Armor	Light	A/B	Cavalry
German		135	110	10		2	1
French	115	104[d]	93[e]	3	3		5

Source: Duroselle, *France and the Nazi Threat*; Goutard, *Battle of France*.
A/B included one airborne and one air landing division.
[a]Estimates by Gamelin in 1935 and 1936 and German numbers are inflated.
[b]Includes equivalent of thirteen fortress divisions.
[c]Two brigades that formed two armored divisions.
[d]Included ten British divisions.
[e]Included ten British divisions and thirteen fortress divisions.

The French troops encountered little opposition as they moved forward several kilometers until they reached the West Wall between Pirmasens and Spichern, in front of Saarbrücken (Prételat, *Le Destin Tragique*, pp. 65–69). Since the reserve divisions lacked sufficient training, Prételat had to use his active and mechanized divisions instead. Faced with merely five German regular and four reservist divisions, the French never attempted to mass their forces for their long-awaited "methodical battle" because they were not ready for mobile warfare. As their AT guns failed to penetrate the heavier French tanks, the Germans fell back on their main line of resistance. However, recalled Prételat, the French tanks failed to breach the obstacles of the West Wall, possibly because they did not receive enough training for this type of operation before the war. In addition, Prételat's heavy artillery was short of the new shells needed to destroy concrete positions. Booby traps and AP mines in the vast minefields of the West Wall took a heavy toll on the French troops.

On 12 September, Gamelin ordered a halt to the lackluster offensive. By mid-September, the Germans, already in the closing stages of the Polish campaign, started dispatching divisions to the Western Front. By the end of the month, Gamelin ordered the withdrawal of the bulk of the forces, letting slip through his fingers the opportunity to smash through the West Wall and move toward the Rhine. France and Germany now settled into a period of uneasy truce known as the Phony War while both sides built up their forces (Tables 5.8 and 5.9).

Public Expectations

Public expectations were shaped by the information spread by the media. Thus, a majority of the public expected a war between fortified lines: the West Wall versus the Maginot Line. It was supposed to be a conflict involving World War I era tactics, new weapons, and "methodical battles." The public's faith in the Maginot fortifications was strengthened by books and articles extolling its strength.

A particularly interesting volume from this period on the subject is *The Maginot Line: The Facts Revealed*, written by an "unnamed" French officer. In it, the author enthused about the line, calling it the "Shield and Buckler" of France, and spread the most extravagant myths with a blithe disregard for fact and details on the ground that he had to maintain the security of the fortifications. The Maginot Line, he claimed, was an "invulnerable underground way" that ensured contact between forts. The author painted a vision of covered concrete trenches with firing positions and extensive lakes of flammable liquid ready to burst into flame at the first alert. A cross section of an *ouvrage* showed a multilevel subterranean fort dug into a mountain. This imaginary fort included turrets, antiaircraft guns, and an "artificial sheet of water" ready to ignite at the approach of the enemy. The Maginot Line—claimed the author—would observe and report the approach of enemy aircraft, and an "aerial Maginot Line" "equipped with photo-electrical defence apparatus and searchlights" and a system of captive balloons tethered by cables would form a gigantic barrier that would deter enemy aircraft. Among the mishmash of absurdities, the author also included some accurate details like the diesel engines in the *usine* and the military-gauge railway in the main gallery.

TABLE 5-8. French army approximately three weeks after mobilization and during the Saar offensive

September 15, 1939 GHQ Reserve			GHQ			SE Front		Army Group		
6th Army (SE FRONT)	7th Army	II Motor	8th Army RF Belfort	1st Army	2nd Army	(6th Army)	DAA	3rd Army RF Metz	4th Army	5th Army RF Lauter
XIV 27 Alp, 28 Alp 31 Alp 64 Alp[a] SD Rhone[a] SF Savo SF Dauph	I Motor		VII SF Colmar SF Mulh	III 51,53, SD Flanders, SD Lille	II		XI 4	VI 42, 2 NA, 5 NA, SF Boulay[a]	IX 18, 4 NA 6 Col, SD Sarre[a]	VIII 15 Mot 9 Mot[a] 23[a] 25 Mot[a] 3 Col 4 Col, SF Rohr[a] SF Vosges SF Rhine
XV 66 29 Alp, 65 Alp[a] SF AlpMar		Cav	VIII	V Mot[b] 1 Col	X		IV 7, 52	XVIII 58, 3 NA[a]	XVII 41, SF Faul[a]	XII 16, 43, 70
XVI 64 Alp 1 NA, SD Rhone		1 Mot 54	XIII 2 Cav	Reserve 2	XXI 10, 20 SF Momt SF Crusnes		Reserve	Colonial 12 Mot 22, 3 NA, 3 Cav, SF Thion[a]	V Mot 9 Mot 21, 23	V Mot[a] SF Rohr
Reserve 30 Alp 65 Alp 2 Col			Reserve 13, 14, 47		CAF 7 Col		1 Cav	Reserve 26, 36,[a] 56, 5 Col	XX 11, 21,[a] 45, 62	Reserve 35
Paris 61, 71			RM 57, 63, 67, 82 Af		Reserve 1 NA[a]					
				GHQ Res. 2 DLM	GHQ Res. 36, 55		GHQ Res. 6, 19, 1 DLM	GHQ Res. 3 Mot 5 Mot	GHQ Res. 24, 25 Mot	GHQ Res. 4 Col*

(continued)

TABLE 5-8. (Contd.)

Oct. 1939 Changes[c]		GHQ Reserve	3rd Army Group	GHQ	1st Army Group				2nd Army Group		
6th Army **XIV**	**7th Army**	**Cav**	**8th Army**	**1st Army** **III**	**2nd Army** **X**	**BEF**	**DAA**	**3rd Army** **Colonial**	**4th Army** **IX**	**5th Army** **XVII**[d]
62		2 DLM		1 Mot, 2	71, 7 Col *SF Mont*	SD Lille and British Div. arriving		36	41, SF Faul	SF Rhine
XVI		5 Col		**V Mot**	**XVIII**[d]					**XII**
9 Mot, 53, 60, SD Flanders		1 Pol			**XXI**					SF Hag
				SF Maub	3 Cav					
				CAF	Reserve 42					Reserve 23

Note: Army Detachment Pyrenees, not listed, had several brigades.
Bold indicates armies and corps; Roman numeral indicates corps; *italics* indicates division.
RM, military regions; CAF, Fortress Army Corps; SD, Defensive Sector; SF, Fortified Sector.
Unit Abbreviations: AlpMar, Maritime Alps; Dauph, Dauphine; Faul, Faulquemont; Hag, Haguenau; Maub, Maubeuge; Mont, Montmedy; Mulh, Mulhouse; Thion, Thionville; Rohr, Rohrbach; Af, Africa; Alp, Alpine (Mountain); Cav, Cavalry; Col, Colonial; DLM, Light Mech Division; Mot, Motorized; NA, North African; Pol, Polish.
[a] Attached 20 to 26 September.
[b] Attached 29 September.
[c] The 1939 section shows only divisions which changed location (unless noted with [d] for a Corps). All other divisions shown in Sept remained with the same unit unless listed in the Oct Changes section. The 6th Army was on the SOUTHEAST FRONT. The DAA (Army Detachment Ardennes) was the XI Corps and in November became the 9th Army.
[d] Attached October. The Colonial Corps arrived from Paris early in September. Southeast front headquarters in October moved north and became First Army Group headquarters.

TABLE 5-9. French army divisions, including Metropolitan and African, by category and type

Divisions	Active Infantry	Active Mot.	Armor & Cav. Arm.	Armor & Cav. Cav.	African Units in France NA	African Units in France Col	African Units in France Af	Type A Infantry	Type B Infantry	Overseas Units Type[a] Active	Overseas Units Type[a] A	Overseas Units Type[a] B
July 1939 regular divisions	10, 11, 13, 14, 19, 21, 23, 27 A, 29 A, 31 A, 36, 42, 43	1, 3, 5, 9, 12, 15, 25	1 DLM 2 DLM	1, 2, 3	1, 2, 3, 4	1, 2, 3, 4						
August/ September 1939					5	5, 6, 7	82 Af	2, 4, 6, 7, 16, 18, 20, 22, 24, 26, 28A, 30 A, 32, 35, 41, 45, 47	51, 52, 53, 54, 55, 56, 57, 58, 60, 61, 62, 63, 64 A, 65 A, 66, 67, 70, 71	81 Af, 82 Af, 83 Af, 1 Mr	84 Af, 85 Af, 86 Af	87 Af, 88 Af, 2 Mr, 3 Mr, 181 Af, 182 Af, 183 Af,
October/ November 1939				6			1Mr, 87Af					191 Af, 192 Af
January/ May 1940	1LM, 2LM[b] 3LM		3 DLM, 1 DCR, 2 DCR 3 DCR 4 DCR	1 DLC, 2 DLC, 3 DLC, 4 DLC, 5 DLC, 6 DLC	7	8	84 Af, 85 Af	8, 44	68			180 Af
Total May 1940	13[c] (+3 LM)	7	7	6	7	8	5	19[d]	19	3 (−2)	3 (−2)	10 (−1)

A, Alpine/Mountain; Af, African; Arm, Armor; Cav, Cavalry; Col, Colonial; DCR, Heavy Armored Division; DLC, Light Cavalry Division; DLM, Light Mech. Division; LM, Light Mountain Divisions; Mot, Motorized; Mr, Moroccan; NA, North African.

[a]Those overseas units considered "active" were Category 1; Categories 2 and 3 equaled Types A and B, respectively.
Underline unit refers to one moved into France from overseas; those *italicized and underlined* arrived in late May 1940. *1, 2,* and *3* DLC were 1, 2, and 3 Cavalry Divisions converted in February 1940. 4 DCR created mid-May 1940.
[b]The First LM (Light Mechanized) and Second LM after returning from Norway re-formed their elements into form the Fortieth Division in late May.
[c]First Polish Division formed in September 1939, and Second Polish Division formed in April 1940. A Czech division began forming in May 1940.
[d]Some sources list the Forty-second Infantry Division as a regular division and others as a Series A that would change the total of types on the above chart. Additional divisions formed after mid-May 1940 along with a number of brigade size units.

He also guessed fairly accurately that the concrete walls were ten feet thick (about three meters). A combined air and ground attack, concluded the author, would very likely fail. If the enemy managed by any chance to penetrate this wide front, the fortresses of the line would stand proudly like "resisting salients," hitting the enemy's advancing supply columns and striking at his flanks. The Maginot Line, he rhapsodized, was "one of the pillars of France's national defence, and it is indeed the active defence of the country...." (Anonymous [a French officer], *The Maginot Line: The Facts Revealed*).

A second English language book of interest is *The Maginot and Siegfried Lines* by James Eastwood, who based his information on early 1939 reports and sometimes fell prey to the rampant misinformation of the period as well. Comparing the Maginot forts to a fleet of battleships on land, he claimed that they were up to six stories deep and mounted "big guns in steel domes." The main forts, Eastwood wrote, were veritable underground cities with cinemas,[8] barbershops, and even cafes. Eastwood absurdities were capped by his description of Germans snipers clad in bulletproof armor that made them look like cylindrical "shining metal objects."

However, unlike the anonymous French officer, Eastwood did not lose complete sight of reality. It is obvious, for instance, that if he never visited the interior of a Maginot fort, he had scouted out their exterior perimeter. Thus, he compared the French and German fortifications with some degree of accuracy, pointing out that the Maginot Line ran the length of the frontier and was more complex than its German counterpart. He also mentioned "asparagus beds" that not even the casual observer could fail to see. These AT rails of different lengths sunk into the ground to create an obstacle would, he claimed, tear a tank apart if it tried to cross them.

In his book, Eastwood also offered a study of the fortress troops, referred to as "*écrevisses de rampart*"(shellfish of the forts) by the media in the late 1930s. Particularly worrisome, he reported, is the problem of "concretitis," a sort of depression caused by extended periods spent in an underground world lined with concrete and devoid of sunshine. A touching detail was man's need to create beauty, even in the most unpromising of environments. Thus, observed Eastwood, both German and French soldiers planted rose bushes around their concrete forts. On a more serious note, Eastwood also reported the creation of the new fortress infantry regiments in 1933 and claimed that each battalion consisted of heavy and light machine guns.

Unlike the anonymous French officer, Eastwood was not blind to the shortcoming of the Maginot Line because he concluded that the Germans might well attempt to take advantage of the weak French antiaircraft defenses using their air superiority. However, Eastwood overestimated Frances's "modern shock army," which he said was working on a decisive weapon, the new eleven-ton Renault tanks.

Overall, Eastwood expressed a great deal of faith in modern fortifications because the German military authorities he interviewed estimated that it would cost them two million casualties to take the Maginot Line. Based on this, he deduced that the Allies would take similar heavy losses attacking the West Wall. Eastwood also insisted that if the Germans made a thrust through the Low Countries, they would encounter a lesser Maginot Line on the Franco-Belgian border; he concluded that "Germany cannot win." All in all, Eastwood's book ranged from the realistic, to the optimistic, to the absurd (Eastwood, *The Maginot and Siegfried Lines*).

THE PHONY WAR

After the abortive Saar offensive, French troops settled in at the border while the divisions of the British Expeditionary Force (BEF) continued to stream onto the Continent. Relations with Belgium remained cool, especially since the Belgian government refused to allow the Allied troops to make preparations for the mutual defense of Belgium. Nonetheless, the Belgian military staff tried to coordinate planning while pretending to defend all their nation's frontiers. The French also carried on some discussions with the Swiss military since they feared a German flanking attack on Belfort through Switzerland. This explains why so many divisions of the Eighth Army were stationed in this corner of the front. Although Italy was not in the war, Gamelin had to prepare for that contingency and continue to commit troops to the Southeast Front.

A look at a situation map shows that a large number of divisions remained committed to the front along the Franco-German border in the area commanded by the 2nd Army Group. The initial covering force had done its job, allowing the French Army to mobilize. Army Detachment Ardennes, covering the Ardennes front, was converted into the Ninth Army and reinforced. In October 1939, General Prételat's Army Group on the Northeast Front received the designation of 2nd Army Group. General Gaston Billotte and his staff transferred from the Southeast Front to head the newly designated 1st Army Group and take over the front covering much of the Belgian border. Late in the month, Gamelin created a new command, the 3rd Army Group under General Antoine Besson that took control of the Eighth Army in RF Belfort. A number of formations shifted their locations during the months of the Phony War because of modification of army assignments. Not long after Billotte and his staff departed, a number of divisions of the Sixth Army on the Southeast Front moved north; in December, General Robert Touchon's Sixth Army moved back into the general headquarters (GHQ). Reserve while the Seventh Army moved into 1st Army Group. The Alpine Army of General René Olry took command of the entire Southeast Front since no other forces were available (Gunsburg, *Divided and Conquered*, p. 95).

That November, Gamelin and his staff considered their options between Plan E (Escaut) and Plan D (Dyle). French and British troops began digging in and building new blockhouses along the Belgian frontier; units on the German frontier continued patrolling operations through the winter. To give the troops of the BEF a taste of war, their units were rotated into the intervals of the Maginot Line, near Thionville. When the German offensive materialized, one British division was still stationed there.

Plan E offered the least risk because the Allies could not know how the Belgian army would resist the German invasion. To execute this plan, forces of the Seventh Army and the BEF would move a short distance into Belgium and occupy the Escaut River line that also included a number of Belgian fortifications built around the Ghent Bridgehead. The Escaut (the Belgian Scheldt River) was wide and deep and took river traffic for much of its length. The only disadvantage of this plan was that it would extend the front a much greater distance than the Dyle Plan would. The French and British leadership, who contemplated a long war, needed another year or two to prepare for a major offensive. In the meantime, Plan E would keep Ostend out of German hands and make it difficult, if not impossible, for the Germans to use Antwerp as an outlet to the sea, assuming they did not invade the Netherlands. While the Allies worked on their

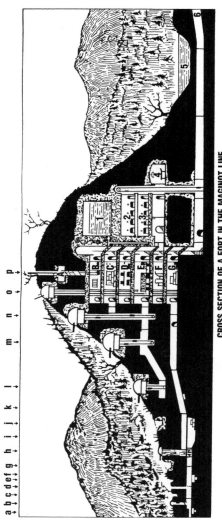

CROSS SECTION OF A FORT IN THE MAGINOT LINE

a b c d e f g   h   i   j   k   l   m   n   o   p

Facing the Enemy

a. Belt of steel spars.
b. Advance machine-gun post.
c. Ditch.
d. Observation post.
e. Ditch.
f. Belt of steel spars.
g. Tank trap.

h. Gun-turret with magazine.
j. Tank trap.
k. Belt of steel spars.
l, m, n. Armour-plated and concreted gun-turrets.
o. Anti-aircraft gun cupola.
p. Periscope concealed in tree.

Facing the Rear

1. Drinking-water tank.
2 and 3. Hospital and first-aid post.
4. Waiting-room and operating theatre for urgent cases.
5. Artificial sheet of water.
6. Subterranean gallery for evacuating the fort.

All the gun-turrets are reached by staircases and service lifts.

A. Observation post.
B. Guard room.
C. Light arms ammunition dump.
D. Barracks.

E. Gallery with rail track linking up several units.
F. Machinery: electric lighting and power, ventilation,
G. Magazine.

The galleries are intersected at various points by armour-plated doors protruding galleries are so constructed that they are not revealed by exploding mines during an enemy advance.

from *Maginot Line: The Facts Revelated* (1939)

FIGURE 5-3. Cross section of a fort on the Maginot Line. [© Tomasz Idzikowski]

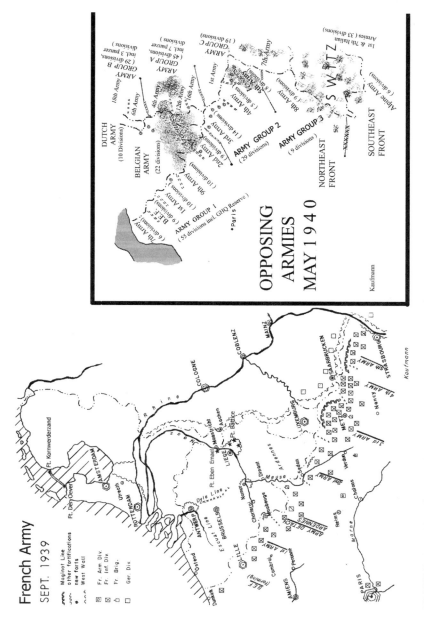

FIGURE 5-4. French army 1939/opposing armies May 1940. The 1939 map shows the location of French armies and divisions after mobilization. The right map shows the location of Allied and German forces in May 1940. [Joseph Kaufmann]

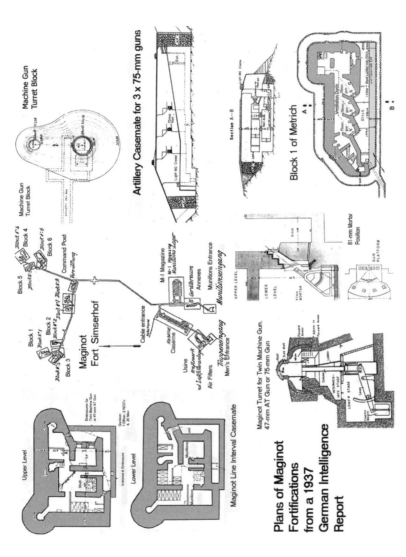

Machine Gun Turret Block

Machine Gun Turret Block

Artillery Casemate for 3 x 75-mm guns

Section A—B

Block 1 of Metrich

Block 5   Block 4

Block 6

Command Post

Maginot Fort Simserhof

Block 1

Block 2

Block 3

Cable entrance

M-1 Magazine

Annexes

Munitions Entrance

Kaserne Caserne

Usine w/ Air Filters

Men's Entrance

81-mm Mortar Position

GUN PLATFORM

UPPER LEVEL

LOWER LEVEL

Maginot Turret for Twin Machine Gun, 47-mm AT Gun or 75-mm Gun

Upper Level

Lower Level

Maginot Line Interval Casemate

Plans of Maginot Fortifications from a 1937 German Intelligence Report

FIGURE 5-5. Plans of Maginot fortifications from a 1937 German intelligence report. German intelligence acquired these plans in 1936/37 and prepared a detailed report on the French fortifications with them. Despite some incorrect areas, most of the details are correct. [Joseph Kaufmann]

strategy, a German officer carrying a copy of the German invasion plan crashed on an unauthorized flight in the Netherlands, and his superiors could not be sure that the Allies had not recovered it.

The disadvantage of Plan D was that it required Belgian cooperation. After secret talks with the Belgians, Gamelin concluded that they would make a strong effort to hold the Albert Canal Line from Antwerp to Maastricht and their main line covering Liege. That would allow the Allies enough time to reach the Dyle. Gamelin informed the government of his plans in February 1940, after he obtained the approval of the British military on 17 November 1939 (Goutard, *Battle of France*, pp. 84–87). Between the end of the KW Line, which ran from Antwerp's ring along the Dyle River, and the Meuse, there was a gap where the Belgian army installed a line of Belgian Gates as an AT obstacle. Although some bunkers had been built along the Dyle Line, they did not constitute a strong defense line because they were less formidable than those built along the Meuse and Albert Canal. The Dyle River itself was not a major watercourse and did not present a serious AT obstacle. The BEF was responsible for occupying much of the river line, but it needed time to prepare a solid defensive position. The French First Army, which had most of the mechanized and armored divisions, would have to cover the gap between the Meuse and the Dyle. It was expected to encounter the German forces in a more fluid action than the other Allied forces. The Dyle Plan offered not only great risks but also a shorter front and greater rewards if it was successful.

The possibility of an invasion of the Netherlands forced the Allies to add the Breda Variant to this plan in March 1940. According to this variant of Plan D, elements of the Seventh Army were to hasten by land and sea to link with the Dutch near Breda. Unfortunately, this plan should have been dropped when the new Dutch commander decided to abandon all territory outside of Fortress Holland between the Zuider Zee and the Maas and Waal Rivers in case of an invasion. In any case, the Breda Variant was a risky maneuver that failed since it had little chance of success once the Germans actually struck.

The Maginot Line made Plans E and D possible because it allowed the French to remove the best and most mobile divisions from its intervals to take part in such an operation. The question remains why the French did not remove more divisions from the sectors of the Maginot Line, along the Rhine, and the Belfort front and send them to the 1st Army Group. French intelligence should have informed Gamelin that German Army Group C, which faced these fronts, consisted of a small number of divisions, mostly of low grade. The high command continued to fear that the Germans would take on the Maginot Line, even when it was certain that the main thrust would come through northern Belgium. Only a minimum number of formations remained to hold the Southeast Front, despite the constant threat of Italian intervention.

A look at the situation for May 1940 reveals serious flaws in French planning. However, even if more divisions had been shifted from the Maginot Line to the 1st Army Group, it is doubtful that they would have taken up position along the Ardennes sectors. Nonetheless, they could have been held in reserve. However, Gamelin continued to believe that the Ardennes were impassable to mechanized formations and that the Meuse, with its steep banks, was a major AT obstacle. In this sector, he claimed, "the terrain would defend itself" (Goutard, *Battle of France*, p. 85).

TABLE 5-10. The Allied Order of Battle May 10, 1940

1940	Army	Corps	Divisions	Brigades, etc.	Notes
GHQ	Reserve	1st Arm Gp	2nd DCR, 3rd DCR		At various points behind the front
		XXI			
		XXIII			
		NC	1st NA, 2nd Polish, 3rd Mot, 5thCol, 7th Col, 7th NA, 10th, 14th, 23rd, 28th, 29th, 36th, 43rd		
NE Front HQ					
Army Group 1	7th Army Air Element	NC	68th		On coast
		I (Mot)	1st DLM, 4th, 21st, 60th, SF Flanders	510th Tank Bd.	Near coast
			25th Mot		
		XVI	9th Mot		
		FA 107			
	BEF	British GHQ Res.	5th	1 Fighter Sq, 1 Rec Sq.	3 divisions on L of C
				1st Tank Bd, 1st Arm Rec Bd, 2nd Arm Rec Bd	
		I	1st, 2nd, 48th		
		II	3rd, 4th, 50th		
		III	42nd, 44th		
	1st Army Air Element	NC	1st DCR, 32nd, SF Escaut	515th Tank Bd	Between Lille and Maubeuge
		Cav Corps	2nd DLM, 3rd DLM		
		III	1st Mot, 2nd NA		
		IV	15th Mot, 1st Mor		
		V	12th Mot, 5th NA, 101st Fort		
		FA 101			
	9th Army Air Element	NC	1st DLC, 4th DLC, 4th NA, 53rd	519th Tank Bd.	Ardennes Sectors
				1 Fighter Sq, 1 Rec Sq	
				3rd Sph Bd, 518th Tank Bd	
		II	5th Mot		
		XI	18th, 22nd		
		XLI Fort	61st, 102nd Fort		
		FA 109			
	2nd Army Air Element	NC	2nd DLC, 5th DLC, 71st, SF Montmedy	1 Fighter Sq, 1 Rec Sq	
				1st Cav Bd, 503rd Tank Bd	
		X	3rd NA, 55th		
		XVIII	1st Col, 3rd Col, 41st		
		FA 102		1 Fighter Sq, 1 Rec Sq	

Army Group	Element	Corps	Divisions	Units	Notes
Army Group 2	AG Reserve	NC	4th Col, 87th Af	1st Sph Bd, 511th Tank Bd	RF of Metz
	3rd Army Air Element	NC	3rd DLC, 6th, 6th Col, 6th NA, 7th, 8th	520th Tank Bd, 532nd Tank Bd	
		Col Corps	2nd , 51st (British), 56th, SF Thionville		Sarre
	4th Army Air Element	VI	26th, 42nd, SF Boulay		
		XXIV	51st		
		XLII Fort	20th, 58th	513th Tank Bd	
		FA 103		1 Fighter Sq, 1 Rec Sq	
		NC	1st Polish, 45th		
		IX	11th, 47th , SF Faulquemont	502nd Tank Bd	
		XX	52nd, 82nd Af, SF Sarre	504th Tank Bd	
		FA 104		1 Fighter Sq, 1 Rec Sq	
	5th Army Air Element	NC	44th	501st Tank Bd, 517th Tank Bd	RF of Lauter
		VIII	24th, 31st Mtn, SF Rohrbach	508th Tank Bd	
		XII	16th, 35th, 70th, SF Haguenau		
			62nd, 103rd Fort		
		XVII			
		XLIII Fort	30th Mtn		
		FA 105		1 Fighter Sq, 1 Rec Sq	
Army Group 3	AG Res.[a]	XLV Fort	57th, 63rd, SF Jura	506th Tank Bd	RF of Belfort
	8th Army Air Element	NC	13th, 27th Mtn	2nd Sph Bd	
		VII	19th, 54th, 104th Fort, 105th Fort		
		XIII			
		XLIV Fort	67th, SF Altkirch, SF Montbeliard	Defenses of Belfort	
		FA 108	8th	1 Fighter Sq, 1 Rec Sq	
South East Front	Army of The Alps Air Element	NC	8th	514th Tank Bd	Swiss Border to Menton
		XIV	64th Mtn, 66th Mtn, SF Rhone, SF Savoy, SF Dauphine		
		XV	2nd Col, 65th Mtn, SF Maritime Alps	SD Nice	
	Defenses of Corsica			1 Rec Sq	

Af, Africa; AG, AG, Army Group; Arm, Armored; Bd, Brigade; Cav, Cavalry; BEF, British Expeditionary Force; DCR, Heavy Armored Division; DLC, Light Mechanized Cavalry Division; DLM, Light Mechanized Division; FA, Aerial Force (organic to army); Fort, Fortress; GHQ, General Headquarters; Gp, Group; Mor, Moroccan; Mot, Motorized; Mtn, Mountain or Alpine; NA, North African; NC, not assigned to a corps or part of the army reserve; Obv, Observation; Rec, Reconnaissance; Res, Reserve; Sph, Spahi (North African cavalry).
[a]Some sources identify this as Sixth Army in May 1940.

At the time, the scattered reserve, with only fifteen divisions—including two *division cuirassée de réserve* (DCRs)—was inadequate because so many formations were committed to the fortified zones. Since the 3rd Army Group consisted of four Series B divisions, two nonmobile fortress divisions, and three active divisions, the French could have diverted two of the active divisions further north. However, General Besson had been ordered to move into Switzerland, Contingency H, in case the Germans violated Swiss neutrality to strike out toward Belfort (Sharp, *French Army*, Vol. 1, pp. 45–47). The 2nd Army Group, stationed in and behind the fortified sectors of the Maginot Line, consisted of thirty-one divisions, including a British one, ten B Series, fifteen Series A, fortress divisions, and one mobile division (a *division légère de cavalerie* [DLC], light cavalry division). Several of the Series A divisions and possibly one or two regular divisions could have joined the reserve or 1st Army Group since these two army groups with forty divisions faced only fourteen, mostly second-rate, divisions of German Army Group C (Table 5.10).

The Maginot Line certainly had not siphoned off the best elements of the French army since the two army groups committed to it consisted mostly of Type A and B divisions. Admittedly, many more troops were stationed there than needed, considering that there were also first class troops that formed most of the fortress infantry regiments on the front. The 1st Army Group, the most mobile force, consisted of nineteen active divisions, only eight Type A and six Type B divisions, and eight BEF divisions. In addition, the General Headquarters Reserve could add another ten active divisions and four Series A divisions.

In summary, the Allies could have deployed fifty-five of their ninety-five divisions of the Northeast Front on the vulnerable Belgian frontier northwest of the Maginot Line. Furthermore, the reserve included thirty-seven of their best divisions and all but one of their mechanized and armored divisions. The problem on the front of the 1st Army Group was not that the best of the French forces were unavailable, but that faulty strategic planning consistently underestimated the capabilities of modern armor that allowed the Germans to strike through the poorly defended Ardennes, which were left wide open.

CHAPTER 6

THE FRENCH ARMY AND THE MAGINOT LINE AT WAR

Twenty-five years and one month after the outbreak of World War I, France was again at war with Germany. The French high command had not prepared for an offensive war, and the diversionary attack into the Saar was a short-lived event. In mid-November, the Allies agreed on Plan D, involving a limited advance into Belgium to take up new defensive positions, but only if Germany attacked first. After the French forces pulled back from the Saar in early October, the Allies and Germans settled in during the Phony War, called *Drôle de Guerre* (Funny War) by the French. During this period, the opposing forces contented themselves with patrolling and some taunting, especially along the Rhine. The Germans also bombarded the French troops with propaganda leaflets and megaphone broadcasts. The British Royal Air Force and the French *Armée d'Air* riposted by dropping propaganda leaflets over Germany at night. The severe winter hindered construction of new defenses and improvements to existing fortifications.

The months of the Phony War gave the French military time to prepare, train, and reorganize. The Maginot Line defenders garrisoning the *ouvrages* or occupying the interval positions had a great deal of work to do on their positions. In several *ouvrages*, some would-be Michelangelos painted frescoes on the walls of the poorly lit galleries and the damp chambers to pass the time and cheer up their surroundings. The commanders also looked for ways to distract their men from the drudgery of a sunless life, to give them time outdoors, and to make the forts livable. In addition, the defenses of the forts had to be finished: Wire obstacles had to be added, and vegetation had to be cleared to keep the fields of fire unobstructed. The harsh winter weather impeded the work, but the spring of 1940 brought back the weeds and wild grasses, obscuring the fields of fire again. The German assault on Denmark and Norway stressed the importance of maintenance work, but time and again during the Phony War the daily routine in the *ouvrages* was disrupted by false alerts and mistaken sightings of enemy forces.

At some of the *ouvrages*, the armored searchlights were finally delivered and gradually installed on several casemate blocks. *Gros ouvrages* (GOs) of Four-au-Chaux and Schoenenbourg were linked to the 0.60-gauge military railroads to improve their supply line, and their truck-type *entrées des munitions* (EMs; munitions entrances) were converted to accommodate the small trains. The remainder of the *ouvrages* were linked to the National Grid, often with underground cables (see Chapter 2). However, since time was running out, the cables leading into some of the GOs had to be buried at a depth of less than one meter instead of the required three meters. The POs remained linked to the small transformer building nearby with aerial cables because there was no more time to bury the cables (Mary, *Maginot*, Vol. 3, pp. 28–29). In addition, in June 1940, the machine gun turrets of a few forts were upgraded to include a 25-mm antitank (AT gun), while other turrets still awaited delivery of these weapons.

Within the forts, volunteer groups called *corps francs* formed, taking the soldiers from their routine activities so they could go out on patrols. In the spring, additional barbed wire and new French "bouncing" antipersonnel (AP) mines were delivered to the forts to complete their defenses. The French AP mines, somewhat similar to the German, were not installed in minefields. Instead, they were planted in front of the wire obstacles to form individual booby traps. Unfortunately, the troops, who had no experience in mine planting, especially at night, were often accidentally killed or maimed.[1]

In some sectors, especially the *Secteurs Fortifiés* (SF) of Crusnes where the AT rail barrier was not complete, AT mines were laid out to form a barrier of one or two lines (Mary, *Maginot*, Vol. 2, p. 54). The mines were stored in a small concrete storage area comprised of several niches near the entrances to GOs, *petit ouvrages* (POs), and some interval and Rhine casemates. They were to be used around the *ouvrages* or casemates to close avenues of approach when an attack was imminent. In many of the casemates of the third line of the Bas Rhin Sector, these niches came in different designs. These niches contained mines like the *Piquet Olivier* but probably few, if any, of the elongated AT mines. Secret instructions from 1934 that came with these elongated AT mines, not for issue until mobilization, indicated that a kilometer-long single line required 1,370 AT mines.

The emplacement of the mines was entrusted to the interval troops. The elongated AT were placed in groups of five and camouflaged. When the weight of a heavy vehicle pressed on the igniter, it triggered the detonator of one mine, which in turn ignited the other four. The *Piquet Olivier*, named for the designer, consisted of a wooden or metal rod that projected above ground and was attached to an old 120-mm artillery shell (sometimes old shells of other sizes were also used). This rod served as the firing device or igniter to detonate the mine. Only a direct artillery hit could cause a mine to detonate according to the instructions supplied with them (Notice sur les mines et piquets anti-chars, *Instructions* from 1934; German Army High Command, *Denkschrift* p. 342).

As the fortress troops readied their positions, the divisions in the intervals began building their own locally designed blockhouses (see Chapter 3). Some labor regiments consisting of older reservists also pitched in. On General Gamelin's order, the *Génie* started to close the gaps between forts and even build a second line known as a Stop Line. The *Commission d'Études des Zones Fortifiées* (CEZF; Commission for the Study of Fortified Zones) was formed under the direction of General Belhague in September 1939. Belhague drew up ambitious plans for up to six hundred kilometers of defenses, divided into four equal sections and intended to include over one thousand casemates and several hundred steel cloches. However, no project of this magnitude could be realized in such a short time period, especially since most work could not begin until spring. That winter, the ground froze solid well below the surface; sleet blanketed many trails, roads, and mud-filled trenches where excavation had been possible. Thus, by springtime most of the work was far from complete.

In addition, early in 1940 Gamelin decided to create a salient around Longwy, known as the Advanced Position of Longwy (PAL; *Position Avancée de Longwy*), to protect its industrial production. Eventually, only seven blockhouses and two emplacements with a 75-mm field gun were built. The 75-mm gun turret of the *ouvrage* of Fermont covered much of the PAL, up to Longwy and along the Belgian frontier, but no other *ouvrage* was able to support it. Much of the planned AT ditch was excavated, but a section several kilometers to the east of Longwy was not finished. CEZF also oversaw construction behind the Sarre front and between Longuyon and the North Sea, creating new lines linking defended areas and reinforcing the main lines of resistance (see Chapter 5).

In the summer of 1939, General Gaston Billotte, the military governor of Paris, proposed a defensive line to cover Paris, an idea already proposed in 1930. On 10 September, after Billotte was assigned to an active command on the front, Prime Minister Edouard Daladier authorized General Pierre Hering, the new military governor of Paris, to take up the project. Work began in October with the goal of creating a major AT obstacle to shield Paris from a German armored thrust. This position, called the Chauvineau Line, was named for the general most responsible for its construction. The line stretched from Corflans (about twenty-five kilometers northwest of the center of Paris), along the Oise River, by Précey, along the Nonette River, to La Ferté-sous-Jouarre on the Marne. General Georges and his staff of the Northeast Theater Command were located at Château Bondon, near La Ferté-sous-Jouarre.

Work on the obstacles and blockhouses continued through April, 1940 when approximately three hundred blockhouses were completed. These positions came mainly in two simple variants without armored protection for their embrasures. One type, known as a shield, was open in the rear and accommodated a 25-mm AT gun; the second was a concrete cupola known as a 7th Military Region Type. A number of old naval 47- and 65-mm guns were placed in open, circular concrete emplacements. Rivers and flooded terrain formed almost half of the AT barrier that was almost twenty-eight kilometers long. In the Nonette River valley, blockhouses covered all the crossings. In February, the Marne River and the canals near La Ferté-Sous-Jouarre were frozen solid, losing much of their defensive quality. On the remainder of the line, the frozen ground prevented the excavation of AT ditches that winter. When finished these, ditches were about two meters deep and two to three meters wide and covered by blockhouses. About a thousand tetrahedrons (obstacles of steel or concrete with four triangular sides) blocked restricted traffic on the roads. These defenses of Paris, which did not include impressive fortifications, were not completed. In addition, its blockhouses were not as strong as those that were built by CEZF work on the Northeast Front.

Drastic changes took place between September 1939 and March 1940 as Gamelin reorganized the front. Between January and March 1940, he converted several SFs into fortress infantry divisions (the 101st at Maubeuge, the 102nd in the Ardennes, the 103rd on the Bas Rhin, the 104th at Colmar, the 105th at Mulhouse). In March, he formed the XLII Fortress Corps to control the elements of the *Région Fortifiée* (RF; Fortified Region) of Metz and the XLIII Fortress Corps to control those of the RF of Lauter and dissolved the RFs. The XLII Fortress Corps occupied the front of the SF of Crusnes, which was dissolved. The XLIII Fortress Corps occupied the area of the defunct SF of the Vosges. Gamelin also replaced the RF of Belfort with the XLIV Army Fortress Corps at the same time. The other SFs remained operative. Early in January, he formed the XLI Army Fortress Corps and assigned it to the Ardennes front. The XLV

Army Fortress Corps replaced the SF of Jura. The last two corps did not control heavily fortified zones but areas where the terrain was believed to favor the defenders. Gamelin also upgraded all the SDs to SFs.

LIMITED ACTION DURING THE PHONY WAR

Between October 1939 and early May 1940, the Western Front was quiet, except in the air. During the Phony War, the French air force, which flew reconnaissance missions over the Saar, lost thirty aircraft by the end of September. Occasionally, French fighter pilots in the MS-406s engaged the superior German Me-109 over the fortified lines. Some squadrons were being equipped with newer Bloch MB-151 but were still awaiting the improved MB-152 fighters early in the war. The De-520 and the American Curtis H-75 were the only French aircraft that could match the German Me-109, but they still were too slow.[2] Some bomber crews still flew the old Amiot-143, a slow, awkward-looking aircraft that looked like a flying observation platform for civilians. It formed a large part of the French bomber force and flew on reconnaissance missions and night bombing raids over Germany, dropping tons of leaflets. The faster and more modern Amiot-351 and 354 that were to replace the Amiot-143s were unavailable in 1939 because of months of production delays. They were finally delivered to the first squadrons in April and May 1940. Ninety-two older Bloch MB-200 bombers, true flying dinosaurs, were still used by a few squadrons, but they had to be withdrawn from front line duty after taking serious losses in September.

Each French army had an air element that included the old Mureaux-113, 115, and 117, which had been used with the bomber, combat, and reconnaissance (BCR) program. However, by 1939 they were so slow and poorly armed that they could barely carry out reconnaissance missions. Of over two hundred of these aircraft serving in the *Groupes Aériens d'Observation* (GAO; or air observation squadron), 75% were lost, most of them before May 1940. The odd-looking Bréguet-270s, one of the slowest French aircraft available, also suffered heavy losses flying reconnaissance missions over Germany and was temporarily withdrawn in early October. It returned to service on the front in 1940 because the Potez-63.11 aircraft had not arrived to replace it (Breffort and Jouineau, *French Aircraft*, p. 56).

While these air engagements were taking place, there was little action on the ground. The French troops on the front became more slovenly, allowing their beards to grow and bundling up against the bitter cold. Observers and reporters observed that some soldiers also seemed undisciplined and poorly motivated, while others were ready and waiting for a fight. After the abortive Saar Offensive of September, they all settled into a routine of patrolling, preparing defensive positions, and keeping warm.

On the night of 8/9 September 1939, the *ouvrage* of Hochwald became the first Maginot fort to fire a volley at the enemy when its turret of 75-mm guns in Block 7-*bis* roared in support of troops of the 3rd Regiment of Moroccan *Tirailleurs* of the 43rd Division in the Schweigen sector. This brief exchange revealed unforeseen problems: The firing loosened the mounting bolts of the gun, sending them flying around the confined turret. Fortunately, no one was injured (Bruge, *Faites Sauter la Ligne Maginot*, p. 67). In addition, the ammunition for the 75-mm guns turned out to be defective, and the barrels of the two cannons were damaged. The replacements were two reinforced tubes with semiautomatic breaches, superior to the older Nordenfelt normally used in this older type of turret (Wahl, *Hochwald*, p. 128). According to Rowe, author of *The Great Wall of France*, the gunners were blamed for the problem for using old ammunition. However, Mary claimed that the damage was caused by the new, more powerful Mle 1929 ammunition that had to be replaced with older Mle 1917 rounds, which reduced the range of the 75-mm guns by about 1,300 meters. When a similar ammunition-related incident occurred at Grand Hohekirkel, it became clear that it was necessary to test fire the guns at other forts. Later, during combat, faulty ammunition caused damage at Rochonvillers and Barbonnet (Mary, *Maginot*, Vol. 3, p. 34; Rowe, *Great Wall*, p. 116). At Rochonvillers, a bad round destroyed the 75-mm gun, wrecking the recoil system in June (Mary, *Maginot*, Vol. 3, p. 222; Vermuellen, email correspondence).

Well into the Phony War, the gunners of the *ouvrages* began test firing their guns into the "no man's land" between their position and that of the Germans. There were also several incidents when German troops were targeted. On 16 October, the 75-mm gun turret at Hochwald and the two 75-mm gun turrets of Schoenenbourg fired over one hundred rounds in support of a patrol moving against a German observation post, but the enemy escaped. In November, the artillery commander of Hochwald ordered his gunners to fire on Germans laying a minefield nearby (north of Wissembourg, according to Jean-Bernard Wahl).[3] On 4 December, the Maginot gunners began firing on an apparent massing of German troops.

The high command did not allow the artillery to fire at targets of opportunity until three months after the beginning of the war. Even then, the Maginot fort commanders were cautioned to avoid important targets lest they disturb the Germans. The 75-mm gun of the GO of Four-au-Chaux dropped eighty rounds on the nearby German village of Northwiler when German combat engineers were spotted working in the vicinity. At the same time, the 135-mm *lance-bombes* were tested for the first time, but their rounds bounced off the frozen ground without exploding because their fuses were damp. After this, all the fuses were replaced. At Hochwald, the range of one of the two 81-mm mortars was less than eight hundred meters, only half the distance of the other. In addition, the ammunition hoists malfunctioned and had to be repaired and adjusted (Rowe, *Great Wall*, pp. 125–127).

As the winter wore on, the boredom of the fortress troops increased. The interval troops, on the other hand, must have felt pleased just to keep warm and wait out the enemy. At this time, patrols of volunteers (*corps francs*) began operating out of the *ouvrages*. The turret gun crews were allowed to test their weapons by firing into the no man's land and to engage enemy targets occasionally. The majority of casemated gunners, on the other hand, had little to do but sit behind their guns because there were fewer opportunities to find a target, and weapon testing could not be done regularly. Although Latiremont had two 75-mm-gun casemates and no 75-mm gun turrets, its gun crews were allowed fire to their guns in the direction of Fermont on 21 October. As Latiremont fired its first volleys, the panicked burghers of the nearby town concluded that the Germans were coming through Belgium. At Hochwald and Schoenenbourg, where the 75-mm casemate guns and the 81-mm mortars had no targets, the gun crews were given batteries of old 120-mm L Mle 1878 guns with a range of 12,000 meters to hone their skills in March 1940. These old guns were set on wooden firing platforms prepared for them inside their fort's perimeter. At Schoenenbourg, faulty ammunition caused one of the 120-mm guns to explode, killing one gunner and wounding several others. However, the other guns remained in use.

Also during the Phony War, a parade of dignitaries and journalists was allowed to visit a carefully selected assortment of positions on the Maginot Line. Some of these visitors included King George VI of England, the Duke of Windsor, Winston Churchill, Lord Gort, Anthony Eden, Edouard Daladier, General Gamelin, and General Georges. On 9 December 1939, the English monarch, accompanied by Generals Gamelin, Pré-telat, and the commander of the 3rd Army General Condé, descended on Hackenberg and Mont des Welches. At another time, the American military attaché Colonel Sumner Waite, who produced a number of intelligence reports for the U.S. Army, visited the fortifications. After the French and foreign media were invited on tours, a number of articles and photos appeared in popular French magazines such as *Paris Match* and *L'Illustration*. American journalist Dorothy Thompson described a French 75-mm gun turret in action at Hochwald (probably Block 7-*bis*). This flow of information served to reassure the French and their allies about the strength of the fortifications. British general Alan Brooke, who visited the French 9th Army, criticized the unmilitary attitude and laxness of the troops and concluded that this was indicative of an army in trouble.

The 11 March 1940 issue of *Life* magazine showcased a soldier with the insignia of the 165th Fortress Infantry Regiment. The bearded, untidy French soldiers staring from the pages of the magazine earned nothing but scorn from British Generals Alan Brooke and Bernard Montgomery. The latter attributed the ensuing defeat to the lack of military bearing and slovenly dress of the French soldiers. The sheepskin "coatee" worn by the French soldiers to keep warm drew particular fire from the *Life* reporter, who wrote scathingly that the troops at the front were "not a chic spectacle" and "are allowed a latitude of dress that the British or German Army would never permit." However, the journalist admitted, "as fighters the French are tops" (*Life*, p. 81). A caption under the picture of a French general swathed in scarves, "his mustache still damp with soup," stated that he was a typical French officer (*Life*, p. 83). Nonetheless, conceded the author, the Maginot Line was "a line of steel, concrete, and men superlatively trained to kill." The great forts were described as underground positions "surrounded by little forts, pillboxes, tank barriers, tank traps and land mines. Inside the fort, reported the article, "elevator operators cry out subway station stops" (*Life*, p. 77). The article went on to mention that the front between the forts consisted of earthworks and trenches, a fact that the majority of other writers failed to mention. The *Life* magazine article also showed a textbook example of a zigzag trench with a makeshift shelter in which the troops sought protection from the fierce winter. Many of these trenches had revetments, usually of chicken wire supported by stakes (*Life*, p. 78–79).

Finally, as the Phony War drew to an end, a chorus of military experts and reporters predicted with trepidation that the big offensive would take place in the spring. The options were clear to everyone: The Germans would either launch a massive assault on the Maginot Line or try a flanking movement through the Low Countries or Switzerland. An invasion of Belgium would not come as a surprise but most, including the French high command, expected a repeat of the old *Schlieffen* Plan.

In the meantime, the Germans conducted a war game in February to test a new plan, the Manstein Plan, which involved the main strike through the Ardennes. When this plan was adopted by the German high command in March 1940, German units, mainly armored, began to mass near the Belgian border in the German Eifel region, along the Ardennes. French air reconnaissance failed to detect the buildup, later blaming the bad weather and the vulnerability of their aircraft for their failure to do so.

The French 1st Army Group, which included the best of the French Army and the British Expeditionary Force (BEF), prepared to leave its newly fortified positions to blunt the German thrust through Belgium, north of the Meuse. General Charles Huntziger, commander of the Second Army, concerned about the weakness of his position along the Ardennes around Sedan, requested four more divisions to build up the defenses but was turned down.

The French Air Force Unprepared?

The April invasion of Denmark and Norway signaled the close of the Phony War as the British and French dispatched troops to Norway. The French air force had received a number of new aircraft, but according to Pierre Cot, the air force was simply considered a supporting arm of the army and many of its squadrons were assigned to the army groups. Almost 40% of its strength was scattered on the Mediterranean fronts, facing Italy. Cot did not blame General Vuillemin for this state of affairs because he said the general "had no idea of modern aerial warfare" and was not suited for his position. Instead, he faulted General Marcel Tétu, the chief of aerial forces and the man responsible for preparing the air force for war, who was an intelligent and energetic person who "hated new ideas." Cot also criticized General Bergeret, the man in charge of the operations section that planned strategy and tactics, for failing to learn from the Polish campaign and held him responsible for the ineffective deployment of aircraft.

Cot's denunciations were not unfounded. Several squadrons of mostly obsolete bombers were concentrated for reprisal raids on Germany, yet the air force was unable to challenge and disrupt the enemy army after the assault began. In addition, since the French were short of antiaircraft artillery, only a few units were placed near the front; the remainder were deployed in rear areas to protect industrial sites, leaving many airfields largely undefended (Cot, *Triumph of Treason*, pp. 304–306; Ellis, *The War in France and Flanders*, p. 25).[4]

Many of the reserve infantry divisions still needed training. The troops of the regular divisions and those of the fortress regiments, including their allotment of reservists, were in relatively good condition and ready for action. The French army engaged in some reorganization during the Phony War as its leaders tried to draw some lessons from the experiences of the Polish Campaign. In most cases, however, France continued to lag behind Germany when it came to adapting to modern warfare. The cavalry divisions became light mechanized divisions, one of which—the 3rd DLC (*Division Légère de Cavalerie*, Mechanized Light Cavalry Division)—occupied the Advanced Position of Longwy. Two DLCs of the Second Army and two of the Ninth were ready to charge into the Ardennes to check the small German infantry force that was expected there. The most significant change was the creation of the first two French heavy armored divisions (*division cuirassée de réserve*, DCR), in January 1940. The DCR consisted of a demibrigade of two battalions with thirty-three Char B-*bis* tanks, a demibrigade of two battalions with ninety H-39 light tanks, a battalion of mechanized infantry,[5] a motorized artillery regiment with twenty-four 105-mm guns, a battalion of twelve 47-mm AT guns drawn by Kegresse or Laffly half-tracks, and a motorized engineer company with other supporting elements.

The light mechanized divisions (DLM, *Division légère mécanique*) consisted of one brigade with two battalions of armor, one brigade with a mechanized reconnaissance regiment, and one mechanized infantry regiment instead of a single mechanized battalion with similar support artillery and engineer units. The two armored battalions of the DLM were equipped with eighty-seven medium SOMUA-35 (S-35) tanks and eighty-seven light Hotchkiss-35 (H-35) or H-39 tanks. The cavalry divisions became light cavalry divisions (DLCs). One of its two cavalry brigades was replaced with a mechanized brigade consisting of 100 H-35 or H-39 tanks and about 180 armored cars.

The most heavily armed tank was Char B, which mounted a 47-mm gun in the turret and a 75-mm gun in the hull. The one-man turret of Char B was also used on the S-35. The tank commander was also the gunner and handled hand and flag communications with other tanks because most of these vehicles still had no radio. All French tank turrets were made to hold one man, which slowed their rate of fire since the commander had to load the gun, locate the target, aim, and fire the weapon. Before the war and the creation of the DCR at the instigation of General Billotte, the Char B was relegated to independent battalions or companies to support the infantry (Sharp, *French Army*, Vol. 2, p. 151). General Louis Keller, inspector general of tanks, who organized the 1st Armored Grouping, later was permanently assigned to this formation. General Bruneau assumed command of the 1st DCR. The 2nd DCR stayed under the command of Colonel Perret until General Bruche took over. The entire force, including the 3rd DCR created in March and the Cavalry Corps of two DLMs, was assigned to the 1st Army Group of General Billotte.

French Tank Doctrine

In August 1939, during a conference on the use of armored units held by the 511th Tank Regiment at Verdun, French and German doctrines were compared. The Germans, it was said, preferred mass engagement on a broad front. It was predicted they would use large tank formations on favorable terrain and try to take the enemy by surprise to prevent the enemy from concentrating mobile AT defenses at the point of attack. Their independent armored divisions—assembled in an armored corps and supported by the infantry and the artillery—would be able to penetrate the front and exploit it to the limit.

The French, on the other hand, preferred using armored units within and subordinated to infantry formations. The role of these units was to break the front, exploiting it to a limited degree, and allow other types of units to complete the breakthrough. The officer who organized the conference attributed the differences between the German and French doctrines on tank usage to the nature of the fortifications facing them. The Maginot Line, which had little depth, and the Siegfried Line (West Wall), which he speculated was up to thirty kilometers deep, required different approaches. After the conference, the French doctrine underwent slight adjustments. Thus, the DCR, intended for attacking well-organized positions and exploitation of breakthroughs, would lead counter-attacks. The assault against a strong enemy position would devolve on a combined force dominated by the infantry. The DCR would be pitched into the battle at a critical moment to penetrate the front. Hot on its heels, the Hotchkiss tanks and the mechanized infantry would pounce on the enemy, reducing the enemy's positions.

In February, despite the freezing weather, the first two DCRs began training and maneuvers. These divisions relied on a radio company for communications, but their tanks still lacked radios, and their tank crews had to rely on hand signals. The crucial radio units had already been designed, but few had been installed in the tanks by the spring of 1940. This infuriated Colonel de Gaulle, who exclaimed "Without radios were are f***ed!" (Ferrard, *France 1940*, pp. 110–113).

Sumner Waite's Account of Tank Maneuvers

During the end of the first week of February 1940, a week after the formation of the 1st Armored Groupement, Lieutenant Colonel (LTC) Sumner Waite, American military attaché in France, was invited to visit the two new DCRs as they began their training at the Suppes maneuver area. He found the area still had German trenches and bunkers from the last war. The colonel in charge of the aviation section informed Waite that two dive-bomber squadrons would be added to the unit.[6] When Waite reached the 37th Tank Battalion of the 1st DCR, the icy conditions were not very conducive to training, but morale was high, and the troops were enthusiastic. The tanks, which were scattered around, had to be started four times every twenty-four hours to protect them from freezing. This weather was ideal neither for training nor for a German offensive. The troops, billeted in farmhouses and barns and trying desperately to keep warm, were looking for small stoves. Despite this, morale was high when General Bruneau, commander of the 1st DCR arrived.

The two new divisions were given two months to complete their training. The bad weather in February seriously hampered training. Sumner Waite, an infantryman, was allowed to take over the controls of a Char B. Later, he wrote that he "was amazed, from a driving standpoint, at the facility with which it was possible to increase speed and change direction" and noted that the tank steered "as easily as an automobile."

Although many of the personnel in these divisions consisted of reservists, they gave "the impression that they had been soldiering for years," noted Waite. The "keenness and enthusiasm of reserve officers as well as regulars throughout for their tanks, guns or what-not, and the pride of the men in their respective organizations make an excellent foundation upon which to build divisional esprit de corps," he reported. These men, he added, were "ready to meet the best the enemy has." This was a far cry form the sorry troops General Montgomery claimed to have encountered.

At the time of Waite's report, about 100 Char B tanks were used in training or held in reserve. Another 189 were assigned to units or reserve in accordance with

FIGURE 6-1. Western front. This map shows all the major and minor fortified lines in 1940 on the western front. [Joseph Kaufmann]

the French policy of keeping 50% of their heavy tanks in reserve. Trucks from a transport company from the GHQ Reserve transported the tanks. The men of this transport company were nicknamed "bandits" by the officers in the armored units because they were undisciplined and sloppy.

Since the French had supposedly lost only one Renault tank in combat during the Phony War, the officers were satisfied that the armor of their tanks could withstand most AT weapons. Their greatest concern was the AT mine. Waite, impressed by what he saw during his visit, was convinced that the French DCR had greater striking power than the German armored units did. He was not aware that the Germans had reduced the tank strength of their panzer divisions to double the number of divisions, and that their supporting services were much more effective (Attaché Report 25,501-W, March 1940, "Organization of Divisions").

FAILURE IN COMMAND

By the time the spring thaw set in, all was ready for war. The Germans had perfected their new plan of attack; the French and British had had months to build up their forces and study the results of the Polish campaign. The French government changed once more as Édouard Daladier was replaced by Paul Reynaud as prime minister. However, with the threat of an imminent offensive as the Norwegian campaign wound down, it was too late for the new prime minister to replace General Gamelin. The failure of the Allies in Norway had left British Prime Minister Neville Chamberlain in such a bad position that he had been replaced by Winston Churchill as the German offensive in the West began on May 10.

General Gamelin established his headquarters in the medieval keep of Vincennes, outside Paris. The ancient surroundings seemed to suit the old soldier's approach to running the French armed forces. He had no radio contact with his subordinates and relied on the telephone or dispatch riders. General Alphonse Georges, commanding the Northeast Theater of Operations, was a good distance away, with his headquarters at La Ferté-sous-Jouare. Georges, noted for his skills as a strategist, did not agree with his commander's strategy for Belgium, so Gamelin was only too happy to distance him from his headquarters in January by giving him the new command. General Joseph Doumenc, the chief of staff, was located at Montry, between Vincennes and La Ferté-sous-Jouare. Colonel de Gaulle, who saw Gamelin in the underground chambers of his headquarters, felt as if he were in a convent, visiting a "savant testing in a laboratory the chemical reactions of his strategy" (de Gaulle, *War Memoirs*, p. 34).

It was during this visit, which took place just before the German attack on Norway, that General Gamelin gave de Gaulle the command of the new 4th DCR, which would be forming in mid-May. He explained to the colonel that he was convinced the Germans would launch a diversionary attack in Scandinavia and later open their main offensive with a version of the *Schlieffen* Plan, which he would successfully blunt (de Gaulle, *War Memoirs*, pp. 34–35). However, Gamelin overestimated German strength, and due to his dispersed command system, he would quickly lose control of the situation when events did not unfold as planned. One of his major mistakes was his tendency to overestimate enemy strength. So, one can only wonder at his reaction when he received a grossly exaggerated report that the Germans had 7,000 tanks in May 1940 (Goutard, *Battle of France*, p. 27).

The fact is that Gamelin was incapable of fighting a modern fast-paced war. General Georges, on the other hand, may have lost his nerve after being wounded during the assassination of the Yugoslav king in 1934. The fact that Gamelin and Georges were at odds over strategy, which was compounded by the squabbling between them and their weaknesses as leaders, diluted their ability to lead decisively. General Weygand was brought back from Syria that spring to try to resolve the problems between the two. When Plan D left the French left wing overextended and the Germans began breaching the Meuse at Sedan on 14 May, General Georges's nerve was gone, and Gamelin was

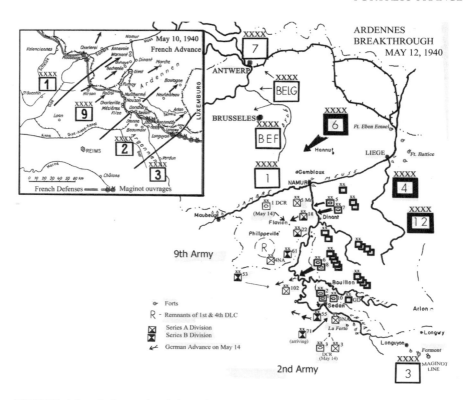

FIGURE 6-2. Ardennes breakthrough, May 12, 1940. The inset shows the advance of the French units on May 10 in response to the German invasion. The main map shows the concentration of German forces in the Ardennes sector and the German breakthrough. Note the location of La Ferte and the other three *ouvrages* of the Maginot Line Extension. [Joseph Kaufmann]

unable to follow the developments, much less take control of the situation. Doumenc went to Georges's headquarters, tried to restore his confidence, and helped formulate a plan to attempt to stem the tide by using the three DCRs in concentric counterattacks. Before that, Georges had already concluded that the junction of the Second and Ninth Armies needed reinforcement and had dispatched additional divisions. When he ordered a major counterattack with the 3rd DCR and other divisions, his subordinates did not obey. Georges let that ride, so by 15 May the situation was lost (Gunsburg, *Divided and Conquered*, pp. 133–135, 193–197). Here lay the greatest weakness in French armed force, not troops stretched from the North Sea to the Swiss border supposedly imbued with the Maginot mentality.

THE GERMAN OFFENSIVE: CASE YELLOW

The long wait finally ended on 10 May 1940, when the Germans launched Operation Case Yellow. Preceding the ground assault, the offensive began when parachute, glider, and other air-landed troops struck at key points. While these special units secured the bridges over the rivers and canals the advancing ground forces must cross, glider troops embarked on a surprise attack on the Belgian fort of Eben Emael, the most modern of the Belgian forts. Their gliders, silently approaching the fort in the early morning hours, skidded across the fort's surface, taking the garrison by surprise. Despite the presence of antiaircraft weapons, the Belgians had no time to react. The German assault troops forced the garrison to surrender the next day thanks to their 'secret' weapon.

The news left a profound impression on the troops of the Maginot Line, especially since no one was certain how the Germans succeeded until well after the campaign. The secret was that glider troops carried a new type of demolitions called the hollow charge. When placed on steel cloche or turrets, the force of the blast is channeled downward, instead of upward, penetrating the thick armor and killing the occupants of the position. At the Eben Emael, the German troops actually blasted their way into an artillery casemate, not much different from those of the Maginot *ouvrages*, and the defenders were soon cornered. The defenders used their own demolitions to block German access into the gallery below. The fact that the Belgian forts were garrisoned by only artillerymen and not infantry troops trained for close combat contributed to the quick fall of the fort. Before long, the other three new Belgian forts of the main line of defense of the Fortified Position of Liege also surrendered.

The Allies had become aware of the effectiveness of an armored spearhead during the Polish Campaign. In the Netherlands and Belgium, an air-landed element forged the way for this spearhead, soon giving rise to the rumor that a Fifth Column of traitors and troops without uniforms behind the lines had helped the enemy. Fear began to spread among the civilian population of France as well as the soldiers. The media contributed to the rising panic by distorting the facts. On the Maginot *ouvrages*, the troops went on alert, assiduously patrolling the surface and anxiously surveying the sky for any trace of the enemy.

As the German forces plowed forward, the French and British crossed the Belgian border, heading for the Dyle Line. The armored force moved toward the gap between the Dyle and Meuse Rivers expecting to engage the German armor. As the Breda option was implemented, some elements of the Seventh Army moved along the coast, while others boarded ships for the Dutch coast. The Allies moved the main elements of the 1st Army Group from Maubeuge to the North Sea coast into Belgium. Thus, everything went according to plan—the German plan.

The light tanks and armored cars of the DLCs raced into the Ardennes to secure advanced positions. However, their efforts were quickly blunted because the Germans had airlifted a small number of troops in small aircraft to secure a few key points to protect the left flank of Guderian's three-division XIX Panzer Corps. This corps was part of the main German force (Panzer Group Kleist) of two panzer corps (including XLI Panzer Corps with two panzer divisions) advancing through the Ardennes. Further north in the Ardennes advanced another two-division panzer corps, giving this combined force seven of the ten panzer divisions in the West. In addition, the two Belgian divisions defending the region had withdrawn toward the Meuse, leaving behind a small force to man the bunkers at key points like Bastogne. In some places, these Belgian troops managed to hold off the German advance for much of the first day. Meeting little resistance from most of the Belgian positions, the main German force clashed with the French DLCs, easily pushing them back. They crossed the Meuse between Dinant and Sedan, outflanking the Maginot Line, the 2nd Army Group, and the 1st Army Group, which had advanced into Belgium.

Together, the French Ninth and Second Armies held a section of front equal to the section guarded by the remainder of 1st Army Group, but these two armies consisted mostly of reservist divisions. The Ninth Army commander, General André Corap, placed his best and most mobile divisions on his left flank to advance to the Meuse from Givet to Dinant. In the meantime, the 61st Division (Series B) and the 102nd Fortress Infantry Division held their positions on the right. These two divisions had fronts of twenty-five and thirty-five kilometers, respectively, when a regular infantry division was expected to hold a front of six kilometers and in some circumstances up to ten kilometers. To the southeast, between Sedan and Montmédy, the 55th and 71st Series B Divisions of Huntziger's Second Army were assigned to the defense of a long stretch of the front. However, they were still moving into position after 10 May. The poorly trained 71st was pulled from the reserve and hardly battle-ready.

On 12 May, General Doumenc ordered the 3rd DCR, the 3rd Motorized Division, and the 14th, and 28th Divisions to move to the vicinity of Sedan. However, on 14 May, before these units even reached their positions, the Germans crossed the Meuse at several places defended by the French Ninth and Second Armies. The previous day, the badly outnumbered 5th Motorized and the 18th Divisions of the Ninth Army, supported by the 1st DLC, had offered the Germans a spirited resistance. On 14 May, the 102nd Fortress Division held the 6th Panzer Division at Montherme and moved back only when it was attacked from the rear. The reservists of the 55th and the 71st divisions broke at Sedan, opening the front, but only after undergoing four hours of intense aerial bombardment and ground assault. At this critical time, General Georges failed to take a personal hand when his subordinates failed to carry out his orders.

Meanwhile, a number of French divisions remained locked in their positions, facing the very weak German Army Group C, which presented no serious threat at that time. The elite troops of the Maginot Line stood impotently by while the best of the French divisions, including many of the mechanized and armored divisions, pinned down in Belgium, were about to be outflanked and cut off.

THE FRENCH MILITARY VERSUS
THE GERMAN WAR MACHINE

The caliber of the French military machine was revealed during the first week of the campaign. The French high command failed dismally, and its military doctrine encouraged poor leadership at a time when independent action was needed. In battle, the French soldiers did as well as could be expected, considering that many were left in an untenable position, facing an overwhelming force. The First Army had taken up position in Belgium in the Gembloux Gap between the Dyle and Meuse Rivers. It was covered by the Cavalry Corps of General René Prioux with the 2nd and 3rd DLMs, which moved forward about twenty kilometers toward Jandrain and Hannut, where they engaged the 3rd and 4th Panzer Divisions of the German XVI Panzer Corps on 12 May. The French SOMUA proved superior to most German tanks, despite its one-man turret that forced the tank commander to do several jobs at once. The French tankers finally retreated toward Gembloux, where the fighting continued through 15 May. The Germans, despite their air superiority, were unable to break the line formed by the First Army's regular and colonial divisions backed by artillery and the DLMs.

Unfortunately, the action at Gembloux was only part of the German diversionary effort to draw attention away from the Ardennes. Only the German breakout along the Meuse and the collapse of the overextended Ninth Army forced the First Army to withdraw. The 1st DCR, which had been sent to aid the First Army, was diverted toward Philippeville against the flank of the German XLI Panzer Corps emerging from the Ardennes and crossing the Meuse at Dinant where the weak divisions of the Ninth Army had been pushed back. Despite the heroic efforts of the 1st DCR and its commander, the attack failed because its support echelon was held back by the masses of refugees clogging the roads.

Troops, especially reservists, needed time to adjust to combat, especially when facing new weapons, tactics, and elements. However, the Germans did not give the French troops any breathing time, pounding them between Sedan and Dinant before they could even move into position. Only the 102nd Fortress Division, which was already in place, stood up to the Germans until it was isolated. The Germans' ability to react quickly and with overwhelming force gave them the impetus to break through the Allies' lines and march all the way to the coast within days, isolating the 1st Army Group and the best of the French army. The fortifications, especially those built during the Phony War, proved too inadequate to check the German advance, especially since they had been left unmanned when the Ninth Army had gone into Belgium.

As the German forces moved forward, they brushed against the edge of the Maginot Extension, at the *ouvrage* of La Ferté. The propaganda value of breaching the Maginot Line was very enticing, so the Germans made an all-out effort against this poorly armed PO, where the heaviest weapon was an AT gun, and the only 75-mm guns were in two separate interval casemates built to cover the approaches to the fort. The German 71st Infantry Division moved against the *ouvrage*, marked on German maps as *Panzerwerk 505*. On 16 May, the 71st Division advanced to Hill 226 and Les Fourches and then to Hill 331 to isolate the fort; the 68th Division moved along its right flank to prevent the French 3rd North African and 6th Infantry Divisions from interfering. The German 15th Division faced the GO of Les Chesnois to divert it from supporting the PO of La Ferté with its 75-mm guns.

On 17 May, the Germans brought to the front nine 210-mm mortars from the Great War (taken from the Czechs in 1939) and began pummeling La Ferté with 135-kilogram shells from a distance of almost 10 kilometers, just out of reach of the French weapons. During the next two days, the Germans, with support from five other batteries, dropped over 2,500 rounds on La Ferté, tearing up the barbed wire network and AT rails. The 210-mm rounds plowed furrows up to 10 meters long and over 3.5 meters deep. The small 25-mm guns of La Ferté's mixed-arms turret had little effect. The PO became totally isolated when the crews of the two independent casemates, each with a 75-mm gun, flanking it on each side withdrew on the night of 17 May when they were left unprotected after the mixed-arms turret of La Ferté jammed while firing at the Germans on Hill 31.

Late on 18 May, a team of German combat engineers worked its way to the small fort; German high-velocity 88-mm Flak guns next opened up on the cloches, and an assault platoon reached Block 2, destroying the *guêt-fusil mitrailleur* (GFM) cloche with a demolition charge. The jammed mixed-arms turret was blown out of its mount with a forty-kilogram charge. The last cloche of the block was destroyed with another charge. Additional charges were dropped into the position, setting the interior on fire.

All along, Block 1 continued to resist, keeping the German assault teams at bay until midnight. By then, the Germans had reached the block and destroyed three of its four cloches, taking out the final one in the morning. Next, the German blasted their way through an embrasure and set the interior of the block on fire. The 75-mm gun turret of the GO of Les Chesnois fired over four thousand rounds to support La Ferté but had little effect. On 18 May, a counterattack by elements of the 6th Infantry Division and Char B tanks from the 3rd DCR failed.[7]

At 5:00 A.M. on 19 May, the telephone lines between the two *ouvrages* fell silent. The Germans finally entered the block and descended to the gallery below only to find the hundred-man crew dead, including the commander, Lieutenant Maurice Bourguignon. It is speculated that they had been asphyxiated by the fumes from the *usine* after the air intake system was badly damaged. After the battle, the Germans celebrated the taking of La Ferté with a propaganda blitz far exceeding the merits of their little victory (Bruge, *Faites Sauter la Ligne Maginot*, 218, 224–239; German Army High Command, *Denkschrift*, pp. 194–195; Hofmann et al., *German Attacks*, pp. 110–117; Pallud, "Maginot," pp. 14–15).

The other three *ouvrages* of the Maginot Extension were ordered to evacuate about three weeks after the fall of La Ferté, after the high command realized that they would be easy picks for the Germans when they became isolated positions, like La Ferté. In any case, by that time, the French high command had formed a new defensive position that did not include these forts.

While the battle was raging at La Ferté, the 101st Fortress Infantry Division and the four POs and casemates it occupied at Maubeuge came under attack from the German 28th Infantry Division and the 5th Panzer Division. Boussois was the first to come under fire on 18 May. Although its 25-mm guns were no match for German 150-mm cannons and deadly 88-mm Flak, the little fort resisted gamely. On 20 May, Boussois and Le Sarts were targeted by *Stuka* dive-bombers. The mixed arms turret of Block 2 at Boussois suffered some damage and was unable to retract, but it was repaired in the dead of night. On 21 May, the powerful interval casemate of Heronfontaine repelled a German assault with its mixed-arms turret. The *Stukas* returned to dive-bomb Boussois that day. The Germans hauled in a huge 210-mm mortar and began pounding the fort, the same way they had done at La Ferté. Undaunted, the little fort's defenders fought back, halting another infantry assault in its tracks. Finally, on 22 May, the crew of Heronfontaine pulled out, leaving the PO of Le Sarts exposed.

The PO of Bersillies came under fire next, followed by La Salmagne. The Germans tried to take the *ouvrages* from the rear, but met heavy resistance. Finally, assault troops using demolition charges took out the embrasures and air vents of Boussois, while troops with flamethrowers neutralized the mixed-arms turret and cloche. While Boussois was on the brink of surrender, the Germans launched an attack on the PO of La Salmagne, using smoke to blind the observers. This allowed the assault force to cross five hundred meters of open terrain, breach the line of obstacles, and reach the superstructure of the fort. The Germans knocked out the mixed-arms turret of Block 1 with demolitions charges. Before long, only Le Sarts was left standing.

Finally, on 23 May, the German artillery destroyed the fort's mixed-arms turret, and assault teams breached the line of obstacles. Thus, Maubeuge and its forts fell but not before putting up stout resistance against the odds. The 1st Army Group was still extracting itself from the trap set by the enemy when the German armored thrust reached the Channel on 21 May (German Army High Command, *Denkschrift*, p. 219; Hofmann et al., *German Attacks*, pp. 47, 119–121; Mary, *Maginot*, p. 190).

As the fight for Maubeuge continued, the 5th Panzer Division moved against the French positions in the Mormal Forest. On 20 May, the German infantry moved toward Fort Maulde, north of Valenciennes, eliminating many of the blockhouses in its way. Whenever the Germans targeted the embrasures of the weak blockhouses in the area, the occupants took to their heels. On 22 May, the two-block PO of Eth, the last of the border forts beyond the Maginot Extension, was confronted from the rear, with German 105-mm guns firing at a distance of six hundred meters. Its exposed façade was hit. All the while, the artillery of Fort Maulde laid down supporting fires until it too came under attack and had to surrender on 25 May. Once its artillery support was thus eliminated, the badly damaged PO of Eth surrendered on 26 May (Hofmann, *Attacks*, p. 44; Mary, *Maginot*, p. 185).

On 17 May, de Gaulle had attempted a counterattack with the hastily formed 4th DCR to break the German pincer isolating the 1st Army Group, but despite some initial success, his incomplete division's effort amounted to too little, too late. Nevertheless, the division stayed in action until late in the month.[8] By the end of the month and the first days of June, the British had evacuated the BEF and the remnants of the 1st Army Group from Dunkirk.

Case Yellow ended as the Germans regrouped for the final assault. By this time, General Weygand had replaced Gamelin as commander, and much of the French army had been lost. Weygand tried to put up a new defensive line from the Channel to the Maginot Line. However, all that was left at his disposal in the way of mobile forces was the newly formed British 1st Armored Division and the remnants of his own armored force that had survived the debacle in the north.

THE FINAL GERMAN OFFENSIVE: CASE RED

The French line stretched along the Somme to the Oise River and from there to the Aisne River, south of Laon—which was in German hands—and along the Aisne to Réthel, across the Argonne Forest where it reached the Meuse. From the Meuse, it linked up with the Maginot Line and then followed the 1939 defensive positions to the Swiss border. The length of this position from the Meuse to the coast was much greater than the position held by the 1st Army Group in 1939, but at this point the French had fewer units to hold the line.

This last, hastily formed line of defense between the Maginot Line and the coast was called the Weygand Line. On this line, the general set up hedgehog positions in an attempt to break up the German's second offensive. The hedgehogs were strong points consisting of various weapons—including at least one 75-mm gun used as an AT weapon—laid out for all-around defense at key villages and woods. Any troops and formations that could be scraped together were assigned the task of maintaining the gaps between the hedgehogs.

About forty infantry divisions and the reconstituted armored formations were deployed to hold the final line of defense; only seventeen of these divisions were behind the Maginot Line. General Besson's 3rd Army Group (Sixth, Seventh, and Tenth Armies) took the front from the Channel to the Oise, and the new 4th Army Group (Second and

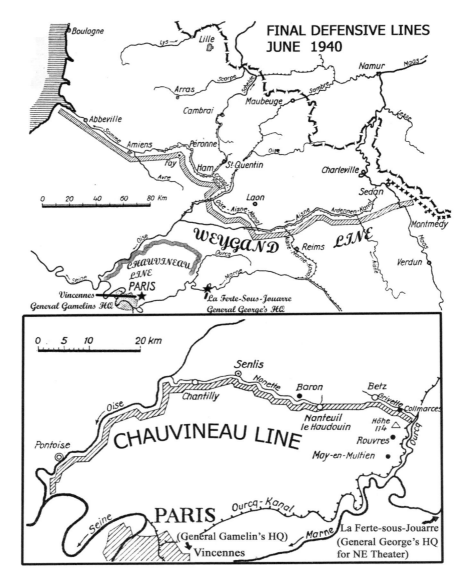

FIGURE 6-3. Final defensive lines, June 1940. The map shows the location of the Weygand Line and where it met the remaining border defenses northwest of Montemedy. It also shows the location of the Chauvineau Line and Gamelin's and George's headquarters. [Joseph Kaufmann]

Fourth Armies) under Huntziger held the remainder of the Weygand Line between the Aisne River and Maginot Line. The divisions of these two army groups held frontages of up to sixteen kilometers, more than twice the normal frontage for these units. Prételat's 2nd Army Group (Third, Fifth, and Eighth Armies) held not only what remained of its old front, but also the Upper Rhine. Reinforcements from the Alpine Army rushed north. Weygand and his superiors decided that this would be the last stand of the French army, and Reynaud's plans for a Breton Redoubt were dropped.[9]

The new offensive began between 5 June and 9 June. The line along the Somme had fallen, and French troops had taken up positions along the Seine. In a matter of days, the Weygand Line began to come apart but not until after putting up a stiff resistance. Units like the reconstituted 3rd DCR even launched a relatively successful counterattack. Nonetheless, the evacuation of Paris began on 10 June, and the capital was declared an "open city" on 13 June. The entire front finally began to break apart. At this time, the First Army of German Army Group C launched Operation Tiger to reduce the Maginot Line, and the Seventh Army undertook Operation Bear to breach the Rhine defenses.

The Advanced Position of Longwy had been abandoned as early as 13 May. By the time operation Case Red got under way, half the divisions defending the Maginot Line and the Rhine had moved to the Weygand Line. The Sarre Gap remained as vulnerable as ever, with four fortress infantry regiments and two colonial machine gun regiments left to hold the line of inundations between the PO of Téting and the *ouvrage* of Haut Poirier. Behind them remained the 1st Polish Division and the 52nd Division. Between 31 May and 3 June, the German 258th Division took on the French at the line of *avant-postes* on the right flank of the RF of Metz in preparation for Operation Tiger, but the French had strongly resisted. The French 52nd Division counterattacked, driving the Germans out of Puttelange on 6 June. Several divisions had already moved off by the end of May to create the Weygand Line, including the British 51st Highland Division serving near the *ouvrage* of Hackenberg, leaving only one regular division with the Maginot Line when the Germans launched Operation Tiger in June.

When the Weygand Line was finally overcome, the old forts of Verdun also joined the action. On 15 June, the German 76th Division attacked Fort Choisel, which mounted a 75-mm gun turret and a new GFM cloche. Before Verdun's defenses fell on 12 May, General Guderian's panzer group was already moving to isolate the 2nd Army Group by advancing toward the Swiss border after managing to push through the Third DCR, 7th DLM, and the 3rd Motorized Divisions near Rheims.

On 2 June, General Prételat asked his superiors for permission to withdraw, but that was denied, so on 6 June he issued General Order Number 2, in which he exhorted his troops to resist:

> Until now, the enemy has not yet attacked you. The position that you have been assigned to defend was covered by an advanced position on which all the divisions of the French Army have become seasoned this winter. This advanced opposition has been voluntarily evacuated in order to permit these divisions to join the battle, where many have already covered themselves with glory. It is your turn now to show that you are worthy of the defenders of Verdun. The Maginot Line, entrusted to your guard, must remain inviolate. The garrisons of the ouvrages, interval troops, everyone must constitute a solid block against which the enemy attack will break. As the proud motto of your insignias says: "ON NE PASSE PAS." (*Lageberichte West*, 1940)

RETREAT, CONFUSION, AND HOLDING THE LINE

Originally conceived to shield the frontier as the army mobilized, the Maginot Line had gradually become a major part of French operational plans beyond the point of

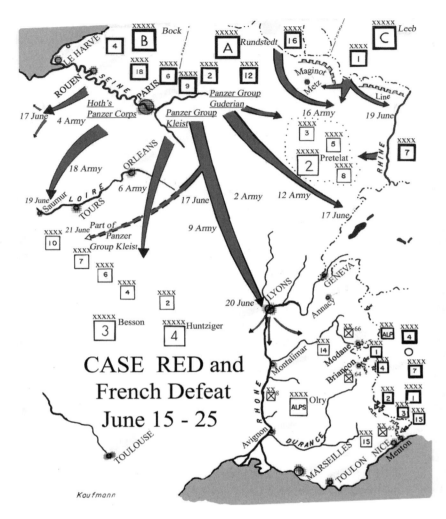

FIGURE 6-4. Case Red and French defeat, June 15–25. The map shows the final German offensive that broke the Weygand Line and brought about the collapse of the French forces in the north. Also shown are the location of Italian and French forces on the southeast front. [Joseph Kaufmann]

mobilization. As the French army stood on the verge of collapse, the Maginot Line again reverted to its original role as a temporary shield, except it was not to cover a buildup, but a withdrawal. On the afternoon of 12 June, General Prételat finally received permission from Weygand to withdraw his forces. He sent out orders to the units of the 2nd Army Group.

As the divisions prepared to pull out of the Maginot Line, many of the fort commanders were accorded command authority over their sectors and fortress troops therein. Since there was no established method of evacuation, Third Army headquarters issued three measures. Measure A called for the withdrawal of the troops and garrisons of the interval positions in the evening of 15 June. Measure B called for

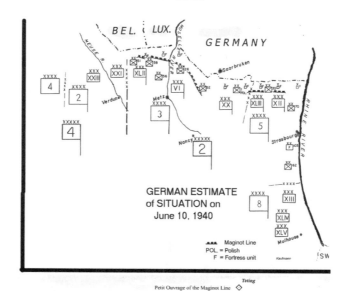

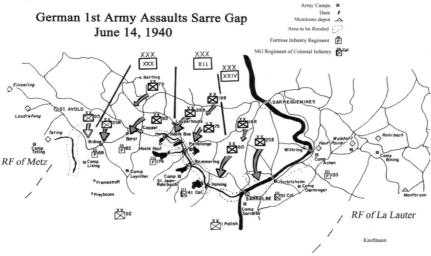

FIGURE 6-5. German first Army assaults Sarre Gap, June 14. The map shows the penetration of the Sarre Gap by the German first Army and the location of the *petit ouvrages* on both flanks. Inset map shows the location of major French units before the second Army Group withdrew. [Joseph Kaufmann]

the pullback of the artillery units in the evening of 15 June followed by the final abandonment of the fortified positions on the next evening after the sabotage of any artillery that could not be carried away. Measure C concerned the abandonment of the *ouvrages*. Every member of the crews, except personnel essential for minimal operations, was to depart in the evening of 16 June. The personnel who stayed behind were to impede the enemy's advance until 18 June, then to destroy supplies, equipment, and weapons in the early afternoon and abandon the forts (Bruge, *On a Livre*, p. 13). The abandonment of the RF of Metz did not take place as planned, and in many cases, the French officers of the fortress troops exhibited the leadership missing in the debacle in the Ardennes.

During the night of 12/13 June, the casemate crews of three of the remaining *ouvrages* of the Maginot Extension (now the bridgehead of Montmédy) began to evacuate. Their positions were becoming increasingly isolated and played no role in delaying a German advance against the retreating army group. Too late, General Prételat and his colleagues realized that, due to the prewar skimping, the new *ouvrages* of the Maginot Extension could not sustain themselves in independent operations. La Ferté had been the first casualty of that policy. The decision was to evacuate the *ouvrages* but not without sabotaging them first. As the *ouvrages* of the Maginot Extension were evacuating, most of the Third Army began to move out of the RF of Metz, leaving the plateau of Marville between Longuyon and Marville undefended. The commander of the German Sixteenth Army of Army Group A took advantage of the situation and sent his divisions around the left flank of the Maginot Line on 14 June.

During the first twenty-four hours of the pullback, three-quarters of the interval troops were gone, except in the SFs of Haguenau and Sarre since the large gaps without *ouvrages* between the two RFs and the RF of Lauter and the Rhine had to remain covered to prevent a quick German breakthrough. The fortress troops of the Maginot Line were aware of the fate of their comrades at La Ferté, but they did not lack confidence in their own positions, and many wanted to fight. As the retreat began, each sector was left with a fortress commander and his staff, who, faced with the order to evacuate the front, had to decide on the procedures to be followed. Due to the rapid German flanking movement around the Maginot Line, the German 161st and 183rd Divisions were soon fanning out behind the SFs of Crusnes and Thionville, and the 169th Division headed toward Metz with four other German divisions on its left flank. In addition, the German 1st Army launched the long-awaited assault on the Sarre sector. The swift action of the German Sixteenth and First Armies prevented the garrisons of the *ouvrages* from evacuating and destroying their forts and gave them the longed-for fight.

When the infantry divisions began to withdraw, several *divisions de marche* consisting of interval troops of the *régiments d'infanterie de forteresse* (RIFs; fortress infantry regiments) were formed in various sectors and began to pull back.[10] The garrisons of the *ouvrages* and some interval casemates prepared for their first and, in many cases, only battle. In the RF of Metz, a portion of some garrisons evacuated their *ouvrages* as part of Measure A, moving toward Metz or Nancy as best they could, but many were overtaken by the rapidly moving German forces and were taken prisoner within a few days.

The German 161st Division went around Longuyon and pull up behind the *ouvrages* of Fermont and Latiremont on 14 June. The 183rd Division had held a large section of the front along the Luxembourg border and had intended to breach the defenses between the POs of Bois du Four and Mauvais Bois. Instead, it moved around Longuyon, behind the 161st Division, and advanced toward Thionville, isolating the SFs of Crusnes and Thionville by 15 June. The French engineers had contributed to the isolation of their own troops by destroying bridges during the initial retreat (Mary, *Maginot*, Vol. 3, pp. 200–202).

Colonel Jean-Patrice O'Sullivan, who was put in command of the SF of Thionville when the 3rd Army retreated, ordered the *ouvrage* commanders in his sector to begin the evacuation on 17 June. As the German 183rd Division approached his headquarters at the old German fort of Illange, outside Thionville, O'Sullivan realized that the troops of the *ouvrages* of Rochonvillers, Molvange, Immerhof, Soetrich, Karre, Kobenbusch, Oberheid, Galgenberg, and Sentzich would be trapped between the enemy and the Moselle River. He decided therefore to countermand his previous order. On 16 June, he moved his headquarters to the GO of Métrich.

On 14 May, when German troops began moving around the *ouvrages* of Fermont and Chappy on the left flank of the RF of Metz, they came under the fire of Fermont's 75-mm gun turret.[11] This GO had first engaged German troops along the Belgian border on 12 May and later gave fire support to Latiremont. A few days earlier, on 11 June, German patrols had tried to penetrate its perimeter but were stopped by the interval troops, which pulled out the next night. As the German 169th and 183rd Divisions moved behind the SF, Fermont's 75s tore up a supply column of the 183rd Division on 15 June, forcing it to find a safer route. On the same day, the Germans cut off the external power source for Fermont and nearby *ouvrages* by taking the transformer station of Xivry-Circourt. From that moment, the *ouvrages* had to depend on their own *usines* for all their power.

On 17 June, the Germans installed a battery of deadly 88-mm guns within two kilometers of the rear of Fermont. While the gunners of Block 4 were at breakfast, one of the 88s began firing on a single point of the casemate, delivering a round every three minutes throughout the morning. Since this face of the block had the weakest concrete protection, the crew was worried, but it was unable to locate the German gun. Later, while the crew ate lunch, a round finally breached the wall at the point that had been hammered all morning. The German gunners, for unknown reasons, gave up; not realizing that one more shot would have opened a gaping hole in the block and hit the ready ammunition near one of the guns. It is probable that they could not see their target and gave up out of sheer frustration. That night, the engineers of the *ouvrage* sealed up the breach with concrete and iron plates under the cover of darkness. Another near-disaster struck Fermont that day: A fire broke out in the *usine* while the ventilation system was being serviced (Bruge, *On a Livré*, pp. 79–82).

Meanwhile, the 1st Army of German Army Group C massed its forces to breach the Maginot Line, according to its after-action report. In reality, it took on the weakly defended Sarre sector. On the front between St. Avold and Sarralbe, three German army corps, totaling seven infantry divisions, faced three fortress infantry regiments (69th, 82nd, 174th RIFs) and two colonial infantry machine gun regiments (41st and 51st (RMIC)) with the 1st Polish and 52nd Divisions in reserve. Since these units lacked the transportation needed to withdraw, there was little question of removing them when the order was given on 12 June. On the left flank, the German First Army deployed a corps of three divisions that extended all the way to the Rhine. Its 215th Division prepared to advance into the Vosges between the two main sections of the RF of Lauter. Seven German divisions had already begun their flanking movement around Longuyon. Behind the troops that would assault the Sarre front on 14 June 1940 came several special batteries that included eight rail gun batteries, a 355-mm *Mörser*, and two 420-mm *Mörsers*. Artillery Group 800 consisted of Battery 810 with one 355-mm howitzer, Battery 820 with a German 420-mm howitzer, and Battery 830 with a Czech 420-mm howitzer.[12]

On the morning of 14 June, the 1st Army opened its offensive on the Sarre front with a barrage of fire from almost one hundred batteries and *Stuka* bombing individual positions. The 93rd Division overcame stiff resistance on the morning of 14 June, but it was stopped at Cappel by a line of bunkers and fortress troops that refused to give up. The German combat engineers tried to use hollow charges against the bunkers, but they were driven back after sustaining heavy losses. The French began withdrawing that evening, each company leaving a platoon behind. The German 258th, on the right flank of the 93rd Division, joined the fray on the morning of 14 June but encountered brief resistance on the Nied. Finally, the German assault units began to bypass the French strongpoints all along the Sarre front, and the front was torn open by evening. Almost a dozen German divisions soon fanned out behind the French front. The 95th and 167th Divisions moved behind the SF of Boulay (Hofmann et al., *German Attacks*, pp. 133–142).

Colonel Raoul Cochinard was left in command of the SF of Boulay and Commandant Adolph Denoix of the SF of Faulquemont. Cochinard had ordered the main part of the fort garrisons to withdraw on 17 June and the remainder on the following night. Denoix had issued similar orders in his sector. Thus, the crews prepared to destroy supplies, armament, and equipment. At the time of the German breakthrough, Denoix, who was moving his command post to the PO of Laudrefang, countermanded his orders. By 18 June, in the SFs of Boulay and Faulquemont, Measure B—the evacuation or destruction of the remaining artillery of the supporting positions—had been implemented because retreat had still been possible, and those positions could not be held. The commanders of the *ouvrages* of the SF of Boulay prepared the forts for evacuation and stood by. The commander of Bousse, who did not receive the counterorder in time, had already carried out the instructions. His garrison was captured near Metz, soon after leaving Bousse. Colonel Cochinard's *ouvrages* in the SF of Boulay were still ready to fight. Like O'Sullivan, the colonel needed a safer command post in the face of the advancing German army, so he moved to the GO of Anzeling. Thus, the question of evacuating the *ouvrages* of the RF of Metz was shelved, and only Bousse was abandoned (Mary, *Maginot*, Vol. 3, pp. 201–202).

On 15 June, as the RF of Metz was outflanked on the left and the Sarre Front was broken, the German Seventh Army launched Operation Bear, an assault on the Upper Rhine. This movement took place south of Strasbourg and threatened to envelop the forces in the RF of Lauter. The casemate garrisons of the Rhine defenses held their positions, while the 45th and 63rd Divisions of the Eighth Army withdrew with most of the artillery. On the evening of 14 June, the 104th and 105th Fortress Infantry Divisions also withdrew, leaving the garrisons on their own. German 88-mm guns made short work of many of the casemates and blockhouses, and the German 555th, 218th, 221st, 239th, 554th, and 556th Divisions crossed the Rhine at Rhinau, Shoenau, near Marckolsheim, and at Neuf-Brisach. The French withdrew from the positions on the river to new positions but continued the uneven fight. At Shoenau, special Germans assault teams broke the resistance, allowing the main force to advance. By evening, the Germans reached the Rhine-Rhone Canal, but the 221st Division was held up by the positions around Marckolsheim, and it did not break through until 17 June. The withdrawal of the fortress divisions allowed the Germans to succeed on the Upper Rhine (Hofmann et al., *German Attacks*, pp. 144–150). Although Operation Bear did not seriously threaten the evacuation of the RF of Lauter, the fortress troops held their positions.

Before the encirclement of the RF of Metz, the *ouvrage* commanders had been ordered to fire off as much ammunition as possible before the evacuation. Although they proceeded right away to carry out these orders, they still had plenty of ammunition left by the time they faced the enemy.

On 15 June, the German 262nd Division moved around the flank of the RF of Lauter through Sarralbe and approached the SF of Rohrbach from the rear. The commander of the PO of Haut Poirier, who had been preparing to evacuate on 17 June, was trapped. Like the commander of the Third Army, the commander of the XLIII Fortress Corps (Fifth Army), had ordered all *ouvrages* to prepare for sabotage and evacuation. However, he had not specified evacuation dates, so the garrisons of the SFs of Rohrbach and Vosges prepared to make a stand (Mary, *Maginot*, Vol. 3, p. 202). On 15 June, Haut Poirier was cut off by the end of the day by the 262nd Division as the 257th Division moved east to seal off the RF of Rohrbach.

Lieutenant Colonel Jacques Schwartz, commander of the SF of Haguenau, had set up his headquarters in the GO of Hochwald. Since the situation had deteriorated only to the west of the Sarre River and the RF of Lauter was not yet encircled, Schwartz's fortress troops could have withdrawn. Instead, they stayed in place, including many of the interval units. When the 70th and the 30th Divisions eventually withdrew, the 70th Division left behind a battalion of light troops (*chasseurs*). Each of the RIFs that pulled out also left behind a battalion. Schwartz received orders to cover the withdrawal of the Fifth Army by holding his positions. His troops, like those of the RF of Metz, were eager to stay and fight.

On 15 June, the German 246th Division launched its assault on the *avant postes* only to find them strongly held and supported by the gun turrets of Schoenenbourg and Hochwald and the old 120-mm guns positioned on Hochwald.[13] Finally, German combat engineers penetrated the line, taking several support points and forcing the abandonment of many of these positions by the evening of 16 June. The German 246th Division, supported by heavy artillery—the Czech 355-mm and the 420-mm *Mörsers*—finally came face to face with the *ouvrages*.

BATTLE FOR THE OUVRAGES

The GO of Fermont engaged in an artillery duel between 15 June and 20 June. On 21 June, the Germans moved against its neighbors (the PO of Chappy, the Casemate of Puxieux, and the Observatory Puxieux), but the guns of Fermont forced them back. The Germans retaliated with a massive fire barrage supplied by three 210-mm *Mörsers*, four 305-mm Czech *Mörsers*, six batteries of 105-mm guns, and two batteries of 88-mm Flak guns. A huge 305-mm round (289 kilograms) smashed against the ouvrage but inflicted a glancing hit against the 75-mm gun turret of Block 1 without causing any damage. During the bombardment, the turrets eclipsed, leaving minimal surface exposed. The enemy rounds left large craters on the fort's surface, including in the vicinity of Block 1. The flanking 75-mm gun casemate of the GO of Latiremont dropped rounds on and near Fermont to thwart a German ground assault. During the battle, Fermont suffered a single casualty when a German AT gun hit a GFM cloche of the *entrée des hommes* (EH; men's entrance), killing the occupant. Fermont's 81-mm mortar turret retaliated, silencing the offending weapon (Bruge, *On a Livré*, pp. 131–1394; German Army High Command, *Denkschrift*, pp. 199–200; Hofmann et al., *German Attacks*, pp. 42, 51; G. Maistret, *Fermont*, p. 23).

Other *ouvrages* in the RF of Metz also saw action. The GO of Bréhain engaged German troops as they advanced on an interval casemate. On 22 June, a German force tried to take the GO of Michelsberg, but it was repelled with the help of the guns of the GO of Mont des Welches. On the right flank of the RF of Metz, the German 167th Division encircled the SF of Faulquemont, and the 95th Division advanced to the rear of the SF of Boulay. The 167th Division laid siege to the PO of Bambesch, and the PO of Kerfent used its machine gun turret in a vain attempt to drive the Germans off its neighbor. These two POs were outside the range of the nearest GO, Anzeling. On 21 June, German 88-mm Flak guns took up position behind Block 2 of Bambesch and blasted away at its façade, penetrating its GFM cloche. German assault troops moved toward Block 3, and after a two-hour bombardment, the garrison surrendered.

The 88-mm gun crews next turned their attention on Kerfent, firing into its Block 2. The nearby PO of Mottemberg tried to intervene with its machine gun turret, but with no artillery support to drive off the enemy guns, Kerfent was forced to surrender. Meanwhile, the PO of Einseling, supported by the PO of Laudrefang, the strongest fort in the SF of Faulquemont mounting 81-mm mortars in casemate, fought off a German assault. Laudrefang also supported the PO of Téting when it came under attack. All the *ouvrages* of the SF of Faulquemont lacked fortress artillery support, and they had been designed to mount 81-mm mortar turrets for that reason. Laudrefang was originally designed to be a GO. Kerfent, in the SF of Boulay, was also planned as a GO with a 75-mm gun turret to support the POs on its flanks. Thus, the German victories over these POs were not remarkable. However, they gave food for the German propaganda machine.

On the RF of Lauter, the PO of Haut Poirier was the first to fall. Like the *ouvrages* of Faulquemont on the other side of the Sarre sector, it lacked the support of a GO. The Germans moved 150-mm guns behind Block 3 and blasted the rear-facing wall of the casemate, killing three men and forcing the garrison of the fort to surrender on 21 June. At the same time, German troops invested the next *ouvrage*, the PO of Welschoff, which was within the range of the artillery turrets of GO Simserhof. Nonetheless, the Simserhof was unable to drive off the German gunners, who blasted a hole in Block 1 of Welschoff. The small fort surrendered on 24 June after two days of fighting. The Germans chalked up another hollow victory. Next in line was the PO of Rohrbach, which withstood the German assault thanks to the support of the artillery of Simserhof (German Army High Command, *Denkschrift*, p. 197; Mary, *Maginot*, p. 190).

On 19 June, the German 215th Division moved through the Vosges toward Lembach. The soldiers in the surrounding blockhouses tried their best to stop the enemy with the support of the guns of the GO of Four-au-Chaux and the 75s of the western combat blocks of the GO of Hochwald. That morning, German aircraft bombed the PO of Lembach and the GO of Four-au-Chaux. The guns of Hochwald fired on the *Stukas* that were attacking Four-au-Chaux. The bombers scored hits on the Lembach and Four-au-Chaux but inflicted no significant damage. Returning in the afternoon, the Germans directed their aerial attacks against Four-au-Chaux and, for the first time, Hochwald Ouest (Hochwald's western group of combat blocks). Late in the day,

German bombers, including *Stukas*, repeatedly directed their ordnance against the entrances of Schoenenbourg and Hochwald Ouest, ending the day with an air attack on Hochwald Est. Block 14 (135-mm *lance-bombe* turret block) of Hochwald sustained several hits but no crippling damage.

On 20 June, the GOs were subjected to another round of enemy artillery bombardment and aerial assault. Hochwald Est and Schoenenbourg came under dive-bomber attack early in the afternoon and again in the late afternoon. The 75-mm casemate guns of Block 12 at Hochwald drove off a ground assault on the PO of Lembach.

The last major air attacks against the two GOs took place on the morning of 21 June. In the late afternoon of 21 June, a 420-mm *Mörser* started shelling Schoenenbourg as the 246th Division engaged the casemates of the main line east of the *ouvrage*. (This was most likely the Czech 420-mm weapon since no sources have actually verified the German 420-mm being in action or at the front. The German mortar is only listed on the order of battle for the First Army's offensive in June.) One of the huge rounds created a crater seventy centimeters deep next to a combat block. Other shells tore through the loamy soil, penetrating twenty meters before detonating as close as five meters above the subterranean galleries and sending a shock wave through the galleries. About fifty 355-mm and 420-mm rounds were fired at Schoenenbourg during these last days.

The *Luftwaffe* rejoined the engagement on 22 June, but the 420-mm *Mörser* did not cease the bombardment until the Armistice (Collin and Wahl, *Basse Alsace*, pp. 40–43; Hofmann et al., *German Attacks*, pp. 53–54; Rowe, *Great Wall*, pp. 279–284). After three days of unrelenting aerial bombardment, about 120 bombs were dropped on Four-au-Chaux, 140 bombs on Hochwald, and 160 on Schoenenbourg. The *Stukas* and *Heinkel* 111s dropped bombs of 250, 500, and 1,000 kilograms on both GOs, almost half of which landed near or on target. Yet, there was no damage so crippling that it hindered operations was inflicted on these forts (Mary, *Maginot*, Vol. 3, p. 244).

The GO of Schoenenbourg underwent the most severe bombardment of any Maginot *ouvrage*. The wall against the *fossé* of Block 6, which was cracked, suffered the most serious damage. During the night, the garrisons had to clean the dirt thrown up on the turrets by the huge explosions. Some other blocks received minor damage, but the garrison soon repaired them. The most significant problem came on 21 June when a 105-mm round hit the 75-mm turret of Block 3, leaving it jammed in the firing position. However, it was also repaired in the evening. On 23 June, a 420-mm round detonated near the turret, creating a fissure in the M-1/M-2 magazine (the unique designation for the large M-2 of the fort). On that day, a couple of these rounds barely missed the poorly protected, unfinished *lance-grenades* cloche of Block 5 and destroyed the armored air vent of Block 6. Another 420-mm round hit Block 3, fissuring the walls (Collin and Wahl, *Basse Alsace*, p. 42; Germany Army High Command, *Denkschrift*, p. 198; Hofmann et al., *German Attacks*, pp. 53–54; Pallud, "Maginot," p. 38; Truttmann, *La Muraille*, p. 210).

Hochwald received a serious pounding, albeit not from the superheavy guns. A projectile broke a section of its AT wall, and rocks and debris covered the crenels of Block 12. A near miss left a huge crater on the corner of its *fossé* wall. Another large bomb plowed into a section of AT rails. Other bombs spewed rock and debris on turrets and cloches. Each evening, members of the crew cleaned up the debris that obstructed the operations of affected blocks, and the fort continued to fire back thousands of rounds

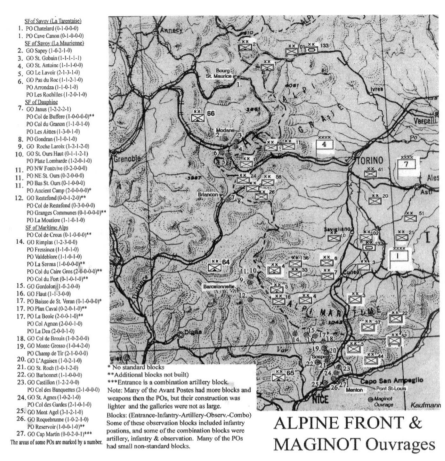

SF of Savoy (La Tarentaise)
1. PO Chatelard (0-1-0-0-0)
1. PO Cave Canon (0-1-0-0-0)
SF of Savoy (La Maurienne)
2. GO Sapey (1-0-2-1-0)
3. GO St. Gobain (1-1-1-1-1)
4. GO St. Antoine (1-1-1-0-0)
5. GO Le Lavoir (2-1-3-1-0)
6. GO Pas du Roc (1-1-2-1-0)
   PO Arrondaz (1-1-0-1-0)
   PO Les Rochilles (1-2-0-1-0)
SF of Dauphine
7. GO Janus (1-2-2-2-1)
   PO Col de Buffere (1-0-0-0-0)**
   PO du Granon (1-1-0-1-0)
   PO Les Aittes (1-3-0-1-0)
8. PO Gondran (1-1-0-1-0)
9. GO Roche Laroix (1-2-1-2-0)
10. GO St. Ours Haut (0-1-1-2-1)
    PO Plate Lombarde (1-2-0-1-0)
11. PO NW Fontvive (0-2-0-0-0)
11. PO NE St. Ours (2-0-0-0-0)
11. PO Bas St. Ours (0-1-0-0-0)
    PO Ancient Camp (2-0-0-0-0)*
12. GO Restefond (0-0-1-2-0)**
    PO Col de Restefond (0-3-0-0-0)
    PO Granges Communes (0-0-1-0-0)**
    PO La Moutiere (1-1-0-1-0)
SF of Maritime Alps
    PO Col de Crous (0-1-0-0-0)**
14. GO Rimplas (1-2-3-0-0)
    PO Fressinea (1-1-0-1-0)
    PO Valdeblore (1-1-0-1-0)
    PO La Serena (1-0-0-0-0)**
    PO du Caire Gros (2-0-0-0-0-0)**
    PO Col du Fort (0-1-0-1-0)**
15. GO Gordolon (1-0-2-0-0)
16. GO Flaut (1-1-3-0-0)
17. PO Baisse de St. Veran (0-1-0-0-0)*
17. PO Plan Caval (0-2-0-1-0)**
17. PO La Beole (2-0-0-1-0)**
    PO Col Agnon (2-0-0-1-0)
    PO La Dea (2-0-0-1-0)
18. GO Col de Brouis (1-0-2-0-0)
19. GO Monte Grosso (1-0-4-2-0)
    PO Champ de Tir (2-1-0-0-0)
20. GO L'Agaisen (1-0-2-1-0)
21. GO St. Roch (1-0-1-2-0)
22. GO Barbonnet (1-1-0-0-0)
23. GO Castillon (1-2-2-0-0)
    PO Col des Banquettes (2-1-0-0-0)
24. GO St. Agnes (1-0-2-1-0)
    PO Col des Gardes (1-2-0-1-0)
25. GO Mont Agel (1-3-2-1-0)
26. GO Roquebrunne (1-0-2-1-0)
    PO Reservoir (1-0-0-1-0)**
27. GO Cap Martin (0-0-2-0-1)***
The areas of some POs are marked by a number.

* No standard blocks
**Additional blocks not built)
***Entrance is a combination artillery block.
Note: Many of the Avant Postes had more blocks and
weapons then the POs, but their construction was
lighter and the galleries were not as large.
Blocks: (Entrance-Infantry-Artillery-Observ.-Combo)
Some of these observation blocks included infantry
postions, and some of the combination blocks were
artillery, infantry & observation. Many of the POs
had small non-standard blocks.

ALPINE FRONT & MAGINOT Ouvrages

FIGURE 6-6. Alpine front and Maginot *ouvrages*. This map shows the location of French and Italian units in the 1940 and also identifies all the French *ouvrages* of the Little Maginot of the Alps. [Joseph Kaufmann]

in response. By the end of the battle, the surfaces of the two *ouvrages* were pocked with craters, giving them a fantastic, lunar appearance, but all the combat positions remained fully operational (Wahl, *Hochwald*, pp. 128–129; Wahl, *La Ligne Maginot en Alsace*, pp. 140–182).

In the meantime, Guderian's armored columns reached the Swiss border and trapped the 2nd Army Group; some of its units crossed into Switzerland to be interned. The remainder of the Weygand Line had fallen like a stack of dominoes, and the French troops were in retreat on all sectors. Although the Armistice took effect on 25 June, some of the *ouvrages* did not surrender until emissaries were sent to inform them of the fact. It took several days to bring about their surrender, and some of the officers, like Commandant Pierre Fabre commanding the SF of Vosges, fervently protested the terms, but to no avail. Thus, no GO actually fell in combat. Some, like Schoenenbourg, took a severe pounding and still survived. In most cases, the garrisons received the honors of war as they surrendered, and their officers were allowed to keep their pistols.

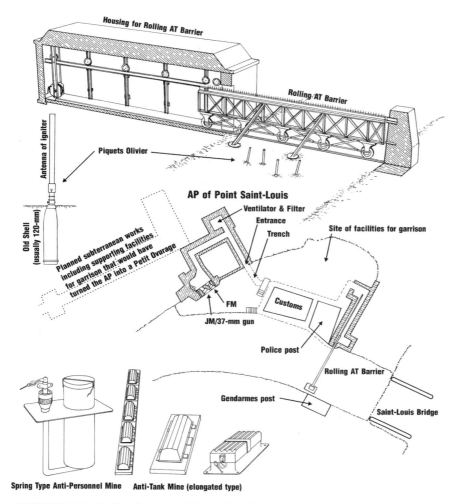

FIGURE 6-7. Rolling barrier, AP Pont Saint Louis, mines. [© Tomasz Idzikowski]

The Maginot troops were sent to prisoner-of-war camps in Germany, an improper treatment, they believed, since they had not been taken prisoner before the Armistice, but nothing could be done.

BATTLE FOR THE LITTLE MAGINOT LINE IN THE ALPS

Before the final German offensive, Mussolini declared war on 10 June, hoping to share in the German victory. Thus, a new front was opened against France just as the Germans were about to smash the Weygand Line and shortly before the withdrawal from the Maginot Line interval positions. The two French army corps of General Rene Olry's Alpine Army with a modest number of troops held the Southeast Front. A few days earlier, the troops of the *ouvrages* been ordered to move from their surface casernes into their forts. With the declaration of war, the border villages and towns—including

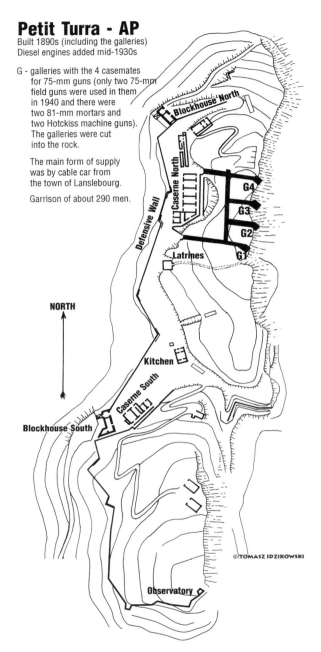

Petit Turra - AP
Built 1890s (including the galleries)
Diesel engines added mid-1930s

G - galleries with the 4 casemates
for 75-mm guns (only two 75-mm
field guns were used in them
in 1940 and there were
two 81-mm mortars and
two Hotckiss machine guns).
The galleries were cut
into the rock.

The main form of supply
was by cable car from
the town of Lanslebourg.

Garrison of about 290 men.

Blockhouse North

Caserne North

Defensive Wall

G4
G3
G2
G1

Latrines

NORTH

Kitchen

Caserne South

Blockhouse South

©TOMASZ IDZIKOWSKI

Observatory

FIGURE 6-8. Petit Turra. [© Tomasz Idzikowski]

Menton on the coast and Modane in the north—began evacuating. By the time the war began in September 1939, the majority of the population of the Menton area had moved to safer locations. The *Génie* destroyed a number of key bridges and tunnels.

Despite the knowledge of the French moving all available formations to defend their collapsing Northeast Front late in May, Italian intelligence greatly overestimated the number of French divisions remaining along the frontier with Italy and Libya and warned the high command that the French and British would assault Libya. The Italian leadership was informed that seven French divisions were near the Tunisia frontier and its Mareth Line, although the number was only three plus several regiments in the Mareth Line (May, *Knowing Ones' Enemies*, p. 351; Sumner and Vaulvillier, *The French Army*, p. 9). The Mareth Line and bad information protected Tunisia and delayed an Italian invasion of Egypt. This gave the British a respite of over two months since the Italian drive toward the Suez did not begin until 13 September 1940.

Both the French and Italians operated under a similar set of orders: hold their positions and their fire unless fired on. The Italy invasion plan, Plan PR 12, dated to September 1939 (Beraud, *Bataille des Alpes*, p. 14). The Italians amassed over twenty divisions, including Alpine units, under with their First and Fourth Armies against the small French force holding the Little Maginot Line of the Alps. However, the Italians only had superiority in numbers and not equipment. Their little L-3 tankettes armed with machine guns offered no advantage, and many of their troops were poorly equipped. The French main line of resistance rested, for the most part, behind the mountain barriers that formed most of the border. It consisted of impressive *avant-postes*, many of which included several small blocks linked to each other by underground galleries. Their main weapons usually consisted of a *fusil mitrailleur* (FM) and occasionally larger weapons, sometimes including an AT gun. In addition, several older nineteenth century fortifications that covered the border region and the mountain passes were incorporated in to the Alpine front, which consisted of the three SFs of Savoy, Dauphiné, and Maritime Alps.

When the war began, the XVI Corps with three infantry divisions and one North African division held the SF of Savoy and part of the SF of Dauphiné. The XIV Corps with two infantry divisions held the remainder of the SF of Dauphiné and the northern end of the SF of the Maritime Alps. The remainder of the SF of Maritime Alps was under the XV Corps with four divisions and the 2nd Colonial Division. In June 1940, General Olry's 185,000-man force was reduced to three Alpine divisions, some Alpine battalions, the Alpine fortress demibrigades, and two Alpine *chasseurs* demibrigades (Plan and Lefèvre, *La Bataille des Alpes*, pp. 23–25, 41–47).

For most of the first ten days of the war, the Italians only launched small-scale operations. On 16 June, the Italian Fourth Army struck in the vicinity of Briançon just north of Mount Chaberton. The old French Fort Olive engaged the Italian Fort Bardonecchia until the next day, when it was silenced by the 149-mm guns of the Italian Fort Chaberton, an imposing structure lost in the clouds at an altitude of 3,130 meters. On 18 June, Chaberton's eight gun turrets directed its fire at the PO of Gondran, a small position merely armed with a *jumelage de mitrailleuses* (JM; twin machine gun). On 20 June, the Italian fort turned on the GO of Janus; its largest guns were two 75-mm and four old 95-mm naval guns that did not have the Italian fort in their field of fire. Italian troops advanced as far as the village of Montgenèvre (Plan and Lefèvre, *La Bataille des Alpes*, p. 70; Castellano, *Distruggete lo Chaberton*, pp. 60–63).

On 21 June, a battery of 280-mm mortars of the French 154th Artillery Regiment began dropping its twenty-kilogram rounds on Fort Chaberton, but adverse weather conditions delayed and interrupted the French bombardments. On 24 June, the badly damaged Italian fort fell silent at last. The French continued to hold the Italian ground forces in check on the Briançon sector.

On the northern end of the SF of Savoy, Italian forces met stiff resistance at Bourg St. Maurice on 22 June. Over 50,000 Italian troops faced 5,500 French defenders but made little headway against the advanced positions. Italian forces also tried to penetrate the Arc Valley through the Mont Cenis Pass and another major route that included the Fréjus Tunnel to the south of Modane. The valley was studded with old Italian and French forts all the way to Modane, where a group of Maginot *ouvrages* closed the valley. Well in front of Modane, to the south of Lanslebourg, French and Italian *ouvrages* and *opere* (forts) lined both sides of the border overlooking the Mont Cenis Pass (Col du Mont Cenis). Here, the French line of *avant-postes* consisted of older forts and faced the Italians *opere* of the Vallo Alpino. The old French fort of La Turra had a gallery cut into the rock with four gun casemate positions that dominated the pass, but it only mounted two 75-mm field guns.

The Italian forces began their advance on 20 June but were held up by the French positions. On 22 June, field artillery positioned at the Italian Fort Paradiso bombarded La Turra for several hours while Italian troops tried to force their way through the pass. The garrison of La Turra used its two 75-mm guns and two 81-mm mortars to such effect that the Italians had to withdraw, leaving behind twenty tankettes that were soon swallowed up by the falling snow. The Italian forces moved toward Lanslebourg to bypass La Turra but failed to penetrate the line of *avant-postes* and to reach the Arc Valley before the armistice.

The Italian *Superga* Division tried to advance via the Fréjus Pass in the direction of a tunnel surmounted by *ouvrages* above the town of Modane. On 24 June, the Italian troops clambered up the snow-covered slopes onto the GO of Pas du Roc and the PO of Arrondaz. The 75-mm guns and the 81-mm mortars of the neighboring *ouvrages* immediately opened fire on the intruders. In addition, the gunners of Pas du Roc and Arrondaz used their weapons to clear each other of the assailants. Thus, a gallant effort on the part of the Italian troops came to naught (Ministero Della Difesa, *La Battaglia Delle Alpi*, p. 85; Plan and Lefèvre, *La Bataille des Alpes*, pp. 61–63).

The Italian First Army held the southern half of the front. During the course of Operation M, one Italian corps was assigned the task of taking the town of Barcelonnette, while a second corps executing Operation R was to advance up the coast against Menton and the Riviera. A third corps between these two was to create a diversion. The offensive began on 20 June as two divisions advanced toward the town of Larche from two directions. They successfully negotiated the pass until they hit the line of *avant-postes*, where they were stopped in their tracks by the 75-mm gun turret of the GO of Roche Lacroix and the casemate artillery of the GO of St. Ours Haut, which bombarded the supporting Italian 240-mm gun battery that was intended to break French resistance (Plan and Lefèvre, *La Battaille des Alpes*, pp. 92–93).

On 15 June, the GO of Monte Grosso, the largest *ouvrage* in the Alps, destroyed a group of Italian mortars, and on 20 June it was bombarded in turn by Italian 149-mm guns. Its 75-mm gun turret took a hit while in the firing position but remained in action, holding up the Italian advance. The situation was no better for the Italians to the north of Monte Grosso.

The main attack on the Riviera began on 20 June with an artillery bombardment of the French *ouvrages*. As the Italian troops advanced on 22 June, they ran into the *avant-poste* of Pont Saint Louis, on the border, and were unable to take it. The small position was a blockhouse built into the rock and outfitted with a filter room, a firing chamber for a JM, and, facing National Route 7, a 37-mm gun.[14] In front of the blockhouse and the small customs and police posts, an AT barrier was rolled out of its housing to block the road. Behind the barrier, several *Piquets Olivier* were buried in the road, their igniters projecting about waist high above the road. The nine-man crew, with the support of the *ouvrages* behind it, kept the road closed and beat off all Italian attempts to break through until the Armistice.

To bypass the position, the Italians decided to use the railroad tunnel below it. The *Coseria* and *Cremona* Divisions attempted to advance on Cap Martin and Roquebrune as they moved through the abandoned city of Menton. The assault began with a bombardment of the GO of Cap Martin with 149- and 210-mm guns. On the morning of 22 June, French artillery targeted the tunnels near the border. Finally, the Italians brought up an armored train that mounted four turrets with 152-mm guns and fired in support of the infantry moving through Menton. The GOs of Roquebrune, Mont Agel, and Saint Agnès joined the artillery duel from their mountaintops. The armored train soon withdrew into the tunnel but returned in the afternoon, at which time the 75-mm gun turrets of Mont Agel destroyed two of its four turrets, forcing it to retreat hastily into its tunnel. The train lost another gun in the process.

Although the *ouvrages* dominated the battlefield around Menton, the Italians refused to give up. An attempted amphibious assault behind Cap Martin turned into a veritable comedy of errors and never reached the French coast. On 23 June, the Italian forces in front of Menton finally received a promise of air support targeted mainly at the GO of Mont Agel. However, bad weather forced the cancellation of the air operation and of a second attempt at an amphibious landing planned for that night. The next day, two more armored trains arrived on the scene—one mounting four 152-mm guns and

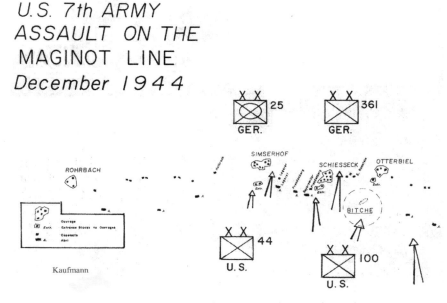

FIGURE 6-9.   U.S. seventh Army assault. [Joseph Kaufman]

the other four 120-mm guns—and opened fire on the GO of Cap Martin. Italian troops moving into Menton at noon were hit by the artillery and machine guns of Cap Martin, but they continued to advance, eventually reaching the *ouvrage*. Block 3, which mounted two 75-mm guns and two 81-mm mortars, suffered damage around some of its embrasures but remained in action. The Italian infantrymen surged onto the surface of the fort, and they could not be dislodged until later in the day, when other French artillery, including 155-mm guns, began dropping shells on the *ouvrage*, forcing the valiant enemy to retreat. On 24 June, the Italians pulled back behind the Carei River in Menton and awaited reinforcements (Ministero Della Difesa, *La Battaglia Delle Alpi*, pp. 76–78, 81–82, 89–90; Plan and Lefèvre, *La Bataille des Alps*, pp. 111, 121).

A little further to the north, the *Modena* Division moved against Castillon in an attempt to take Sospel from the south while the battle for Menton took place, but it failed to get beyond the line of *avant-postes*.

Throughout this campaign, the Italian army could measure its gains in meters, while the French forces remained firmly in control of the battlefield. However, German troops advanced down the Rhone Valley, and after the fall of Lyon, they soon threatened to isolate the Alpine Army. General Olry held his positions until the Armistice went into effect on 25 June. The Italians had about 5,500 casualties, including 631 men killed and another 600 missing; the French losses totaled about 275 men, including 40 killed (Andrew, *The Italian Army*, p. 5). The victory on the Alpine front did not change the course of the war but preserved French honor and demonstrated the effectiveness of the fortifications of the Maginot Line when properly employed.

CHAPTER 7

CONCLUSION

After the French surrendered, the fortifications they had built were taken over by the Germans in the northeast and the Italians in the southeast. Later, after Vichy territory was invaded by the Allies in 1942, the Italians and Germans also took over the Mareth Line in Tunisia. This line in the desert, although modified by the Axis forces, saw action in 1943. Many of the Maginot fortifications were stripped of their removable weapons and components that the Germans installed in their Atlantic Wall. The breech-loaded 50-mm mortar was much prized for that purpose. However, the Axis powers got more use out of captured French armored vehicles, artillery, and other weapons than they did from the concrete positions.

Some forts, such as the *gros ouvrage* (GO) of Hackenberg, served the Germans as underground munitions factories. They used some for testing and practice. When the Allies invaded Normandy and South France in the summer of 1944, the Germans still had little use for the French fortifications. Few in the Alps were put to use. However, in Alsace and Lorraine, the Germans put the old German forts at Metz, which had been used by the French as headquarters and fire-support positions, back into service against the advancing American forces. It was here that the Allies learned firsthand about the combat potential of a fort, even one from the World War I era.

After a prolonged battle, American troops reached Thionville and soon found themselves facing the guns of GO Hackenberg, where the Germans had put one of the 75-mm gun casemates back into service. The fort represented a significant obstacle for the Americans until a French officer led a self-propelled gun to the blind side of the block and blasted its façade, putting it out of action. Near Bitche, the Germans engaged the Americans from GO Simserhof and GO Schiesseck, giving a good account of themselves. Simserhof, many of its weapons gone, changed hands more than once during the winter months, and the Americans had to use demolition devices to destroy some of the positions. In some places, the casemates and blockhouses of the Maginot Line were used by the Germans for defense, but they were not incorporated into a solid position.

After the war, the French military repaired many of the damaged *ouvrages*. By the 1960s, those of their expensive battleships that survived the war became scrap, none of their tanks from the 1930s presented any value, and most of the weapons became sadly outdated. Only the FM-29 remained in service for many years. When the French generals claimed that it was best to wait until war came before building new offensive weapons, they may have been correct from an economic point of view because most of their weapons became worthless within ten years. The fortifications of the Maginot Line, however, have endured. Some *ouvrages* became command centers, but their combat block sections were closed off because they had lost their military value. Thus, Rochonvillers became a headquarters for the army, and Hochwald still serves the Air Force to this day. The forts provide excellent, well-hardened sites in the event of a nuclear war. Taking into account inflation, they still offer real value when considering the costs of building new positions for the same purpose.

When all is said and done, the Maginot Line did not fail to accomplish its original mission, neither on the Northeast nor the Southeast Front. It provided a shield that bought time for the army to mobilize. In the case of the Northeast, the fortifications allowed the French army to concentrate its best troops along the Belgian border to engage the enemy. When the army failed in its encounter with the Germans, the Maginot Line covered the retreat before the advancing German armies.

NOTES

CHAPTER 1: MARCHING TO THE WRONG TUNE

1. The French had pioneered the use of divisions during the middle of the eighteenth century, when Napoleon instituted the corps and perfected the entire system. By the beginning of the twentieth century, the size of divisions had grown, and the role of the corps was modified.

2. In 1928, Doumenc had proposed to the General Staff the formation of armored divisions (Gorce, *French Army*, p.275).

3. Germany only annexed part of Lorraine in 1871. Lorraine had the largest reserves in Europe. France's other major reserves were located from Normandy through Brittany, far from its eastern border. The return of Lorraine also increased French coal reserves by 20%.

4. *Ouvrage*, which means "work" in French, is a general term applied to almost any type of structure or fort. In reference to the Maginot Line, it refers to the actual forts.

5. Two chambers formed the Parliament of the Third Republic: the Chamber of Deputies and the Senate.

6. The *Conseil Supérieur de la Guerre* or Superior Council of War had a vice-president who would become commander in chief of the French army on mobilization.

CHAPTER 2: THE MAGINOT LINE

1. The *lance-bombes* is a weapon that falls between a howitzer and mortar and has been identified in English as both.

2. This has led to some sources, especially during the war and soon after, to describe Hochwald as two *ouvrages*.

3. Historians partially attribute the loss of Ft. Vaux at Verdun in 1916 to the lack of a water supply.

4. During the Cold War, the army and air force let the combat blocks fall into disuse, adopting the support area as underground headquarters. The Swiss, on the other hand, kept their combat forts in full operation during the Cold War, modernizing their weapons as time passed. The Czechs redesigned the entire fort system after the war but gave up most of the combat blocks.

5. In an artillery casemate, the M-3 usually was the ready supply of ammunition stored on the side of the gun chamber. In an artillery bock, it consisted of a separate room aside from the ready supply in the control room.

6. In most cases, French writers refer to the upper level as an intermediate level and consider the turret itself as occupying the upper level in a turret block.

7. The French term for this type of weapon is *cannon-obusier*, but a few French sources list it as an *obusier* or howitzer, although both 1932 R models (short barrel for turret and casemate) are actually howitzers. The first of these fortress weapons was the 75-mm Mle 1929.

8. Strangely, in the *ouvrage* of Billig these guns served in two artillery casemates.

9. The smaller models of Type A had only a 0.20-m thickness equal to Type 1 or 2 protection, while the other models of both types had 0.25 or more, equal to Type 3 or 4 protection;—see section on protection thickness.

10. An older type of transmitter manufactured by Doignon had a much larger rectangular-shaped board that lit up the commands. This was not as efficient as the other designs and was not put into general use.

11. Only a few GOs in the Northeast, like Schoenenbourg, had no M-1.

12. The largest block in the Northeast, and with mixed artillery, was Block 5 at Rochonvillers, with three 75-mm guns and a 135-mm *lance-bombes*.

CHAPTER 3: CLOSING THE GAPS FROM THE NORTH SEA TO THE MEDITERRANEAN

1. In the *ouvrages*, these niches were usually near an entrance block.

2. These obstacles were named for the French general who designed them in 1937; they are better known as Belgian Gates.

3. According to Truttmann, there were to be two 75-mm turret blocks, whereas Mary mentioned two turret blocks and a casemate for 75-mm guns.

4. The West Indies, with the naval base at Martinique, had not been a priority site since the previous century because these positions were no longer a prey to France's traditional enemies.

5. A *wadi* is a dry river that only flows with water during a period of heavy rains.

6. An *erg* is a sea of sand, largely impassable to normal traffic.

7. This type of armored door was commonly used in Germany and other countries in Europe for the same purpose.

8. The designation of fortified region (RF) was not applied until after the war began.

9. Chott Djerid is the largest salt depression in North Africa; in the winter, it becomes a lake almost 1 m deep.

10. According to Dallier, two Char 2C 75-mm gun turrets were used. Since Dallier served as an army captain in Tunisia at the time, he may have actually seen these turrets. He may also be incorrect about their origin because only ten of the three hundred of these monster tanks on order were actually built. All ten remained with the same battalion in 1940. Each had one 75-mm gun turret and a machinegun turret. The 75-mm turret of one of these tanks was replaced with an experimental 155-mm howitzer turret, which turned up in Tunisia, according to Dallier. The other three tanks were being repaired and modified in 1940, but there is no mention of any of their gun turrets being removed. A Mle 35/37 turret used in France is found in the Mareth Museum, but no sources mention its use in the Mareth Line.

CHAPTER 4: SEA AND AIR DEFENSES

1. When Germany invaded France in 1940, the *Paris* and *Courbet* escaped to join the Free French.

2. The planners of the Maginot Line had briefly considered using these large naval guns in the forts.

3. Morocco's Atlantic Coast was a separate region.

4. This method also employed in the construction of most Maginot blocks, but not for the subterranean galleries.

5. By comparison, a typical Maginot turret block, like the one at the GO of Monte Grosso, measured about 28 by 14 meter using as the example.

6. The description of the defenses is further detailed in Jean-Jacques Moulins' *Les Défenses de Bizerte*, which is the only secondary source available on the subject to date.

7. It appears that the French army used the terms *blockhouse* and *casemate* interchangeably in Tunisia, and there is little to distinguish them.

CHAPTER 5: THE MARCH TO DEFEAT

1. General Alphonse Georges was also severely wounded when this happened, and it may have affected his abilities to act decisively in 1940.

2. A French corps was to operate in Yugoslavia and serve as a buffer between hostile Yugoslav and Italian forces while its logistical support came across Italian territory.

3. The Char B and Somua both had a one-man turret with a 47-mm gun. The Germans had only a few hundred modern Panzer III and IV tanks in 1939 and had to rely on a large number of captured Czech tanks that were better armed than their Panzer I and II tanks; see Table 5.1.

4. The first French armored division, the DLM (*division légère mécanique* or light mechanized division), was formed in 1933–1935. In addition, Weygand also had five divisions motorized. Gamelin formed a second DLM in 1937 and partially motorized his five cavalry divisions. In 1939–1940, three DCRs—*divisions cuirassées de réserve* (heavy armored divisions)—and additional DLMs were created.

5. French engineer officers also advised the Swiss on these fortifications during the 1930s.

6. The French had no AP minefields until after the war began.

7. At this time, Prételat's Army Group was responsible for the entire northeast front and was not yet given the designation of 2nd Army Group.

8. The only cinema found in an *ouvrage* was a relatively small chamber with regular chairs and a portable screen.

CHAPTER 6: THE FRENCH ARMY AND MAGINOT LINE AT WAR

1. At this time, only the Germans were preparing true minefields. The French did not have either the facilities near the *ouvrages* to store the number of mines needed to create true minefields or enough AP mines available.

2. The RAF Spitfire was the only fighter superior to the Me-109 on the Allied side.

3. He was "severely reprimanded for believing himself to be at war," according to Rowe. Wahl described the same incident in Hochwald but mentioned no reprimand, only that the high command was curious about the episode. Wahl also mentioned that the 75 and 135-mm weapons were fired on Germans during the winter to prevent them from moving too close (Wahl, *Hochwald*, p. 128).

4. During the war, many airfields consisted of open fields without concrete runways. Although these airfields were adequate for many aircraft, there were many accidents nonetheless.

5. According to Sumner Waite's report of March 1940, the DCR was initially supposed to have a demi-brigade of two battalions of mechanized infantry.

6. In the event, the squadrons were not added because the French air force refused to use dive-bombers, and the few built in 1940 went to the navy.

7. The battalions of the 3rd DCR had been parceled out for infantry support and no longer presented a force that could assault the flanks of the German break-through.

GLOSSARY

Alpine   Refers to mountain troops.

Anti-char (AC) or antitank (AT)   Weapons.

Armes mixtes   Mixed arms position. In the Maginot Line, these referred to a position that mounted a 25-mm cannon with twin machine guns.

Avant postes   Advanced posts or outposts.

Blindé   Tanks or armor or armor plated.

Caserne   Garrison area.

Char   A armored fighting vehicle; a tank.

Chasseur   Light infantry troops; many times, they served in mechanized and motorized units.

Cloches   Literally, a bell-shaped dome. These were fixed armored turrets.

Demi brigade   A half brigade that was generally equivalent to a reinforced regiment.

Division cuirassée de réserve (DCR)   Armored divisions of the reserve (referring to the fact initially they were assigned to the General Headquarters Reserve)

Division légère de cavalerie (DLC)   Light cavalry division; formed of both cavalry and mechanized units.

Division légère mécanique (DLM)   Light mechanized division.

École de Guerre   War College.

Entrée des hommes (EH)   The troops' entrance or men's entrance.

Entrée des munitions (EM)   The munitions entrance.

Ferroconcrete   Reinforced concrete; concrete reinforced with iron bars.

Fossé   A ditch or moat.

Fossé diamant   A diamond moat is angular.

Fusil mitrailleur (FM)   A light machine gun or automatic rifle.

Génie   Army Engineers; those that handled signal communications in the French Army are also listed under this heading but with a specific title under "transmissions."

Gros ouvrage (GO)   A large fort in the Maginot Line.

Guêt-fusil mitrailleur (GFM)   Lookout or observation and automatic rifle. Refers to a GFM cloche.

Jumelage de mitrailleuses (JM)   Twin machine guns.

Lance-bombes   Bomb thrower; a weapon with qualities that ranged between a mortar and howitzer.

Lance-grenades   Grenade thrower; a special mortarlike weapon that showered the immediate area with grenades.

Ligne d'arrêt   A stop line behind the main line of resistance.

Obusier   A howitzer, but not all artillery pieces identified as such were true howitzers, and those of the Maginot Line were a combination cannon-*obusier*.

Métro   Subway or underground railroad when referring to the Maginot forts.

Monte-charge   Usually refers to a small lift or a conveyor that carries ammunition up to the guns.

Mörser   German term for a heavy mortar that is sometimes best identified as a howitzer.

Offensive à outrance   An all-out offensive.

Ouvrage   A fort or, in more general terms, almost any type of works (civilian or military).

Petit ouvrage (PO)   A small fort in the Maginot Line without artillery (except for 81-mm mortars in a few cases).

Régiment d'infanterie de Forteresse (RIF)   Fortress Infantry Regiment.

Région fortifiée (RF)   Fortified region.

Secteur fortifié (SF)   Fortified sector.

Transmetteur sans fil (TSF)   Wireless or radio.

Usine   The powerhouse or engine room.

BIBLIOGRAPHY

*Denotes primary sources.

†Recommended secondary sources readily available through bookstores or libraries with inter-library loan.

Aime, Jean-Christian. *39–45 Magazine*, no. 190 (May 2002): 44–57 *Ligne Maginot Des Alpes: L'Ouvrage Du Mont Agaisen*.

†Allcorn, William. *The Maginot Line 1928–45*. Oxford, U.K.: Osprey, 2003.

Andrew, Stephen. *The Italian Army 1940–1945 (1)* Oxford, U.K.: Osprey, 2000.

Association des Amis de la Ligne Maginot d'Alsace. *La Ligne Maginot en Basse Alsace*. Reich-shoffen, France: Delbecq, 1981.

Beraud, Henri. *Bataille Des Alpes Album Memorial Juin 1940–1944/45*. Bayeux, France: Éditions Heimdal, 1987.

Bigoni, Sylvie. *Montgenèvre de l'Infernet au Janus*. France: Editions Tur, 2002.

Blatt, Joel, ed. *The French Defeat of 1940: Reassessments*. Providence, R.I.: Berghahn Books, 1998.

Borsarello, J. *L'Arméd Française de 39 à 41 Ou le Conflit Deux Ans Tro Tôt*. Do Bentzinger Editeur, 1998.

Bragadin, Marc Antonio. *The Italian Navy in World War II*. Annapolis, MD: U.S. Naval Institute, 1957.

†Breffort, Dominique and André Jouineau. *French Aircraft: From 1939 to 1942*. Paris: Histoire and Collections, 2004.

†Bruge, Roger. *Faites Sauter la Ligne Maginot*. Paris: Fayard, 1973.

———. *On a Livré la Ligne Maginot*. Paris: Fayard, 1975.

Buffetaut, Yves. *De Gaulle, Chef de Guerre*. Bayeux, France: Editions Heimdal, 1990.

Bull, Stephen. *World War I Trench Warfare: 1914–1916*. Oxford, U.K.: Osprey, 2002.

Burtscher, Jean-Louis. *1940 Au Coeur de La Ligne Maginot*. Strasbourg: Editions Ronald Hirle, 1999.

Centre de Documentatin sur les Engins Blindés. *Les Chars Français Du Musée Des Blindés, Catalogue*. Saumur, ND.

Chazette, Alain. "Le Secteur Fortifié de Fort Lapin/Blériot-Plage." *39–45 Magazine*, no. 166 (April 2000): 52–61.

Christienne, Charles and Pierre Lissarague. Francis Kianka, trans. *A History of French Military Aviation*. Washington, DC: Smithsonian Institution Press, 1986.

Cima, Bernard and Raymond. *Ouvrage Du Barbonnet*. Menton, France: Auto-Edition Cima, 1988.

———. *Sospel: Ouvrage de Saint Roch*. Menton, France: Auto-Edition Cima, 1989.

———. *Ouvrage de Sainte-Agnes*. Menton, France: Auto-Edition, 1990.

———. *Ouvrage de L'Agaisen*. Menton, France: Auto-Edition Cima, 1994.

———. *Ligne Maginot 2000*. Menton, Auto-Edition Cima, 2000.

Cima, Bernard, Raymond Cima, and Michel Truttmann. *La Glorieuse Defense Du Pont Saint-Louis*. Menton, France: Auto-Edition Cima, 1995.

———. *Ouvrage Du Cap Martin: OTCF Type 1939*. Menton, France: Auto-Edition Cima, 1996.

Claudel, Louis. *Ligne Maginot: Conception—Réalisation*. Switzerland: Association Saint-Maurice pour la recherche de documents sur la fortresse, 1974.

*Cot, Pierre. *Triumph of Treason*. New York: Ziff Davis, 1944.

Daillier, General Pierre. *Terre d'Affrontements: Le Sud-Tunisien La Ligne Mareth et Son Etrange Destin*. Paris: Nouvelles Editions Latines.

Denkschrift: Über die Französische, Landesbestigung. Berlin: Oberkommando des Heeres, 1941.

Depret, Julien. "Le Secteur Fortifié de Maubeuge Face à l'Invasion de Mai 1940 (1)." *39–45 Magazine*, no. 155 (May 1999): 52–61.

———. "Le Secteur Fortifié de Maubeuge Face è l'Invasion de Mai 1940 (2)." *39–45 Magazine*, no. 156 (June 1999): 52–61.

———. "Le Fort de Maude, Centre Résistance Organisé Ou Simple Ligne de Blocks (1)." *39–45 Magazine*, no. 172 (October 2000): 51–60.

———. "Le Fort Maulde, Centre de Résistance Organisé Ou Simple Ligne Blocks (2)." *39–45 Magazine*, no. 173 (2000): 52–61.

———. "La Batterie de Zuydcoote." *39–45 Magazine*, no. 189 (April 2002): 46–56.

†Doughty, Robert Allan. *The Seeds of Disaster: The Development of French Army Doctrine 1919–1939*. Hamden, CT: Archon Books, 1985.

Dupuy, R. Ernest. *World in Arms: A Study in Military Geography*. Harrisburg, PA: Military Service Publishing Company, 1940 (revised 15 March 1940 edition).

Duroselle, Jean-Baptiste. *France and the Nazi Threat: The Collapse of French Diplomacy 1932–1939*. New York: Enigma Books, 1985 (2004 reprint).

Eastwood, James. *The Maginot and Siegfried Lines*. London: Pallas, 1939.

Ellis, Major L. F. *The War in France and Flanders 1939–1940*. Nashville, TN: Battery Press, 1953 (1996 reprint).

†Evans, Martin Marix. *The Fall of France: Act with Daring*. Oxford, U.K.: Osprey, 2000.

Ferrard, Stéphane. *L'Armament de l'Infanterie Française 1918–1940*. Paris: Argout Éditions, 1979.

†———. *France 1940: L'Armament Terrestre*. Boulogne, France: ETAI, 1998.

*First Army Staff. *Report #16: Durchbruchsschlacht der 1. Armee from Jun 1–25*. Germany: First Army Photo Department, 1940.

*Fischer, Karl, ed. *Die Wehrmacht*. Berlin: Oberkommando er Wehrmacht, 1940.

*Flandin, Pierre-Etienne. *Politique Française 1919–1940*. Paris: Les Éditions Nouvelles, 1947.

"The French Front: 2,000,000 Men in Arms Wait for the Great Assault." *Life*, 8, no. 11 (11 March 1940): 77–85.

*A French Officer (Anonymous). *The Maginot Line: The Facts Revealed*. London: Duckworth, 1939.

Gaber, Stéphane. *Le Secteur Fortifié de Montmédy 1935–1940*. Metz, France: Editions Serpenoise, 2000.

*Gamelin, General Maurice Gustave. *Servir*. Paris: Librairie Plon, 1946.

Gamelin, Paul. *La Ligne Maginot: Hackenberg—Ouvrage A-19*. Nantes, France: AMIFORT, 1979.

*Gaulle, Charles de. *The Complete War Memoirs of Charles de Gaulle*. New York: Simon and Schuster, 1959 (1968 reprint).

*General Staff, War Office. *Handbook of the French Army*. Nashville, TN: Battery Press, 1940 (2004 reprint).

*German Army High Command. *Denkschrift: Uber die Belgische, Lnadesbefestigung*. Berlin, 1941.

*———. *Denkschrift: Uber die Franzoische, Landebestigung*. Berlin, 1941.

*———. *Denkshrift: Uber die Tschecho-Slowakische, Landesestigung*. Berlin, 1941.

*German High Command. *Grosses Orientergungsheft*. Berlin, 1936.

*———. *Grosses Orientergugnsheft*. Berlin, 1937.

Gorce, Paul-Marie de la. Kenneth Douglas, trans. *The French Army: A Military-Political History*. New York: George Braziller, 1963.

Goutard, Colonel A. and Captain A. R. P. Burgess, trans. *The Battle of France, 1940*. New York: Ives Washburn, 1959.

*Grosses Orienterungsheft Frankreich: Ausgabe 1935/1936. Berlin: Oberkommando des Heeres, 1936.

*Grosses Orienterungsheft Frankreich: Ausgabe 1935/1937. Berlin: Oberkommando des Heeres, 1937.

†Gunsburg, Jeffery A. Divided and Conquered: The French High Command and the Defeat of the West, 1940. Westport, CT: Greenwood Press, 1979.

*Hart, Liddell. The Defence of Britain. London: Faber and Faber Limited, 1939.

†Hiegel, Henri. La Drôle de Guerre en Moselle 1939–1940. Editions Pierron, 1984.

*High Command of the Wehrmacht (Armed Forces). Die Wehrmacht. Berlin: Die Wehrmacht, 1940.

*Hofmann, Rudolf, et al. German Attacks Against Permanent and Reinforced Field Type Fortifications in World War II. Germany: Historical Division, HQ U.S. Army Europe.

Hohnadel, A. and R. Varoqui. Ligne Maginot: Le Fort Du Hackenberg. Metz, France: AMIFORT, 1986.

Hohnadel, Alain. "Le Toit de la Ligne Maignot: Les Ouvrages de Restefond." 39–45 Magazine, no. 160 (October 1999): 52–61.

———. "Au Coeur Du Brançonnais, le Petit Ouvrage Des Aittes sur la Ligne Maginot." 39–45 Magazine, no. 176 (February 2001): 58–61.

Hohnadel, Alain and Jean-Louis Goby. La Mémoire Des Forts: Peintures Murales Des Soldats de la Ligne Maginot et Des Forts de Metz 1914–1940. Metz, France: Éditions Serpenoise, 1990.

Hohnadel, Alain and Jean-Yves Mary. "Au Coeur Du 'Bitcherland,' l'Ouvrage Maginot Du Schiesseck." 39–45 Magazines, no. 210 (March 2004): 48–57.

Hohnadel, Alain and Jan Yves Mary. "Au Coeur Du 'Bitcherland,' l'Ouvrage Maginot Du Schiesseck (2)." 39–45 Magazine, no. 211 (April 2004): 50–57.

†Hohnadel, Alain and Michel Truttmann. Guide de la Ligne Maginot—Des Ardennes au Rhin, dans les Alpes. Bayeux, France: Editions Heimdal, 1988.

Holstein, Christina. Fort Douaumont: Verdun. Barnsely, U.K.: Leo Cooper, 2002.

Hood, Ronald Chalmers. Royal Republicans: The French Naval Dynasties Between the Wars. Baton Rouge, LA: Louisiana State University Press, 1985.

†Horne, Alistair. To Lose a Battle: France 1940. Boston: Little, Brown and Company, 1969.

Howard, Michael, ed. Soldiers and Governments: Nine Studies in Civil-Military Relations. London: Eyre and Spottiswoode, 1957.

Hughes, Judith. To the Maginot Line. Cambridge, MA: Harvard University Press, 1971.

———. "Inside France's Maginot Line and Outside the Siegfried Line." Life 5, no. 14 (3 October 1938): 13–22.

Ireland, Bernard. Jane's Battleships of the 20th Century. New York: Harper Collins, 1996.

†Jackson, Julian. The Fall of France: The Nazi Invasion of 1940. Oxford, U.K.: Oxford University Press, 2003.

Johnson, Douglas W. Topography and Strategy in the War. New York: Henry Holt and Company, 1917.

Kannik, Preben. Military Uniforms in Colour. London: Blandford Press, 1968.

Kaufmann, J. E. "The Maginot Line—German Intelligence Before the War." FORT 26 (1998): 199–231.

†Kaufmann, J. E. and H. W. Kaufmann. The Maginot Line: None Shall Pass. Westport, CT: Praeger, 1997.

Koch, Oliver. Le Petit Ouvrage de Rohrbach. Sarregueminoise, France: Association Fort Casso, 1997.

———. "La Tourelle Mitrailleuse Modèle 1935 sur la Ligne Maginot." 39–45 Magazine, no. 153 (March 1999): 54–61.

———. "La Tourelle Mitrailleuse Modèle 1935 sur la Ligne Maginot (2)." 39–45 Magazine, no. 154 (March 1999): 56–61.

———. "Le Petit Ouvrage Du Welschof (1): Le Block 1." 39–45 Magazine, no. 201 (May 2003): 54–59.

Komjathy, Anthony T. The Crises of France's East Central European Diplomacy 1933–1938. New York: East European Quarterly, 1976.

Kupka, Vladimir. *Pruvodce: Po Maginotove Linii.* Prague: FORT Print, 1997.

*Lageberichte West Vom 10.Mai Bis 30. Juni 1940. Berlin: Oberkommando des Heeres, 1940.

Lambert, Pascal. *TM 32 Le Téléphone dans la Ligne Maginot.* Thionville, France, 1998.

Lannoy, François de. "Une Capitale Sous la Menace: La Défense Passive è Paris (1935–1939)." *39–45 Magazine,* no. 154 (March 1999): 15–29.

Leurquin, Robert. "Crust of Gunpowder Guards France." *New York Times,* 4 September 1938, IV-3.

Martin, William. *Verdun 1916 "They Shall not Pass."* Oxford, U.K.: Osprey, 2001.

Mary, Jean-Yves. *La Ligne Maginot.* Cueno, Italy: SERCAP, 1980.

———. "Retour sur la Position Avancée de Longwy." *39–45 Magazine,* no. 177 (March 2001): 52–60.

†Mary, Jean-Yves and Alain Hohnadel. *Hommes et Ouvrages de la Ligne Maginot.* Vols. 1–3. Paris: Historie and Collections, 2000–2004.

May, Ernest R., ed. *Knowing One's Enemies: Intelligence Assessment Before the Two World Wars.* Princeton, NJ: Princeton University Press, 1984.

†McNair, Ronald. *Mai—Juin 1940: Les Blindes Français.* Bayeux, France: Éditions Heimdal, 1990.

**Ministero Della Difesa. *La Battaglia Delle Alpi Occidentali: Giugno 1940.* Rome, 1947.

**Ministry of the Army, Historical Service. *Les Armées Françaises Dansla 2éme Guerre Mondiale Campagne 1939-1940: Atlas Des Situations Quotidiennes Des Armées Alliées.* Paris: Impression Nationale, 1964.

*———. *Les Grandes Françaises.* Paris: Imprimerie Nationale, 1967.

†Moulins, Jean Jacques. *Les Défenses de Bizerte 1881–1963.* Paris: Éditions Historie et Fortifications, 2001.

———. "La Batterie d'Artilerie Secondaire de Couronne à Marseille." *39–45 Magazine,* no. 203 (July/August 2003): 66–75.

Musée des Blindes. *Les Chars Francais Du Musee Des Blindes Catalogue.* Saumur, France: Centre de Documentation sur les Engins Blindes, circa 1985.

"New Methods of Attack in the War of Position on the Western Font." *Life* 7, no. 13 (28 September 1939): 38.

Ogburn, William F. and William Jaffé. *The Economic Development of Post-War France: A Survey of Production.* Social and Economic Studies of Post-War France. Vol. 3. New York: Columbia University Press, 1929.

Paillole, Paul Colonel. *Fighting the Nazis: French Intelligence and Counterintelligence 1935–1945.* New York: Enigma Books, 2002.

†Pallud, Jean Paul. "The Maginot Line." *After the Battle,* no. 60 (1988): 1–48.

Parkes, Oscar and Francis McMurtrie. *Jane's Fighting Ships 1924.* Trowbridge, U.K.: David and Charles Reprints, 1924 (1973 reprint).

†Plan, Genral E. and Eric Lefevre. *La Bataille Des Alps: 10–25 Juin 1940.* Paris: Charles-Lavauzelle, 1982.

Prasil, Michal. *Skoda Heavy Guns.* Atgen, PA: Schiffer, 1997.

**Prételat, General André-Gaston. *Le Destin Tragique de la Ligne Maginot.* Paris: Éditions Berger-Leverault, 1950.

†Raybaud, Claude. *Les Fortifications Françaises et Italiennes dans les Aples-Maritimes.* France: Serre Éditeur, 2002.

Rimington, Critchell. *Fightng Fleets: A Survey of the Navies of the World.* New York: Dodd, Mead and Co, 1944.

†Rocolle, Pierre. *La Guerre de 1940: La Défaite—10 Mai—25 Juin.* Paris: Armand Colin, 1990.

†———. *La Guerre de 1940: Les Illusions—Novembre 1918—Mai 1940.* Paris: Armand Colin, 1990.

†Rodolphe, LTC René. *Combats dans la Ligne Maginot.* Vevey, Switzerland: Editions Klausfelder, 1975.

Roton, G. *Années Cruciales: La Course Aux Armements 1933–1939: La Campagne 1939–1940.* Paris: Charles-Lavauzelle and Co., 1947.

†Roudier, Jean-François. *Le Cap Aux 340*. Guilherand Granges, France: Le Plume du Temps, 2000.

Rowe, Vivian. *The Great Wall of France: The Triumph of the Maginot Line*. London: Putnam, 1959.

Salmond, J. B. *The History of the 51st Highland Division*. London: Blackwood and Sons, 1953.

Schwartz, Serge and François Klein. *Simserhof: Ouvrage d'Artilerie de la Ligne Maginot*. Paris: Citedis, 1998.

†Sharp, Lee. *The French Army 1939–1940*. Vols. 1–3. London: Military Press, 2001–2003.

Stehlik, Eduard. *Lixikon Tvrzi: Ceskoslovenskeho Opevneni z Let 1935–38*. Prague: FORT Print, 1992.

Sumner, Ian. *The French Army 1914–18*. Oxford, U.K.: Osprey, 1995.

†———. *The French Army 1939–45 (1)*. London: Osprey, 1998.

Tarnstrom, Ronald L. *Handbook of Armed Forces: France Part II*. Lindsborg, KS: Trogen, 1983.

*Thompson, Dorothy. "The Maginot Line: A Fort in Action." *Current History* (June 1940): 51–52.

Truttmann, Philippe. "La Fortification Française de 1940 Sa Place dans l'Evolution Des Systems Fortifies d'Europe Occidentale de 1880 à 1945." Doctoral thesis. Metz, France: University of Metz, 1979.

———. *La Muraille de France Ou la Ligne Maginot*. Thionville, France: Gerard Klopp, 1985.

†———. "*La Muraille de France Ou la Ligne Maginot*." Woippy, France: Gérard Klopp, 1992.

*U.S. Army. Military Attaché Reports. Individual reports posted by attaches to Berlin and Paris in the National Archives, 1939–40.

Varin, Jacques. *Été 40: Cent Jours Qui Ébrandèrent la France*. Milan, Italy: Editions de la Courtille, 1980.

†Vermeulen, Caspar and Vincent. *Maginot Line: Atlas CORF*. CD-ROM. Netherlands, 2004.

Wahl, Jean-Bernard. *La Ligne Maginot en Alsace*. Steinbrunn-le-haut, France: Editions du Rhine, 1987.

———. *39/40 dans le Sundgau*. France: Société d'Histoire de la Hochkirch, 1995.

†———. *Il Était une Fois la Ligne Maginot: Nord—Lorraine—Alsace*. France: Do. Benzinger Editeur, 1999.

†———. *Hochwald—Une Forteresse en Alsace*. Ostwald, France: Editions du Polygone, 1999.

———. *Chemins de Fer Militaires à Voie de 60 Du Système Péchot à la Ligne Maginot*. Strasbourg: Les Éditions du Polygone, 2002.

Windrow, Martin. *French Foreign Legion 1914–1945*. Oxford, U.K.: Osprey, 1999.

Worth, Richard. *Fleets of World War II*. Cambridge, MA: Da Capo Press, 2001.

Young, Robert J. *In Command of France: French Foreign Policy and Military Planning 1933–1940*. Cambridge, MA: Harvard University Press, 1978.

INDEX

ABOUT THE AUTHORS

J. E. KAUFMANN is a freelance researcher and a retired public school teacher. He has published several books on fortifications and is the founder of Site O, an international group devoted to the study of fortifications. His numerous articles have appeared in Military Affairs, Fort: the International Journal of Fortification and Military Architecture, and Strategy and Tactics.

H. W. KAUFMANN is an instructor in the Romance Language Department at San Antonio College. She has a Ph.D. in Medieval Spanish, and is fluent in French, Spanish, Italian, Polish, and Amharic. She is the co-author of numerous books on fortifications and has translated articles on fortifications for foreign-language magazines.